PRAISE FOR
animal house

'*Animal House* is great at conveying the social changes of
the 90s and the buzz at the time. Reading it is a bit like being
strapped into the passenger seat of a speeding sports car'
Guardian

'A boisterous and often touching autobiography. What shines
through most of it is that Brown really did love the trade
of journalism, a sort of Harry Evans with a habit'
Financial Times

'James was at the very epicentre of all the carnage, chaos and
hedonism of the 90s. I'm impressed he can remember enough about
it to fill a book'
Sarah Cox

'Brown doesn't skimp on the wild tales but it's
the backstory that gives this book its heart'
US Vogue

'James Brown was a hard-drinking, brilliant loudmouth
and I loved those early *loadeds*'
Josh Widdicombe

'A gripping read . . . A brilliant memoir!'
Closer

James Brown started his career producing his own fanzines, joined the *NME* staff aged 21 and wrote over 50 cover stories, championing Beastie Boys, KLF, Happy Mondays and many others. He created the award-winning and hugely popular *loaded* magazines, and went on to edit British *GQ* where he launched the Man of The Year Awards. He floated his own publishing company on AIM and became an in-demand public speaker and creative consultant for leading brands, agencies and publishing houses. He wrote the best-selling book *Above Head Height: A Five-A-Side Life.*

animal house

James Brown

QUERCUS

First published in Great Britain in 2022 by Quercus Editions Ltd
This paperback published in 2023 by

QUERCUS
Quercus Editions Ltd
Carmelite House
50 Victoria Embankment
London EC4Y 0DZ

An Hachette UK company

A CIP catalogue record for this book is available
from the British Library

PB ISBN 978 1 78747 794 0
Ebook ISBN 978 17 8747 792 6

10 9 8 7 6 5 4 3 2 1

Typeset by CC Book Production
Printed and bound in Great Britain by Clays Ltd, Elcograf S.p.A.

MIX
Paper | Supporting
responsible forestry
FSC® C104740
www.fsc.org

Papers used by Quercus are from well-managed forests and other responsible sources.

For my boys, Billy and Marlais

'Was it over when the Germans bombed Pearl Harbor?'

Bluto, *National Lampoon's Animal House*

Foreword

Treasure Island, Mustique, 2001

Me: 'These look like the pirate islands from the books I read as a kid.'

Felix Dennis, the magazine publisher: 'These *are* the pirate islands from the books you read as a kid.'

Felix and I are looking out across the Caribbean Sea from Mandalay, the stunning traditional Japanese house he bought from David Bowie. I'm a long way from home. It's seven years since I launched *loaded* and my life exploded. (The title was always lower case – we didn't want to be pompous like magazines had been before.)

Felix followed *loaded* into the market with *Maxim*, making it the biggest-selling magazine in America. He's made so much money he is perfectly happy to give me half a million quid to add to my own quarter of a million to start my new company.

It's not without expectations though. He hands me a fax (yes, a fax) of the latest US *Maxim* cover image and asks me to write the cover lines, which I do. I don't know if they get used but I calculate it's £100,000 per word.

Me: 'What are we doing today?'

Felix: 'We're going for lunch with Patrick Lichfield.'

Suddenly, despite all the success I've recently enjoyed, I feel like the kid on free school dinners in Leeds again. Lichfield is a top society photographer and member of the royal family; I used to do paper rounds to buy Jam singles.

We set off in a golf buggy down the manicured lanes and bamboo fences that keep the super rich and famous away from each other. I can feel a nervous, nagging tension that was there so often when I was growing up. It's the first time I've felt it in a while but I know what it is now.

The rehab counsellor who recently helped me kick my drug and drink problem explained it's common among addicts – a sense of feeling less than. As if to amplify the moment, Felix points out Princess Margaret's house.

Me: 'Does she ever come round?'

Felix: 'Yes, but I won't let her in any more, she's a nightmare. She points at my ornaments and says, "Oh, this is nice, can I have it?" Some of the idiots on this island say yes but when she phones I just say, "No I have the builders in."'

We swerve into a drive and a smiling Patrick Lichfield is there with his famous bouffy white hairdo and a crisp, sky-blue shirt.

Barely acknowledging Felix's roaring greeting he immediately strides over to me, shakes my hand and warmly asks: 'James, how on earth did you manage to sell all those magazines while taking so many drugs?'

I laugh. The childhood fear disappears.

Me: 'Well you should know, Paddy, in the nineties we were just trying to outdo what you did in the sixties.'

Lichfield: 'Yes, but in the sixties we were trying to outdo the thirties.'

This book is my own answer to Lichfield's question – how I managed to sell so many magazines while taking so many drugs. And not just me but what seemed like a generation. How, by the end of the twentieth century, the world not only allowed me to do both and stay alive but actually give me awards for it. It is a book about two childhoods.

Part 1

Just what is it that you want to do?

Who the hell is going to employ you, Brown?

Mr McCreadie, PE teacher,
Lawnswood School, 1982

It was the last great era of print publishing, when thousands of people queued up to buy magazines from corner shops, news-stands and travel points. Music, film and fashion companies paid publishers and publicists fortunes in adverts and PR contracts to make sure their famous clients and products appeared on the front covers and pages of the world's most influential magazines. Journalists flew round the world to hang out with stars of music, film, football, sport and fashion, and for the first twenty years of my adult life at *Sounds*, *NME*, *loaded* and *GQ* that was exactly what I did. From a van in Holland with Pop Will Eat Itself to Elvis's Vegas suite with U2 to dancing with Prince in Rio de Janeiro, I was getting paid to travel the world, meet amazing people and try and stay sober long enough to interview them.

People simply loved magazines. For many they were a gateway to the world, for others they felt like a club to belong to, something that informed them, made them laugh and feel good, that guided them towards things to buy and places to go. A good magazine was like a good friend, they would tell letters pages and market researchers.

I was lucky enough to work on magazines where I could do pretty much whatever I wanted, what I would be doing anyway without being paid. From road-testing crisps and vodka at *loaded* to standing onstage with Happy Mondays in front of 150,000 people at Rock in Rio for the *NME*. I was able to have as much fun as possible but I also made a career of it. I learned to be a professional writer on *Sounds* and *NME* and then an editor on *loaded*. Eighteen months into that job I was voted the Editors' Editor of the Year by the British Society of Magazine Editors, the Champions League of publishing.

By the end of my time at *loaded* in 1997 a third of a million people would buy my final issue with a yet to be 'Saturday night TV famous' Harry Hill sitting on a stuffed badger. Ours were not your typical magazine stars but *loaded* was far from a typical magazine. Harry was one of the twenty-six male lead covers in my three years since launching *loaded*.

Despite modern media misconceptions of what sold *loaded* there was barely any cleavage in sight on my thirty-six covers. It was mainly just guys we loved like Vic and Bob, *The Simpsons*, Gazza, Gary Oldman, Prince Naseem Hamed and Jimmy White. When we did feature women on the cover it was usually people like Uma Thurman, Kylie or Elle Macpherson, people with notable success and careers to talk about. The two times we featured famous Page Three girls, Kathy Lloyd and Jo Guest, we shot them *in* clothes and interviewed them about their lives. They became our friends and went on to appear on Channel 4's *TFI Friday* and in Blur videos. It was a time when boundaries and preconceptions were crashing left, right and centre. A new era of talent had roared into that final decade of the twentieth century and *loaded* was at the heart of capturing it. I was aware of the publishing past as much as my need to alter the present. My ambition was to compete with the impact the original *Rolling Stone* had had, not *Playboy* or *GQ*, which meant nothing really to young British men. My most basic requirement was a magazine that created generational tension, crossed music and football. And to have somewhere to write about the things I liked.

Loaded created a multimillion-dollar global magazine genre and captured the excess and joy of the 1990s. Readers loved it, most of the media loved it, the publishing industry loved it and World Cup footballers told us if they didn't play for Liverpool and Leeds United they'd want to work on it.

Before then, as the 22-year-old features editor of the *NME* I had spent four years choosing the features content and cover stars for almost every issue of Britain's biggest-selling music weekly. Beastie Boys, Stone Roses, the Pixies, Morrissey, De La Soul, Guns N' Roses, KLF, Morrissey, Primal Scream, New Order, U2, Happy Mondays, Sinead O'Connor, Public Enemy. From acid house to Manchester to the re-emergence of punk rock with the Manic Street Preachers, it was a fantastic period to be a music fan and an *NME* editor. I wrote over fifty cover stories myself.

Despite being only third in command I also edited two issues before I even had facial hair or owned a shirt with collars. Just a young boy armed with a Sony Walkman, an Amstrad word processor and a big, confident gob.

The first was the Clash special featuring Paul Simonon smashing his bass on the cover when they hit the top of the charts with 'Should I Stay or Should I Go' after it was used on a Levi's ad. The second was the iconic cover of Happy Mondays' Shaun Ryder climbing on a giant E during the making of the 'Step On' video. For me and my friends and colleagues they were both important moments in music. Punk had been over long enough for the advertising industry to consider it safe and cool enough to use in commercials. And a new generation of reprobates was walking out of Manchester and into the charts. When the boss came back and asked me where the main Mondays cover line was I just replied, 'It's the E.'

The *NME* was a legendary title. We were influential enough to be able to bring lyrical mavericks like Mark E. Smith, Shane MacGowan and Nick Cave together for a cover just to see what would happen. I still have the tapes of them talking and jamming – we shot half the photo session in my kitchen. Music fans post about and share images of these issues and others to this day.

I was barely two years out of school when I joined the *NME* and before long I was being trampled underfoot by teenage female Public Enemy fans in San Diego, taking Beastie Boy Adam Yauch's liquid acid, and snogging female singers heading to the top 30. It was an amazing job, my first, and set a standard I aimed to improve upon when I came up with the idea for *loaded*. Free tickets to football for a start.

Coming to the end of the century it felt like we could do anything, and often did. It was an inclusive time – the biggest band in the world looked like boys you'd see at the football. The best films were about the lives we led after the pubs closed and extra stimulation was required. The best book was about our holidays spent in search of dreams on the beaches of Thailand.

Having been lucky enough to find a way into the *NME* myself I made sure I left the door open. I wanted as few barriers between magazine staff and readership as possible. I opened the door for a generation of writers and musicians.

The readers, writers and photographers of these late eighties and nineties publications felt like one group in love with the raving, rocking, clubbing, festival-going, heavy drinking, Ecstasy- and cheap-flight-taking world. A period of endless adventures and great laughs. The whole, Labour-voting, shark-floating-in-formaldehyde decade felt like one mad scramble before last orders were called on not only the century but the millennium. As the calendar clicked from 1999 to 2000 many believed that the new digital world was going to end. Who wouldn't want a long drink, only to wake and find little had changed in our computer lives at all? And yet in a way it had.

And if that meant the staff of *loaded* chose to row about whose turn it was to collect and open the champagne? So be it. As Mrs Merton, the premier TV interviewer of her day once said, 'Would George Best have drunk all that champagne if he hadn't been so thirsty from all that running around?' Between 1985 and 1999 I did an awful lot of running around.

A place of work, apparently

London, autumn 1994

'**N**o you fucking get it. It's your turn, I organised the trip.'
'Fuck you, I'm telling you to get it.'

An actual row in the *loaded* main office is so rare I put down the article I am editing and edge round my desk, which is covered in vodka bottles from a *Sunday Times* Life in the Day photo shoot the day before, and I make my way across my office.

On the wall is a large *Scarface* film poster: 'Written by Oliver Stone'. Next to it is a blown-up clipping of a newspaper article highlighting 'the ten traits of a social psychopath' on which someone has placed a red tick next to each entry then stuck it on my door.

The huge blue Habitat sofa that I have brought in from home, which sometimes doubles as an office bed, is at an angle filling the whole of the small room so I have to half climb over it to get out of the office.

At the far end of the sofa is a pile of brand-new outdoor wear from Timberland, North Face and Henri Lloyd that our fashion department swagman Reece has blagged for a forthcoming week on a deserted Scottish island. Opposite my office the four-man art department is all faces to computer screens laying pages out and calling in photographs. Their area has two broken fans hanging off the desk, there are shrink-wrapped piles of our latest issue with Frank Skinner on the cover, and freshly used poppers bottles are scattered across the floor.

To their right is the Internet department – 'nerdsville' – where *up-loaded* website editor Adam Porter and writers Mike Karin and Pete Stanton are starting on what will turn into a weekend-long Carmageddon computer game marathon fuelled by pizza. Not for the magazine, you understand, just for themselves. *Loaded*, the office people don't want to go home from. While the game loads, one of them writes a column in the character of a glove puppet monkey and another is reviewing music pretending to be a duck. The third is thinking about blowing a car up to put on our fledgling website.

Behind them there is a circular meeting table covered in over forty boxes of breakfast cereal from our recent Breakfast Cereal World Cup which was filmed for the E! channel in the US and Canada. The nerds appear to be living off the leftovers.

Elsewhere in a hidden corner of the office someone is emptying a cellophane cash bag of cocaine wraps, carefully opening each and scraping some of the white powder into one bigger wrap. He puts the tightly folded new, smaller wraps back in the bag and puts the larger wrap of siphoned overmatter into his wallet for personal use.

Fashion editor Beth walks out of her department with a beautiful looking black sheepskin coat which she hands me. 'John Rocha says you can keep it.' Her big brown eyes roll in disbelief. When she's not styling the fashion pages of the magazine, Beth's increasingly having to explain to fashion PRs why their clothes have gone missing. Most of them don't seem to care and are actually sending us more stuff to wear in our own editorial photos all the time.

Trainers, sunglasses, coats and T-shirts keep coming in for photo shoots and not going back. None of the staff are buying clothes any more. This morning twelve brightly coloured shrink-wrapped button-down shirts from the recently relaunched Ben Sherman company arrived as gifts and disappeared in minutes.

There is so much product coming our way we start a column called What We Want to try and streamline it. Martin Deeson, the great *loaded* staff writer, has just secured some much-needed dental work. The man himself is slumped across his desk by my office door talking to the infamous New Orleans Police Department about a chance to spend a week with them 'You have a reputation you need to improve, and to be honest so do I, so we're in the same boat. This won't be a stitch-up. I'll send you some magazines and then you'll see why it will be a good idea.' You cannot fault his reasoning.

Across the office in the subs' room there's a burble of low-volume chat where people are actually working. It is the engine room of the magazine, the reason it comes out on time every month without a single world misspelled. Every now and then someone laughs and then reads out loud the amusing copy they are working on. The subs are writing the smart, self-deprecating headlines, blurbs and captions that have made the magazine so appealing to the readers. They are partly the reason *loaded* feels like 'a very funny mate', as readers keep telling us.

By the subs' room door at the gateway to the office, Gaynor, a hippy-ish looking woman, is opening a mountain of mail and answering constant calls while scribbling my name on Post-it notes and sticking them onto the top of letters which she then places inside a clear ziplock envelope along with plane tickets and travel documents. Behind Gaynor there is a tall wall of boxes of Staropramen beer and Moscow Mule vodka cocktails we have been sent. On the office floor a portable TV with video player is playing a soon-to-be-released song called 'Wannabe' by a new band called Spice Girls. The record company want us to go to Japan with the band who they think are 'very *loaded*'. 'LOOK, JUST FUCKING GO TO THE OFFIE!'

The source of the raised voices is the writers' area. The tall junior writer Michael is propped at an angle, like an unused javelin, between his desk, chair and a pile of travel bags. He is playing double devil's advocate and winding up the argument as he takes opposite sides in consecutive sentences. He is waving around a salt and vinegar crisp and grated cheese sandwich (his own invention). The contents are flying everywhere.

He catches my eye and shrugs his arms and shoulders as if to say, 'What can you do?' As I have already heard, the assistant editor Tim Southwell and commissioning editor Adam Black are stood up amid the hand luggage rowing about whose turn it is to buy champagne from the off-licence just a hundred yards away. It's an unusual dispute, given that in my office there are numerous crates of Cloudy Bay white wine with which I pay our back-page columnist, my landlord Vic Reeves. But there is a giddy excitement underpinning the apparent fall-out. I watch in disbelief and think that one day I will look back on this chaos, this second childhood, and wonder if it all actually happened.

Outside are two cars waiting to drive five of us to Heathrow Terminal 4 to fly to New York, for no other reason than I now have a company credit card and as soon as it arrived we immediately decided we should do a travel story there. Within twelve hours of this row we will be in a Manhattan hotel room drinking shots of vodka and fluorescent mouthwash.

I look down at Little Piers, the latest waif and stray to wash up on our freelance desk, who is making a living out of a basic IPC Magazines work experience day rate, product freebies and fees for short articles in the mag. I give him the credit card and ask him to go to the off-licence.

Despite only having had it for a few weeks the signature on the back is already virtually worn off because of the amount of assorted cocaine chop powders it has come into contact with. These include baby laxative, speed and almost certainly bath-cleaning products. When Little Piers asks about signing for the card I tell him to copy the signature from my Ed's Letter page in the mag, which was actually written by Christian the production editor anyway. 'Get four bottles of cold champagne and some Marlboro Lights.'

'Four bottles of champagne just for the car journey to Heathrow?!'
He hasn't quite got his head round the way things are yet.

'Yes, you are right, it's not enough – make it six but give two of
them to Gaynor to put in my bag without the others seeing. Get whatever you want for yourself, get a receipt and be quick.'

I look at Tim and Adam and say, 'You know, guys, it will probably
never be like this again in our lives, so just enjoy it.'

I am twenty-eight years old and have created my perfect job editing
a magazine that has absolutely exploded into public life. No one is
telling us what we can or cannot do, pretty much anything we want
is coming good, but who knows how long it can possibly go on for?
It's five months since *loaded* launched and for me there are thirty-one
more to go. A thousand nights of chaos await.

Sniffer Clarke lives next door

Collingham Bridge, 1970

If *loaded* was to become my second childhood, this was my first. I was born on 26 September 1965 in Hillingdon Hospital, west London, which had a great music and football heritage: Ronnie Wood of the Rolling Stones and Butch Wilkins, the England footballer, both of whom I would later have the pleasure of spending time with, were born there. Strangely, so was the man who would change my life twice, my publishing mentor at *NME* and *loaded*, Alan Lewis, although I only discovered this at his funeral.

My parents were from Leeds but my dad, Ray, was down working for Lyons Maid at Park Royal industrial estate testing ice cream. My mum, Sue, was at home in a semi-detached house on Dawley Road in Hayes looking after me. Within a couple of years my sister Sally would join us. During my first months, my mum was hospitalised with bad postnatal depression. That started a history of mental health problems for her which lasted the rest of her life.

The first memory I have is of seeing her shiny, brightly coloured two-tone capsule pills spilled out on the kitchen table. I couldn't get hold of them but I made do with a bottle of sickly-sweet orange drink with the consistency of medicine. You were supposed to dilute it, but I happily hid myself away under the kitchen table, necking it neat. It tasted great. Underneath tables would become great places for dens and sanctuary in the years that lay ahead.

My second memory is seeing the vision of Arthur Brown, the God of Hellfire, with his smoke-painted face and flaming crown singing on *Top of the Pops*. It was absolutely terrifying. These are not selective memories; they are all I can remember from our time in London. Drugs, drink, music. Like markers to return to later.

My dad tells me there were weekly appointments with *Doctor Who*, where I was terrified of the Cybermen, the Rolling Stones' 'Satisfaction' was top of the charts and Liverpool had just beaten Leeds United in the FA Cup final – my dad later told me he'd heard the cheers as he was out buying me a pram.

After a couple of years we moved back north to the outskirts of Leeds where my parents had met. Despite being brought up in a small, Charlie Bucket-style stone cottage in the village of Thorner with his five older brothers and sisters, my dad had passed his eleven-plus, experienced grammar school as the poor kid, became the first in his family to go to university, and then made enough in the ice cream game for us to be able to move to Collingham. Many of Don Revie's Leeds United greats lived in the area and plenty of current players do too. This is where my childhood really began.

On an idyllic day in Collingham I'd be out in the back field, lying on prickly hay bales staring up at Vulcan bombers in the sky or with my mum and her friend Margaret in her living room, trying on her husband the Leeds United striker Allan Clarke's soft blue full England caps, waiting for him to come back from a game. I had a white, long-sleeve shirt with his blue 8 on, an ancient pair of second-hand football boots, and a plastic ball to boot around. Having my hero live opposite didn't seem weird, but I guess subconsciously it made anything seem possible.

I'd spend hours on my bedroom floor engaging in mini theatres of war with my little plastic Airfix soldiers and Action Man. The end of the sixties was one generation on from the end of the Second World War, and every film on TV seemed to be a war film. If Leeds United were our heroes in real life the Germans on TV were always the baddies. The bent 1975 European Cup final, which I watched in tears, did nothing to later change my opinion.

On the way home from our frequent holidays to Filey on the North Yorkshire coast we'd stop at the Sledmere First World War memorial and I'd look at the engravings of pointy-hatted German soldiers doing terrible things with bayonets. I'd no idea half my mum's family were German, nor that her grandfather had been forced to flee his country during the late 1930s for marrying an Englishwoman.

The other TV 'baddies' were shirtless Indians with warpaint and feather headdresses; they were probably the first people I thought were cool, without realising why. Our street and gardens were full of little boys running around with sticks for guns yelling 'wah-wah-wah-wah-wah-wah' war cries by hitting our open screaming mouths repeatedly with our hands.

Going to places I'd specifically been warned not to held an over-powering sense of excitement and attraction. At the bottom of the avenue we would crawl on forearms, stomachs and knees through a large garden of mowed lawns and well-kept flower beds until we came to two old punts half submerged in the rust-brown, sunlit pools of the River Wharfe. The smooth, dark water flowed quickly past us, tiny eddies spinning beneath overhanging trees. All the kids in the road were told to keep away because of dangerous undercurrents but I liked currants, and raisins, so I couldn't see the problem. I wanted to go and sit in those old submerged rowing boats with water in the bottom, push off and drift wherever this inviting river was going. Then two brothers from school drowned in the Wharfe and we never went back.

I lived in fear of the school dinner hall because I was terrified of eating. I had what's now known as anorexia nervosa, but back then it was called 'being faddy' and was considered being bad or playing up.

There would be adult sieges to try and get food into me. The moment I could smell the school dinner being cooked my stomach was just gripped with tension and it worsened when I sat nervously staring at the food trying to outlast the teachers trying to make me eat. Most of my schooldays I was super skinny and really hungry. With the exception of crisps, fish and chips, white bread, cheese and sweets, this fear of food remained with me for decades. Apart from peas and apples nothing green or healthy passed my lips until the late eighties.

The diet of a five-year-old may seem a long way from a future life of rock 'n' roll journalism but from the off it gave me a weird relationship with how I fuelled myself. I had no sense of balance, and when I did get something I liked I'd want as much as possible to cover what I'd missed at meal times. That need for more would replicate itself across sugar, music, adrenaline and other substances throughout my life.

Although we had plenty of good times at home I'd have no idea why my parents rowed or why my mum would become tense, upset and then ill. There was too much shouting and upset for two little kids to be subjected to. When it happened I'd lie with my face on the carpet in the front room, feeling the fibres against my cheek, listening to the sounds coming out of the long cabinet record player.

They had some fantastic singles. They came in torn paper record company sleeves in black, white, orange and pastel colours and would shape my life. My parents' names were handwritten in the middle of the singles next to the printed info: 45 rpm, Lennon/McCartney, the Beatles. Their Small Faces and Beatles singles sounded mysterious and childlike; even a child could sing along and pick out the words and feel the rush of excitement at the sound effects and building rhythms of the recordings. When I heard a song I liked I would listen to it on repeat. Watching the needle rising and falling on its journey through the groove I'd lie there and ponder if the Beatles' walrus was the same one as in *Through the Looking Glass*, and think about Lady

Madonna's children and what Bert Jones's lumbago was. I had no idea why someone would say 'hello' only for someone else to say 'goodbye' but it didn't matter because the songs had stories and characters. I wasn't to know then but they were some of the greatest pop music ever recorded.

As well as the Beatles, and the Small Faces' 'Itchycoo Park' and 'Lazy Sunday', I loved 'Judy in Disguise' by John Fred and His Playboy Band, Elvis Presley's 'I Got Stung' and 'Jennifer Juniper' by Donovan. I was in the right place at the right time, on the living room floor by the record player, shutting out real life. The music changed the way I felt; it took me away from the nervousness around eating and the tension in the house. Seeking distraction was a habit I'd get used to.

The best album they had was *Sgt. Pepper's Lonely Hearts Club Band*. It was a kid's dream – loads of faces on the sleeve, the band dressed as brightly clothed bandsmen. I would lie there thinking about the pictures and stories portrayed in the lyrics, visualising the colours of the songs as I imagined them.

On a Rolling Stones double compilation album with a pair of giant white plaster-cast lips on the sleeve I listened to 'Satisfaction' over and over again. I didn't understand how the big electric fanfare sound was made but I liked how it bounced out of the record player and into me. That's what I really liked, when the energy of the song took over.

Despite these super-hip mainstream hits my favourite album was the *Trumpton* one from the animated model series on TV. Like some of the Beatles' songs, those on the *Trumpton* album were simple portraits of everyday life in a model town where factory workers went straight from a long shift to waltz in front of a bandstand. As you do. I couldn't detect any difference between 'Time goes by when you're the driver of a train' and 'Wouldn't it be nice to get on with your neighbours?'

These songs took me somewhere else, though, and at times I needed that. Even as a kid I felt things weren't right; you don't really know what is going on when adults shout – you don't want to ask, not when you're four or five. I used to watch my mum's fingers trembling and sense her nervousness and tension. I'd take that feeling and hold it inside and try not to be on the receiving end of how upset she'd be soon after. That atmosphere was just there, and as I got older I came to recognise it might mean she had to disappear to hospital. But in general, life seemed nice and comfortable.

The other world I loved was comics like *Whizzer and Chips* and *Cor!!* with its expanding logo bellowing out of a chimpanzee's mouth. I never got my head stuck in a fence or found a hot pie on a kitchen window ledge like the heroes of the comic strips but the stories kept me engaged for hours. My Granny Lamb later told me I could read a newspaper aged five; I'm not sure about that but I read every word in those comics, right down to the names of the publishing companies like Fleetwood, IPC and DC Thompson. Comic day was a big day; my dad (*Beano*), sister (*Dandy*) and I would sit round reading them then swap. Then after a year of school we upped and moved from the country to inner city Headingley in Leeds, where my mum had grown up.

The Kirkstall Lane end

Headingley, 1971

At the bottom of our red-brick streets, with goalposts sprayed on terrace ends, were the enormous Yorkshire Country Cricket and Leeds Rugby League grounds. Easily accessible via a lamppost in a ginnel they were a constant invitation to trespass. The best thing about the new house, though, was just how many kids and sweet shops there were. Four shops alone in the ten-minute walk from home to my new school. From that moment on my childhood tasted of ice pops, kali, sherbet, McCowan's chews, Black Jacks and fruit salads, Mojos, kopp kops, Mars bars, Mint Cracknels, Texan bars – sugar. I grew up on a diet of the white stuff. The streets were alive with the slap of plastic footballs on gable-end walls and the occasional almighty roar of adults down the road when test wickets fell.

Bennet Road School was a big stone inner city northern primary school, it was 1971, play time was endless games of British Bulldog and kicking a tennis ball around. Lessons were often led by ancient teachers who would slap you on the legs for some mild misdemeanour, or even go full vigilante, once making a kid put a piss-soaked tennis ball into his own mouth because he'd thrown it at a girl.

Maybe it was loneliness or maybe she was just on her way to work in the local hippy shop, Paraphernalia, which smelled of joss sticks and played Procol Harum's 'Whiter Shade of Pale', but my mum would sometimes come and say hi to Sally and me through the iron railings at playtime. It was thrilling seeing her there but occasionally I could sense a sadness I didn't understand. It's only since becoming a parent that I get that need to see your children when you're low.

Acid on the floor so I walk on the ceiling

Park Lane, London, 1996

You know you're getting blasé about success when you're eating sheets of acid before a Park Lane awards evening. In the two years since the launch of *loaded* we had been men's magazine market leaders, creating a new mainstream mass market in sales and readership, winning most of the awards going, busting all sales and advertising targets by miles and becoming one of the most discussed cultural phenomena of the decade. We were over 700 days into an exercise in childish behaviour and things were going well. Almost too well. So by the third major publishing awards I figured that despite the ever-increasing sales and popularity of the magazine I'd probably not be disgracing the stage any more – I just didn't see how we could keep on winning every year. There were two major publishing awards every year, the Periodical Publications Association and the British Society of Magazine Editors Awards. I hadn't expected any when we started and I still didn't expect to win any each time we attended, and yet we had.

Anticipating imminent industry rejection I decided to change our agenda for the night and encouraged the staff attending the evening to take a load of blotter acid.

The A4 sheet of acid was in my desk as a gift from a guy I knew who'd needed a reference to explain where his unexplained income was coming from. You can probably imagine where. I'd written him a letter saying he was a marketing consultant for the title and was paid in cash. Tim Southwell, Michael Holden, and I took the acid at six and the reception was due to start at 6.30. At seven we were still fannying around in the office when the hotline went. This was the only phone in the subs' room where we actually put the magazine together. No one but the staff had that number so I picked it up, thinking it was a writer. On the other end, redirected there by the switchboard, was a reporter from *Daily Express* wanting a quote from someone about me winning Editor of the Year again.

I explained that they must be mistaken as the awards hadn't taken place yet and that they wouldn't be announced until later that night. She explained that the ceremony had already started and it was assumed all entrants would be in the Grosvenor by now. Consequently the organisers had sent the results out to the media. This was before everyone carried phones and could message info around like now so they were safe in assuming no one at the event would find out. I felt my mouth going dry.

I looked across my desk in the subs' room at the A4 sheet of acid which was smaller than it had been an hour before. I put the phone down. 'Fuck!' I explained to the others what had happened, and what was about to happen. They seemed to collectively turn white and looked at the sheet of acid, then at each other, and we all shouted, 'Fuck!'

Even on a normal day Adam Black fancied himself as a bit of a flash bastard; he looked and dressed like Lewis Collins, and had offered to drive us to the ceremony in his second-hand Karmann Ghia. We squashed ourselves into the tiny, open-topped vintage sports car, and as we paraded like tits in a dodgem around Waterloo roundabout, Trafalgar Square and then Hyde Park Corner, my body began to feel unusually uncomfortable inside the metal frame of the car. The air flying through my hair felt nice but my limbs felt awkward and I could feel my face tingling and my teeth tapping. The car started to feel like a restrictive metal coat.

From the screaming, big grins and compulsive desire to wave bottles at strangers I guessed the others were experiencing a similar transformation. We got out at Park Lane and the first thing I did was stand by the entrance with my arms out, gathering the coats of other late arrivals rushing in. Once there was a nice pile I walked back across the two lanes of traffic and dumped them in the tulips.

Back in the hotel's scarlet-walled Red Bar, Tim and Michael were staring at themselves in the mirrors that adorned every surface and pillar. It was the worst possible place to be on acid but they couldn't get out. Everywhere looked like blood was dripping down the walls and all we could see were loads of repeated images of ourselves curving off into a distance in the mirrors. The more you scowled or laughed at what was going on the more frightening it looked.

The reception area was empty and the people whose job it was to hand out champagne were hastily taking down the serving tables and removing the tablecloths. We charged through into the ballroom which looked like a floating ocean of candles, cutlery, chandeliers, ice buckets, wine bottles and glasses. All twinkling away, lots of chatter and excitement, everyone really looking forward to an evening of free booze and food and maybe some acclaim from their peers or their bosses.

Thankfully our table was stuck right beneath the staircase we were heading down so we didn't have far to go, and at this point I could still walk and my arms hadn't started spasming and lashing out involuntary like they sometimes did on acid. 'Keep those irresponsible bastards as far away from the stage and sponsors as possible,' seems to have been the brief for the table planners.

Our bosses, Alan Lewis and Andy McDuff, looked particularly relieved to see that we'd arrived as they were thinking we might not show up. 'I've got good news and bad news,' I said. 'The good news is a woman just rang up and told us we've won.'

Andy and Alan looked delighted but a little confused. 'What's the bad news?'

'We've all taken quite a lot of acid.'

Alan just laughed and poured himself another drink and said, 'Well this should be fun.' Andy the publisher seemed to think we were joking.

The BBC presenter hosting the night had a yellow skintight dress covered in black handprints. 'She looks like she's been groped by a gang of printers,' observed Alan loudly with his usual candour. She'd barely got through her opening remarks when Tim started howling like a wolf. Not a little one-off, lots of it – he couldn't stop. People started giggling and a couple of other wolves joined in around the room, until she made some sort of reference to it in the hope he'd calm down. He didn't. He carried on; he'd slow down and then start again. In fact I don't think he had any awareness he was in a room with 1,000 other people. He was so far under the stairs and facing the wall he probably thought he was in a cell, which is exactly where he should have been.

For even the most patient person any industry awards night can take ages, with disappointment and drunkenness increasing as the night goes on. My own relationship with time had totally disappeared. After the starter of deep-fried Brie I noticed Alan's head had become the shape of the cheese and his face one big cubic beard. He looked like Oddbod from *Carry On Screaming!* I didn't like his new look at all and it was even stranger when he started talking to me. I retreated to my increasingly natural habitat at awards evenings – underneath the table. No one could talk to me there. I could do lines and kiss people. Anyone who also climbed under was usually worth the visit. To this day I occasionally meet people who say, 'We were once under a table at the PPA Awards.'

I re-emerged for tea and coffee and, more importantly, the chocolates, which arrived on a platter of smoking dry ice. Being totally fucking stupid and childlike we started taking the dry ice in handfuls, dropping it into our glasses and grinning like imbeciles as we drank smoking wine. This was the sort of cheap victory that kept us very happy for a long time.

By the time they announced I had to go to the stage I was back under the table and shouted up that Alan would have to go. He refused and said they were waiting for me. I came out and looked towards the stage and it seemed such a long way through a battlefield of spotlights. The whole room looked like one of those solarised camera shots from seventies *Top of the Pops*. Alan eventually agreed to walk me to the stage. I should have made Howling Tim go. He held my arm all the way, guiding me through the chairs like I was a frail pensioner. All I could see were red velvet and gold-sprayed wooden chair backs and the black dinner suits and women's naked shoulders. People were smiling and thrusting their hands out at me; their faces looked like boiled sweets, their cheeks drooped like bingo wings, their bingo wings were like long towels of skin. It seemed to take hours to get there.

When I got to the stage I had lipstick all over me and I was spending a lot of time thinking about how weird my teeth felt in my mouth. I was given the award and then was guided back down to the side of the stage. The roar of clapping and the wolf howling was rushing round and round my head. At the photograph spot a man with a grey beard whose face looked like a budgerigar told me he was called James Dean. Another gruff hairy boulder of a man said he was called Felix, had a ranch in Connecticut and another in Worcester and that I should come and work for him. I didn't understand what ranching had to do with publishing. It was the first of three times he would try and hire me.

I couldn't fathom why these people were talking to me; mentally I wasn't with them, I was busy examining how everything felt and looked. My temperature, my glasses on my face, the touch of the award in my hand. And I still had to get back to the other side of the room.

I've no further memories of that night. Many years later fellow editor Barry McIlhenny, who became the head of the Periodical Publishers Association, told me he'd come across me in open view at a table on the balcony just cutting out long lines of cocaine and giving them away like free magazines to anyone who wanted some. It was like this so often. If it wasn't an awards evening it was an event, a festival, a pub or a party. It was like one of those documentaries where they lock little kids in a house for a week and leave them to it, only we were making millions of pounds in the process of such dicking about. People seemed to like it.

The smiley badge years

Headingley, 1974

Childhood jumped forward playtime by playtime, day by day, night by night. The moment I got home from school I'd cover thick white slices of bread with jam and throw myself into the street football as Lorimer, Bremner and the rest. On international duty we'd always be Scotland because we'd actually seen these Leeds heroes play for them in the televised '74 World Cup when England hadn't qualified.

The wider world appeared in televised astronaut splash-downs and colour supplement spreads of bloodied American soldiers in Vietnam. These were a world away from our own nine-mile summer bike rides to Otley and rumbling skateboard trips into the brutalist concrete university campus where discarded fluorescent tube light bulbs made for great lightsabers.

Big-screen excitements like *Rocky*, *Jaws* and *Star Wars* were enjoyed at the Lounge cinema. *Jaws* kept me out of deep water for decades. The best night of the year was Mischievous Night which occurred the day before Bonfire Night when we spent the evening knocking on doors and legging it, hedge-hopping and creating mayhem with Brock's bangers. Our daily conversations involved the Banana Splits, Harlem Globe Trotters, piranhas, tarantulas, hernias, Eddie Merckx, Mark Spitz, Muhammad Ali, bubblegum football cards, and how stunt rider Evel Knievel had broken every bone in his body – 'including his cock, twice' – all informed by the scantest of knowledge. TV gave us awareness of America but no one ever considered we might go there. The height of our ambition was to make a great den in the woods. This all took place in our flares, non-brand pumps, Adidas striped-shoulder T-shirts and yellow Aertex Leeds United shirts with the famous smiley badge.

I read Biggles, *Just William* and Enid Blyton books my parents had saved from their own childhoods, but while totally engaging they never featured anyone sitting on a brick wall playing kerby, swigging a shared bottle of Tizer and trying not to drink someone else's phlegm.

I devoured *Tiger and Scorcher* comic with the *Roy of the Rovers*, *Billy's Boots*, *Nipper* and *Hot Shot Hamish* strips where football and adventure were intertwined. *Viz Comic* would famously parody this genre years later with *Billy the Fish*. With Seminole wrestler *Johnny Cougar*, racing driver *Skid Solo* and *Martin's Marvellous Mini*, it was *Grandstand* in comic format. Diverse subjects united by a common sense of adventure and tone of voice laid the way for when I was publishing features on cult films, crisps, football and acid house twenty years later in *loaded*.

My favourite book was Barry Hines's *The Blinder*, the story of a schoolboy striker who was the big hope for his town's professional side. It could have been set in my own 1970s secondary school where one teammate was playing with future heroes David Batty and Brian Deane for Leeds City Boys, the Leeds United youth team, and another was actually already fully signed for LUFC. Hines wrote *A Kestrel for a Knave* which became peak Yorkshire film, *Kes*, of which I was a lump-in-the-throat fan. When his book *The Gamekeeper* was published in 1979, my dad, sister and I went to meet him opening a nearby housing estate and the local paper published a photo of him signing our books.

That a great writer could not only come from Yorkshire but actually make a living writing about kids and football impressed me. My dad regularly mentioned local writers like Stan Barstow, whose poems and short stories we read at school, and Keith Waterhouse who wrote the book *Billy Liar* which was also on TV. On a family trip to London we saw Michael Crawford in a musical version called *Billy*. I was so excited 'Frank Spencer' was in it but the early exposure to composer John Barry, lyricist Don Black and writers Clement and La Frenais also made an impression. That's Bond, *The Italian Job* and *Porridge* all in one hit, or half the *loaded* screen section. I'd listen to the soundtrack album thinking about the young undertaker's assistant with three girlfriends and dreams of a writing job in London. It was a road sign for what lay ahead, although I was yet to work with the dead.

It did make me aware that you could actually get more from life than was on offer. Standing outside the walls of the YCCC where, in a reference to a famous criminal trial, 'George Davis Is Innocent' had been sprayed mid-test match a couple of years before, my friend Paul Munden turned to me and said, 'You're going to change the world one day.' I had no idea why he thought this – maybe the cocky intensity of how I swore, spoke or behaved, but with an increasing interest in politics I allowed myself a momentary Billy Fisher or Citizen Smith-style fantasy of leading a revolution, totally unaware that my finest moment would be inventing the Crisps World Cup.

At home my dad pointed to the terrace house behind us and said, 'You can do anything in life, you could jump over that house if you wanted.' It was well intentioned but unfortunately the house in question was home to a Hell's Angel and soon afterwards one of them tried out my dad's theory on acid for real, was hospitalised and then impris-oned for possession. His girlfriend and son, my friend, moved into our self-contained basement flat and from then on I was babysat by a real Hell's Angels girl, which is something I wished I'd remembered when I was later being asked what had influenced *loaded*. The thing that really changed my life, though, was music. Masses of it. I could never have known I would end up in Elvis's suite in Las Vegas with U2 though.

Attention, baby

In the warm desert air Bono sings 'Mysterious Ways' to 28,000 people. He looks like a child's drawing of black-leather Elvis in Velvet Underground wraparound shades. His sweat flies off his face and splashes across the Zoo TV cameraman and me. Without being in the band or fucking them you cannot get closer to the action than to be hit by the bloody singer's perspiration. Strangely, it's where I want to be – not receiving his bodily fluids but right there in the shadow of the backlit rock 'n' roll singer himself. It makes for better copy, a faster thrill. There's only a crash barrier separating me from that crush of bodies where I'd spent my teenage years watching punk and post-punk bands from. The crazed swampland rockabilly of the Cramps, the lean, speedy revolution-themed soul of the Redskins, the booming distorted feedback of the Jesus and Mary Chain, the endless sounds I'd discovered through late-night Radio 1 and whose trail I followed to halls and cellars and pubs and bars: Skids, the Ramones, Depeche Mode, the Teardrop Explodes, the Banshees, Spizzenergi, the Jam, Stiff Little Fingers, the Stranglers, the Undertones, the Specials and so many more ... U2 even. I'm somewhere beyond that now, a rarefied atmosphere; I no longer have to try and talk my way backstage as I have Access All Areas laminates.

I know I'm far from being alone in this love of the gig – all big music fans have it, you can add your own lists of bands you go to see and hear again and again. Throw in the songs that mean everything to you. It doesn't matter if it's Motörhead or Mantronix, Johnny Cash or the Clash, it's just a case of how far you'll go to be a part of it.

When I read how, as a child, Jerry Lee Lewis sneaked into segregated Black dancehalls in Louisiana to see these mysterious men who played the music that inspired him, I understood that need to go wherever you can to get that hit. I've been there again and again, the same bands night after night. Which is how I'm on tour with U2 for the *Sunday Times* magazine, somewhere between my time on the *NME* and *loaded*, flying around the world from Manchester to Berlin to Vegas to Los Angeles to Dublin. I'd liked them when they first appeared with 'I Will Follow', and then didn't like them quite so much when Bono started with big hats, sweaty sleeveless T-shirts and pompous pronouncements. Now suddenly with the energy flash, the multimedia gigs and, most importantly, the songs of *Achtung Baby*, I like them again.

At this point in time, in the Nevada desert, they are the biggest and most attention-grabbing live band in the world. Bill Clinton's on the phone talking to them halfway through the set, there are huge fast-edit montages of political global imagery flashing across their many screens, East German Trabants rotate above them. It's like the graffiti on the Berlin Wall has come alive and danced its way across the stage.

Their creative resurgence is a surprise to the band themselves, especially as they know how close they came to splitting up during the recording of the album. That's why *Achtung Baby* seems so good – it's a record with four people fighting for their own bit of it and with an underlying belief in the bigger picture making that work.

I'm down the front, with a massive grin on my face, singing along to this unexpectedly flamboyant music that has brought the band back from the brink of death and crashing into the midst of their most productive period ever. What the huge open-air Las Vegas crowd sees on the screens is a metre away from me. And I love it. It's where I want to be; there is nothing between me and the music. Nothing in my head but the sound running through me. No fear, just joy. Bono's image is in my eyes and the noise is everywhere. It's all right it's all right. It's allllll right. Life works in mysterious ways. My dad was right saying anything is possible; by the end of the night I'll be in Elvis's old suite watching Bono walking into a full-length mirror.

Summer is heaven in '77

Headingley

Radio 1 pumps pop music out of the windows of cars, kitchens and homes into the streets where my friends and I stand around chanting glam bootboy choruses as we play Wembley doubles. The ice cream van has its own siren call of Tudor pop, 'Greensleeves', but looking back the creamy 99s and cones with bubblies at the bottom were a much-loved cheap thrill in comparison to the forthcoming promise of a musical revolution.

At home Mum had moved on to Neil Diamond and Hot Chocolate and my dad Bob Dylan and Toots and the Maytals. When my schoolfriends came round they'd think it was hilarious he was in the front room singing along to 'Mr. Tambourine Man'.

We'd sit in front of the gas fire after Sunday lunch listening to Jimmy Savile's *Old Record Club*. No idea what you were supposed to do with the points he'd offer if you could guess the name of the song, artist or year. Predictably the big TV moment came on Thursdays straight after *Tomorrow's World* in the form of *Top of the Pops*. The nation was in thrall to the Led Zep theme and the bestselling singles charts and the weekly sight of solarised musicians playing their hits. Only *It's a Knockout* came close in terms of spectacle.

The best bands had clothes that made the special effects even better. The singers wore sunglasses, the drummers leathers and chains. Tinfoil trousers, sparkling hats, star-shaped guitars covered in glitter. Silver double drum kits, stack heels, drape coats, high collars. Real-life astronauts of the day looked so cool in their white suits and bubble glass helmets but pop stars really did look like people they might find out there where the Clangers and Captain Kirk did their thing.

I loved Sweet, Slade, Mud, Gary Glitter, Suzi Quatro and David Essex. My mum took me to see *Slade in Flame* at the local Lounge cinema. There was no sophistication; this was pop music for the masses, and millions listened to the same songs over and over again throughout the Radio 1 day. The glam songs had clap-along accompaniments and choreographed dances. The lyrics were about gangs and fights. The performances were menacing. Sweet, Slade and Glitter were singing anthems quick to be adopted by football crowds, even Terry Jacks's mournful tribute to a lost friend, 'Seasons in the Sun', was quickly corrupted to 'We had joy we had fun, we had Man U on the run.'

Sweet looked rougher and tougher than the rest. Their songs sounded like it felt racing down a hill on a bike. I'd no idea what adrenaline was but these bands made me feel happy and excited. For Christmas my parents bought me *Blockbuster*, a Music for Pleasure compilation of cover versions of songs written and produced by 'Chinnichap' – Nicky Chinn and Mike Chapman, the men behind these dazzling songs – featuring bowling pins being smashed apart on the sleeve. The first time we played it the slow start-up grind of the title track's air raid siren made my dad stop and start it twice, thinking there was something wrong with the turntable. I liked that. The music was mine, it wasn't for parents.

OK, let us speed this up because much as I like meandering through my childhood like an episode of *The Waltons* I know we need to press on. I'm nine and my Marc Bolan-loving older mate, Pete Masters, is playing me the *Slider* LP by T. Rex and another local kid is showing us the sleeve of Bowie's *Diamond Dogs*. Bolan is amazing and seems like everything a pop star should be. There's also some hair recognition going on as Pete, Marc and I all have long curly dark hair.

My dad takes me and a friend to see Showaddywaddy live at a theatre in town, my first gig. The highlight isn't Dave Bartram's doo-wop and rock 'n' roll classics but a full-on brawl of drape coats, quiffs and brothel creepers as the tightly packed crowd of Teddy boys fights over Romeo Challenger's drumsticks.

At middle school my friends and I are becoming increasingly interested in pop music. It's still the days of stack heels, tank tops and star jumpers, and city-centre pub and football violence trickles down to the playground where scraps with big crowds of onlookers occur regularly. My mate Mario is perhaps unfairly chinned for announcing that Village People are gay.

During registration David Hassell jumps up and does the Heatwave 'Boogie Nights' dance he's seen on *Top of the Pops*. My Afro-sporting West Indian table tennis teammates Desmond and Ian impress the school assembly by singing a new crisps advert: 'Rock rock, Rock 'n' Rollers, / New from Golden Wonder they're called Rock 'n' Rollers.'

In the music lesson the teacher, Miss Bamforth, plays classical music records and explains what is going on within them, what the different passages of music mean. How the *1812 Overture* with its cannons is a musical representation of a battle between Russia and Napoleon. This analysis surprises me and stays with me.

Leeds is twinned with Dortmund and our headmistress, Miss Pinnel, is optimistically keen on cementing this relationship through school exchange trips celebrating folk dancing. She has boys trained in morris dancing and Northumberland sword dancing with real blades and the girls doing Scottish and Irish folk dancing. (Yes, I was the morris-dancing fool in case you were wondering.)

Sending a coachload of kids armed to the teeth with sticks and swords dressed in cricket whites and kilts seemed a curious way to make amends for dropping over 2,000 tons of high explosives on the city during the Battle of the Ruhr. But they were great trips and we weren't complaining. In return Dortmund sent us a large brass statue of a fat bloke holding a beer barrel which was erected outside Lewis's department store. This perhaps showed a better understanding of the men of Leeds than wave after wave of prepubescent English folk dancers did for their counterparts on the Rhine. With a tour bus and gigs to perform this was my first taste of life on the road, and just like in *Spinal Tap* there were frequent opportunities for things to go wrong.

On a jaunt to a folk dancing festival in Baumholder, south-west Germany, a teacher, Mrs Ward, was reduced to tears when she got ten of us lost for three hours in an enormous forest. Rescued by actual GIs in a jeep from a nearby American forces base, we rejoined the school party in a traditional inn and were necking Fanta and huge salty pretzels when I was beckoned over by three gnarled old men who took my hand, said something in German about 'soldat' and gave me a ten-mark note.

It didn't occur to me that these were the very Germans who were the baddies in war films we watched and games we played. On seeing the cash Mrs Ward cheerily announced, 'Oh James Brown, you could fall down a toilet and come back with something good.' When I think about the hours I'd later spend leaning over bog seats with a rolled-up note in my hands it's hard not to consider she may have been clairvoyant.

I was in Germany prior to the 1974 World Cup and two years later in Dortmund which was totally plastered in posters for the Rolling Stones at the Westfalenstadion. A visit to the stadium during the day resulted in my mate and me coming away with Black and Blue tour stickers – and yellow Borussia ones. In the huge posters the Stones appeared utterly ravaged. All cheekbones and long, thin, drawn-out faces, their black hair was all over the place and they looked threatening but also really alluring. They looked like they were having a good time. Most of my childhood I was being corrected for having jam on my face or stains on my knees, adults were forever impressing upon us the need to look clean and presentable, and here were these guys looking absolutely fucked. The Rolling Stones were clearly allowed to behave differently to other adults.

In the summer of '77 a band in leather and spiky hair appear on the *Rock Follies* TV show whipping an inner tube about, and when I asked my dad what they are he says, 'They are punk rockers.' Photos of punks in ripped clothes, dyed hair and safety pins appear in a Sunday colour supplement and then along come Johnny Rotten and Sid Vicious of the Sex Pistols looking even more menacing in a straight jacket and mohair and crazed eyes on the evening news explaining why they're doing a concert for striking firemen's kids. They look mesmerising, like real Bash Street Kids with sea-urchin hairdos and trouble in their wild-eyed leers. I'm twelve years old but I can see quite clearly that something is afoot.

And then, *bang*! Nine months later the teenage starter pistol fires and instead of just getting my kicks by climbing railway embankments, running through allotments and lying around on garage roofs, I suddenly discover the new music from new bands pouring into the charts. Then I find the night-time Radio 1 shows that champion more bands like them, find where I can buy their records and eventually discover the magazines that featured them.

Once I realise I can buy my own singles from the local Headingley record shop that sells everything from Stravinsky to the Stranglers, I spend every morning of the week running round Beckett Park doing as many paper rounds as possible. I later upgrade to a far more lucrative milk round which means getting up at 5.50 three days a week, just so I can buy these amazing singles.

Bernie Rhodes
knows – don't argue!

Leeds, 1979

My teens started in 1978 and within ten years I was features editor of the *NME*, so I was probably right to just let music grab me and drag me along. It accompanied everything that was important to me and overshadowed my traditional education. When Kevin Rowland and Dexys burst into our living rooms with 'Geno' and prompted young boys to go topless and whirl their shirts and jumpers above their heads at school discos, it expressed something I already knew. The line 'This man was my bombers, my dexys, my high' was what I got from music: a high, a sense of exhilaration and identification I didn't get elsewhere. Songs did something to me inside that just made me connect; they inspired and soundtracked emotions I wanted more of.

Liking singles as a thirteen-year-old is not big news, I know, but I loved them. I loved the music, I loved the sleeves, the coloured vinyl, the fact I could buy a couple every week and with so much good music pouring out, well, you never knew what you would buy. They were the physical connection with the bands my friends and I loved and, whereas doing anything remotely exciting on a bike or a rope swing was of the moment and then gone, with singles the adrenaline was right there and ready to go again two or three minutes later. Repeat, repeat, repeat. Just as I had experienced as a five-year-old.

I liked that different singles would give me different feelings as well as different sounds. If a band could write great singles they could convince you pretty easily to then buy their album and see them live.

And there were so many bands like Buzzcocks and the Undertones who made great singles. Every week another band emerged through the airwaves.

With punk, new wave, the mod revival, 2 Tone and loads of great pop groups the end of the seventies was a truly brilliant time to be a music fan enjoying the constant change and creative freedom that inspired generations. Leeds city centre was full of record shops; once I'd discovered Scene and Heard, Virgin, HMV and, most importantly, Jumbo, I'd be in them every week. 'Killing an Arab', 'Love Will Tear Us Apart', 'Oliver's Army', 'Reward', 'Bankrobber', 'Doors of My Heart', 'Turning Japanese', 'Suspect Device', 'Jimmy Jimmy', 'Echo Beach', 'Cool for Cats', 'Promises', 'Germ Free Adolescents'; everything the Jam or the Specials released. Just writing those song titles and band names down makes me happy over thirty years on.

I liked the hustle and bustle of the record shops. Jumbo Records in the Merrion Centre became like a second home; the owners and staff didn't mind you being in there even if you didn't have any money. They'd regularly say, 'Have you heard this?' and play some interesting new track.

Round the corner was Bostock Records which sold discounted imports – my first Specials and Undertones albums were Canadian and had slightly different track listings. They sold anonymous bags of thirty singles for a pound which were unlucky bags, really, as you'd buy them once and not find anything you wanted. You could have bought the Penetration or Orchestral Manoeuvres in the Dark single with the money instead. Maybe they were for old soul fans, not little punky kids.

In the old Merrion Centre market was a second-hand record stall, an open-fronted skateboard outlet that smelled of big polyurethane wheels, and a badge stall selling masses of little punk, heavy metal and pop badges. You could make your own badges too. On a trip to

London I found even smaller ones being sold from a doorway off Piccadilly Circus and spent all my money on half-pence coin-sized Pistols and Blockheads badges.

The record industry was huge, the number one entertainment industry, and it was changing as the new bands I loved climbed into the top 40, an alternative to the Brotherhood of Man and Boney M. Listening to music with mates was a social event. Going to my friend Craig Roy's to hear the Monochrome Set for the first time, and his TRB, Damned and Stranglers albums. Or visiting another kid's house to look at his many-coloured punk records hanging in clear plastic display pockets on his bedroom wall.

Albums followed singles; my mum went and bought me Blondie's *Parallel Lines* with my paper round money and I loved it – still do – the heartfelt urgency of the lyrics, the move from punk to disco. Maybe it was because it was the record I had at the same time as my first girlfriend, or maybe everyone feels like this, but Blondie stood at the heart of all that was good about music. Poring over the lyrics and writers' and producers' credits I realised there was a connection with those glam bands I'd loved, as Chinnichap were the producing duo. When Barbara Ellen and I convinced Alan Lewis to put Debbie Harry on the *NME* cover in the late eighties, that decision was based purely on our love of them as kids, not adults.

The impact of these years has stayed with me. Years later, in 1997, as dawn spills into our north London living room, my wife Kaz and the legendary Back to Basics club runner Dave Beer are having a loud discussion about who 'the best band/singer ever' was. Given the two candidates they are suggesting it's a bizarre debate, like comparing cheese and tractors. Kaz genuinely believes it is eighties *Smash Hits* type Nik Kershaw and Beer is touting the Clash (which made sense to me), but she argues so passionately I realise then that the best band in the world is simply the band everyone loves when they are thirteen, when they're falling in love with music, or maybe have a crush on or are going out with someone for the first time. We all have our own best bands in the world.

That's what music had meant to me in my teens. It occupied my mind from before the schoolday started when I was sitting round a portable box record player in the living room listening to the Teardrop Explodes' *Kilimanjaro*, to night when John Peel would keep us awake with his droll drawl and endless sonic surprises. That was my true education, not what was going on in the classrooms at Lawnswood. And then later when I made the connection between music and music papers I realised it was something that could take me somewhere. A route out of unemployment and boredom and into somewhere I could thrive.

At some point in the mid-seventies my dad decided to pack his job in and become a full-time writer, which made a significant change to the household's financial situation. My mum worried more and more about the lack of cash, and this caused more tension. But on the up side I got to see my dad typing all the time, which I guess was instructional. Had he been plumbing I'd have probably become a plumber.

Sensitive about my mum's illness, I used music as a drug, constantly playing singles over and over again as a way to blank things out, to project, to cultivate the feeling of love or anger or frustration. If Blondie made me feel good about having a nice girlfriend so the Jam subsequently reflected my own awareness of socio-economic disparity and how the political battle lines were drawn. Weller's lyrics were teenage lyrics and teenage lyrics are the best for teenagers. He was at the end of his teens when he wrote 'The Eton Rifles', 'Strange Town' and 'In the City', and they vibrated with the hopes, energy and frustration of teenage life. 'Strange Town', 'When You're Young', 'The Eton Rifles', 'Going Underground/Dreams of Children', 'Start', 'That's Entertainment', 'Absolute Beginners' and 'Town Called Malice' is a run of consecutive singles that mattered to me as much as Motown, the Beatles, the Stones and Bowie at their peak did to the previous generation. Every new release was vital and inspiring.

Years later when I joined the *NME* I would be talking to my best mate from school, Geoff, and he would always ask, 'Have you met Weller yet?' Meanwhile sitting right next to me behind his own beaten-up metal desk, my colleague Paolo Hewitt would be on the phone to his best mate, Paul Weller. It was a strange set-up. I never once asked Paolo if he could introduce us because I believed in the Redskins' warning that you should 'Take no heroes, only inspiration', but you could still be excited by or even in awe of those who had inspired you.

The Jam conquering the charts with repeated number ones, and at one point having something like eight reissued singles in the chart, made knowing what was in the chart, and where, even more important – the ups and downs, new entries and non-movers. Like everyone else obsessed with this, I'd record the Radio 1 rundown on a little Philips cassette machine.

In 1995, high on grass and drink on Marie Peyton's sofa with our *loaded* swagman Reece, I find myself reciting one week's late-seventies Radio 1 top 30 rundown commentary word for word. As if the DJ's patter had lodged itself in there after repeated listenings and was just escaping. Marie ran the door of her family's amazing Atlantic nightclub in Piccadilly which was one of the flagship venues of London nightlife in the mid-nineties. She and Reece were just looking at me wide eyed as this torrent of information tumbled out of my mouth. Not that the full chart rundown was full of gold – the opposite, in fact.

Lots of chart music was utter rubbish: showbands from the chicken-in-a-basket working men's club scene, Eurovision entrants, novelty TV show spins-offs, bland mainstream acts. Much of it was hyped into the charts by an old-boy network and payola that passed between the major record labels and the broadcasters. So once the new wave of music crashed in among this rubbish I knew the battle lines were drawn.

And drawn they were, with lots of bands' names scrawled in biro on our schoolbooks, desks and school bags. The more artistically gifted painted album sleeves and band logos on their rucksack covers. From Tangerine Dream and the Pistols in the sixth form to Tubeway Army and Adam and the Ants in the third year.

After the Pistols, Clash, Jam, Buzzcocks, Gen X and Co. had shaken everything up, the music just kept coming, a current that swept me along beyond my teens and into adult life. And I needed the music because it provided a high to counterbalance the pain and shame and upset and confusion of things going on at home.

Alan Bennett didn't behave like this

Lawnswood, 1980

Lawnswood High School, a big old red-brick place with two buildings and massive playing fields on the northern ring road of Leeds, had once numbered the writer Alan Bennett and *Newsround*'s John Craven among its pupils. Not that the teachers told us about either of them.

It was no place for an increasingly politicised, disruptive, bored, cocky, smart-arse with enough intelligence to get by but not enough manners or commitment to shut up and do the work. Much to the annoyance of the teachers and amusement of my friends, arsing around and getting laughs were what I liked best about being there; stuffing Brock's bangers into cake, leading an escape through a first-floor window after being locked in for detention and distracting affable teachers were all groundwork for my second childhood at *loaded*. At home there were other things going on that made sitting still and quiet in a classroom seem pointless.

My parents decided to get divorced when I was in my early teens. Separations are common now but back in the late seventies I didn't know too many people whose parents had split up. The rows and my mum's upset seemed relentless. When I explained it to my mate who I sat next to in biology, on the verge of tears, he didn't seem to understand what I was saying. I'd come into school upset but had no leeway to communicate anything was wrong to the teachers because of my mouthy behaviour, which the home situation was only exacerbating. The same thing would happen in my early years at *NME*.

I felt increasingly at odds with the world. 'You're at an age when you question everything, James Brown,' the irritating diminutive deputy head told me one day, like there was something wrong with asking questions.

I'd feel like saying, 'Well, yes, my mum's spent the last week in Menston, the place where they electrocuted her, the place everyone laughs about.' But that wasn't going to get me anywhere.

In the array of playground insults that included spacker, spazz, doilum, mongy and puff, calling someone mental was a brutal short-hand to heat up any row. Usually it was prefixed with 'fucking' for added severity. In Leeds you could also be called, or call someone, a Menner, which was an abbreviation of Menston. Describing someone as a Menner implied they should be in the High Royds mental hospital situated in Menston to the north-west of the city. Neither the name of the hospital nor the location sounded particularly nice. Look it up now and you'll see old black and white shots of what was once the High Royds Pauper Lunatic Asylum; a heavy stigma attached to residents/patients/inmates long before its name entered my vocabulary.

High Royds in Menston was the worst possible place you could allude to in Leeds, more than Chapeltown which was a byword for 'prossies'. High Royds in Menston was where my mum would go whenever her paranoia overtook reality and she experienced a breakdown. She'd be away for a couple of weeks and when she came out she was never happy about having been in there, but would have shakily regained her normal loving personality and life would go on again.

She never went openly, publicly crazy like most people assumed the residents of High Royds were, but her nerves would go and she'd lose a sense of reality and that was that. No one outside our family and her close friends knew. There'd be tears and shouting and then she'd just go away. Beyond my parents I never spoke to anyone about this but the fear and dread and worry for her built up inside me as a little boy and beyond. Mostly I felt shame.

There weren't any therapists at school in the mid-seventies. One time my mum told me, in tears, that the first time she'd gone in both my dad and her had insisted they didn't try electric shock therapy but they held her down all the same and shot electricity through her head and body to try and cure her. I knew then that the hospital wasn't like other hospitals – it wasn't a place where they cared for people.

So that undiscussed, painful knowledge sat inside me. I winced whenever she was in there and I heard the words at school. It was compounded by not knowing when she would be better or back at home or what was really going on. She didn't want us to visit when Sally and I were so young.

There's something deeply overpowering about fear; it stays with you and manifests as weakness or aggression. Ironically the sensitivity I felt about what was going on made me cockier, angrier and more provocative and confrontational, less sensitive to other people's feelings. I wasn't a tough kid but I wasn't too scared of other kids my own age, even bigger ones who challenged me. If someone wanted a fight I wouldn't run away, and anyway I had big, older mates I played football with. I became a chippy, mouthy kid, someone projecting a force field of noise that some saw as cheek and others aggression. Some of it was funny, some of it bravado, often it was insensitive and a lot of it was just a product of the anger I didn't really understand. I certainly felt a resentment that others didn't know about what was happening in my family, that they didn't have the same disruption, didn't have to see their mum in meltdown and be unable to help.

My mum was either ill or she wasn't, and when she wasn't she was great; it wasn't an ongoing day-by-day state of affairs. She was loving, funny, had friends, she looked after us well. And we loved her very much.

Having a prolific serial killer the Yorkshire Ripper in our midst didn't help anyone's state of mind. The Ripper had murdered one of his first victims on the playing fields I walked home across from playing table tennis at the Prince Philip Centre, and his last, Jacqueline Hill, was murdered behind our local shopping parade, the Arndale Centre, on the route my morning milk round took me on. During the weeks that followed the discovery of her body the three of us – the milkman, myself and my mate, the other teenage helper – were allowed up into the multistorey car park levels which overlooked the scene. We were there to deliver pints to offices but we stopped and peered down as detectives in moustaches and macs stomped around on an overgrown wasteland, separated from the path on Alma Road by a thin line of tape. Too little, too late.

My dad had walked down Wood Lane at the other end of the Arndale on the night of the attack, past the Kentucky Fried Chicken shop where the attacker had waited and watched. They both had black curly hair, a beard and a moustache, but unlike the suspect my dad didn't carry a ball-peen hammer or knives. The police arrived and interviewed him at our home half a mile away for a third time. He wasn't a strong suspect, just one of thousands of men interviewed and catalogued in a sprawling card system. Before that murder there had been another attempt, even nearer to our home. A doctor visiting the city from Singapore was attacked outside my girlfriend's family guest house in Chapel Lane where she was staying. Elizabeth's adult brother and father were both interviewed. Despite giving a description that matched the wanted man's photofit, the victim, Upadhya Bandara, wasn't a prostitute and hadn't been stabbed so she wasn't considered a Ripper victim. Such was the clunkiness of police thought. My mother and her friends knew though; they sensed the ever-present threat and endured the fear.

My mum stood in our living room in Escort Avenue, five minutes' walk from the attack, predicting he would kill in our immediate vicinity. She pointed to the plain-clothes cops who had begun to appear in our streets as proof he was moving his hunting ground from Harehills to Headingley. I watched my mum as her little finger juddered with nerves as she said this. She was petrified. The whole city was in a state of paranoid terror and tension. When he was caught not long after this last murder, my paper rounds took two hours as I read every word in every paper about the man.

Down the front

Any venue, 1980

When I was finally old enough to go to gigs, they gave me a sense of euphoria and escape from my feelings. I loved being down the front in the thrashing pit of bodies, plastic glasses flying around as a band erupted into another number, having a leather jacket banged into your face, being pulled up from the floor if you were knocked over. All while singing along to Stiff Little Fingers, the Stranglers, the Teardrop Explodes or whoever. It was hot, soaking wet with sweat, super loud, and absolutely exhilarating.

Getting to the gig, going in, feeling the buzz of excitement in the place, seeing the support act and finally the main band coming on to screams and shouts, uttering some brief words or perhaps none at all and going straight into the first song and the place going crazy. The whole thing was a ritual and it didn't matter if it was a huge venue like the Queens Hall or a tiny dive like Brannigan's, the routine was always the same. The same build-up of expectation, delight and satisfaction.

It took a while to get there though. By the time I was thirteen I really wanted to go to Leeds's premier punk rock venue the Fan Club, run by John Keenan. There were hand-drawn flyers for its amazing line-ups in every record shop I went into. Any time I heard someone on night-time Radio 1 they were already on those flyers. The problem was I'd only just hit my teens and still looked about nine. Case in point: when their first album came out I had a ticket to see U2 at the 400-capacity Warehouse but my dad wouldn't let me go as it said they went on at 10 p.m. and there were no late buses. My classmate Ashley put his dad's suit jacket on to look older and got in no problem. It was a gig – they didn't really care who came through the door. His dad simply drove down and collected him once it was over. I got to see U2 next time around at Tiffany's.

The first gig I went to with my mates was Skids at Leeds Poly in December 1980. I'd just turned fifteen and after that I was off – saving up, getting tickets and hunting down news of whoever was coming. There were so many venues: the uni and the poly had a pretty broad booking policy, the Warehouse had cool bands, there were various post-punk cellar bars, not to mention the Queens Hall I'd see the Jam and the Boomtown Rats. Even plastic palm tree nightclubs like Tiffany's and Cinderella's, taken over by Keenan for the night, put on great bands. I saw groups that ranged from the truly amazing (the Cramps) to the bloody 'offal' (King Kurt).

I'd get to see loads of bands at the Warehouse as I got older: Depeche Mode, the Fall, B-Movie and Neubauten, who had burning braziers either side of the stage and tried to drill the wall at the back of it until the owner rushed on to stop them. I saw Depeche Mode in a really small wine bar opposite the station. Their micro Casio pop debut 'Dreaming of Me' suited the clean lines of the place and instantly made them accessible to the John Peel crowd, the older mainstream chart lovers and *Smash Hits* kids. Peel was pretty much the seedbed for all the new bands from Sheffield, Liverpool, Manchester and beyond that eventually stormed the charts.

I didn't always have to pay to get into gigs. When the Stones played Roundhay Park in the summer of '82 it was a huge event and people went regardless of having tickets only to be confronted by a tall wooden fence. As I arrived I saw this fence open and two stewards walk into it carrying a police-style crash barrier. A total stranger and I clocked it, picked the nearest one up together without saying a word and just walked straight in after them and got away with it. I did exactly the same thing with a merchandise box when the Monochrome Set played Leeds Uni. These university places had security but they were largely just students. When the Pogues played the Riley Smith Hall at the uni it was a running battle between the audience climbing onstage and student security. After being in the thick of it for half a set I climbed a ceiling-high scaffold lighting rig and watched from up there.

The Ramones and the Cramps were the best bands I saw. Chuck Brown and the Soul Searchers performed for hours and were brilliant, as was Kid Creole. On their first big tour Wham! were so funny and cocky – they were singing the hits and sticking shuttlecocks down their shorts then whacking them out into the audience with badminton rackets.

After catching so many of the bands who'd gone from punk to mainstream I started to see smaller bands. Nick Toczek had his Natural Disasters nights which brought so many underground and hardcore bands to Leeds and Bradford. My mates and I met Henry Rollins backstage when Black Flag played at the Bierkellar and some no-brain big Mohawks were having a go at him because of the American nuclear weapons on British soil. 'It's not our fault,' drawled Henry, hanging like an orangutang from some football changing room style coat hangers. We met Dead Kennedys' singer Jello Biafra and support act Millions of Dead Cops in their dressing rooms at the poly after we'd talked ourselves in.

My mate Craig and I were so excited about the Monochrome Set playing at York University that we got tickets, took the train over and didn't really think about getting back. We were a few miles out of town, walking up a ramp onto the main road back when a lorry picked us up and dropped us back on the Leeds ring road close to home half an hour later. It's twenty-seven miles; without him we'd have got home at dawn.

King Kurt were the most insane band you could ever see, pouring snakebite through funnels into punters' mouths, shaving heads and encouraging people to bring in dead animals and offal to throw around. All the while chanting 'ooh walla wallah' to a tribal beat and encouraging the Gap Band's 'rowing dance' on a floor thick with goo.

At the Astoria in Roundhay on the night my own band, the Butter Cookies, supported James the gig ended with cars being turned over and a full-on brawl between the Leeds United Service Crew and the biker security. This gig has gone down in music/football hooligan folklore in the city. From the off, pint glasses were skidding towards us across the empty floor and I quickly changed all the lyrics to the songs to mention Leeds players. It was only when some of the tearaways recognised me from school that it let up and they started asking for Clash covers. While peace-loving vegetarian yoga-pop heroes and future stars James were onstage singing their fantastic 'Hymn from a Village' the assembled casuals – who loved the band – formed a flying V of windmilling fists and mowed through the largely student audience. I watched in shock from the safety of the back with the Wedding Present's Dave Gedge, and driving home in his van we still couldn't get over how bizarre and unnecessarily violent it had been. At James's next gig in Leeds at Cinderella's, a smaller venue, Tim Booth lulled the audience into sitting down by quietly cooing 'sit down, sit down' to them; I often wondered if that was the seed for the hit that they wrote years later.

I saw Public Image Ltd, the Folk Devils, the Newtown Neurotics, Gary Glitter, Sonic Youth, Julian Cope and so many more. This was my world and that's before you even got into local bands, or later the fanzine-level indie bands like the Membranes, Bogshed and Yeah

Yeah Noh. Walking home in soaking clothes with my ears buzzing was a great life but as ever I always wanted more. And I found that I could accelerate that dive into the world of music with a fanzine.

Career opportunities

Leeds, 1981

I am in the small, inconspicuous career room at Lawnswood School with my dad because I have to plan what I will do now I am almost at the end of my final compulsory year. I'm sixteen and so far in life I've dyed my hair, got an earring, had a pregnancy scare, been on some marches, scored some goals for the school football team, read George Orwell and been to loads of gigs. I haven't been very productive in lessons.

My parents' divorce has left me with the sort of anger with the world that's visible in *Quadrophenia*, which my friends and I watch endlessly on video at house parties, but less so in this year's big TV show *Brideshead Revisited*.

There's an assumption from my expected grades that I am unlikely to be staying on for A levels, so the choice in the summer of '82 is simple: go to FE college and resit O levels or go on the dole. I explain to the careers teacher and external careers adviser that I would like to be a music journalist. They look at me, then at each other, then the teacher looks down at my file and says: 'I see you haven't done music O level.'

'I don't need it,' I reply. From what I've observed walking past the music room this largely involves playing the steel drums and large recorders.

'And,' she continues, looking down at my grades, 'you will probably need to do English A level and then a journalism degree.'

'I don't think you need those,' I answer.

They look at each other, nonplussed, like I've just suggested I want to be one of the heart surgeons who have recently been breaking new scientific ground. I can feel my dad sort of simmering, and am acutely aware he feels the door of opportunity isn't even going to open for my generation.

I explain about the *NME*. How I read it every week and how it just seems to be written by people with an ability to explain which bands they like, and why. Which is pretty much what I do with my mates.

She continues, 'I have a friend, Peter Ball. He writes for the *Guardian*. He has a degree in journalism.'

'Yes but all you seem to have to do is know their music and be able to ask them about it and write.' I know what I'm talking about – a guy I met on a march, who I'll tell you about in a minute, has recently got a job on the *NME*.

The teacher looks at the external careers officer. 'Any suggestions?'

He looks at his papers and brings out a leaflet.

'Have you considered printing?'

This is about the stupidest fucking idea I've ever heard. The bloke is either an idiot or they have such a low opinion of me and my mates that they shouldn't really be giving us guidance. It's not as if there are actually any jobs anyway. Just Youth Opportunity Schemes which will shortly be replaced by Youth Training Schemes. The meeting ends and we get up and leave.

'What the fuck would I need to become a printer for to get on the *NME*?' I ask my dad.

He agrees. 'They go to school, go to university then go back to school to be a teacher. I guess they just have to lower people's expectations,' he says. 'You better make sure you get your O levels so you can stay on.'

I realise I'd better pull my finger out so I immediately ask my mate Kengi to finish my art sixteen-plus coursework for me. It's technically the first time I ever commission anything. He's good at art and I'm shit at finishing things, so it's an early realisation that asking other people to do things they are talented at makes sense. He effortlessly applies a wash to the background of a Lou Reed portrait and hands it in himself to the art teacher who likes him. It goes with my ink-dot copy of Robert Capa's famous Spanish Civil War photograph of the dying soldier and a coloured pencil copy of John Lydon of Public Image Ltd on the cover of *Smash Hits*. I'm excelling at copying other people's work or, as Damien Hirst calls it, photorealism.

Then I do two weeks' revising, fuelled by Seabrook's crisps, Lilt and Rowntree's Fruit Gums, sit the O level exams, and then expecting the worst, don't bother going to school to get the results when they are published. A friend rings from his house to tell me, in disbelief, that somehow I have managed to pass five O levels, a maths CSE and the sixteen-plus in art. Which means I don't have to leave school. Some of my mates I've been endlessly fucking about with have got Us and have to resit or leave. However, my real education is already occurring elsewhere.

Do you wanna buy a fanzine?

Menwith Hill air force base, 1981

It seems strange now in a world of hand-held digital immediacy and instant global connectivity to be writing about starting a printed fanzine in the early eighties.

When I started *Attack on Bzag!*, I had no concept that it would whirl me off into a career as a writer, editor, publisher and then CEO of a plc during the final golden years of print publishing which would have been seen as a total sell-out by my fellow editors and me back then.

I was a comprehensive schoolkid who felt resentful about the apparent calm my friends enjoyed in their own home lives compared to the emotional and mental turbulence in mine. When I discovered these punk-influenced magazines they were an entry point into something I knew I could do, which was telling people about new music I liked. I realised I could reach more people in print than the same old school-mates I tried and failed to encourage to come and see then-unknown local bands like the Sisters of Mercy or the Three Johns.

The only place I could meet like-minded music fans was at gigs or in record shops. So fanzines operated as a chain connecting the people listening to John Peel and keen to track down the bands he had in session, who you could only contact if they had put their address on the back sleeve of their independent, usually self-funded records.

The first fanzine I ever bought was *Knee Deep in Shit*, produced by the 1 in 12 Club, an anarchist music collective from Bradford. It was A4, stapled together, scrappily illustrated and laid out with headlines in the punk ransom demand style. The location where I came across it was typical of where I was spending my time – a succession of noisy, angry, fun day trips to far-flung places like London, Manchester and Greenham Common on coaches full of flags, leaflets, collection buckets covered in stickers, punks, anarcho-hippies, people in neon coats, girls in striped tights, tartan skirts and mohair jumpers, feminists knitting blankets, placards from the SWP, CND, IMG and MFI. I loved it. The ghetto blaster was full of Pigbag, Bow Wow Wow, Gang of Four, the Clash, theSpecials, the Drummers of Burundi, Killing Joke and Heaven 17's '(We Don't Need This) Fascist Groove Thang'. My camera was full of overexposed shots of rolls of barbed wire and policemen scowling.

The furthest we ever marched was the thirty-three miles from Bradford to Manchester on a trans-Pennine anti-war march, four days of walking through *Last of the Summer Wine* country, sleeping on the floor of Hebden Bridge Trades Club, seeing Crass play, and playing the first Clash album over and over again on a ghetto blaster. I'm not sure any wars were stopped as a result of this slog but it got me out of the house and it was something I believed in. My friends in this world were student age and I had no trouble mingling in with them to drink in pubs. It was great.

I bought my second fanzine, *Molotov Comics* – a collection of ranting poetry and Steadman-esque illustrations – from its editor, the local punk poet Seething Wells. The third and fourth, *Kill Your Pet Puppy* and *Panache,* came from a political bookshop and had the luxury of coloured pages and print.

One day I was mooching around an exhibition of music photography at a community centre near the university when I saw a poster for a weekend course explaining how to create your own magazine. The participants included one of the Mekons and Seething Wells. As I wrote my name down on a list of people interested in attending, two students waiting behind me noticed my name and said, 'Great name.'

This was the first ever 'Godfather of Soul' reference I heard; I didn't know what they were talking about, much to their amusement. I took an application form, half filled it in and stopped when I saw you had to pay to take part and then forgot about it. Then in the post one day there was a letter confirming my place on the course. My mum had found the leaflet I'd half filled in and posted it for me. I was so grateful.

I went down to the community centre with my mate Ben from YCND. He had a punk band called Toxic Waste and his band name was Sik O'War. He was infamous in the area for his unicorn hair spike which he fashioned by shaping his long fringed quiff into a point and putting varnish on to make it stick. He'd be a total pin-up now, what with the rise in unicorn stock, but back then people either admired or laughed at him.

We came back from the two-day event with a basic knowledge of Letraset, Rotring pens, and how to print a fanzine. We recruited two other mates, Little Andy and Sean, all pooled a fiver each and created our fanzine which we called *Attack on Bzag!* This was a parody of a Sven Hassel Second World War novel we came up with while hanging around on top of the school goalposts during the summer holidays.

If we'd written about what occupied our collective time it would have been a mixture of football in the park, TV, home brew, glue sniffing, political marches and Andy's role as an extra in Pink Floyd's film *The Wall* which they shot on a nearby vintage railway station. That would have made a far better fanzine than just local punk bands but we just followed the formula and stuck to the latter. I drew the front cover with a Rotring pen in the style of a *Victor* comic and we printed some Toxic War lyrics, interviewed a Mohawk-sporting anarchist singer we had met on a march, commented on the number of CCTV cameras going up in Leeds, interviewed Seething Wells and ran with the back-page headline from the Specials.

Attack on Bzag!

Harehills, 1983

*A*ttack on Bzag! issue 1 was really rough and flimsy. We printed it on a fairly basic Roneo Gestetner machine in someone's cluttered basement in Harehills, Leeds, where our YCND leaflets were produced. It was fascinating watching the printing templates being burnt from the art layouts which we'd strapped round a long thin drum. Then we'd attach the negative skin onto the print barrel and turn it round and round with the paper feeding automatically into the process. The drum wasn't automated and we turned the handle to print each page ourselves. Attention soon turned to the thinners which allowed you to correct anything on the negative skin, and more care was spent making sure we all got a sniff and didn't spill it than making sure we weren't soaking the pages in too much ink. As it was, the layouts were far too dark, and once printed on both sides it was quite hard to read, which was probably no great loss.

These printers have long since been confined to history but I recently came across one in the amazing Solidarity trade union museum in Gdansk where they'd been used illegally to print anti-government leaflets.

We collated the pages with one staple in the top left corner and went out and attempted to sell them. Jumbo Records in Leeds were very encouraging and, unbelievably, a guy called Dave Blackman, the ents secretary at Leeds Uni, came up to me one night and offered me a pass to get into any gigs I wanted to sell them at. I don't know where he ended up or what he does now but thanks, Dave.

It made a massive difference being able to just go and hang around the Riley Smith Hall and the student bar and the entrance to the refectory where most of the big bands you'd want to see like the Stranglers and the Banshees and the Cure came through. We sold all 200 copies of the first issue and I found I quite liked selling them.

We all made our money back and enough to print a second issue. For junior anarchists and communists we'd very quickly become adept capitalists, doubling the investment and making a 100 per cent profit. Andy and Sean dropped away from the editorial and after five issues Ben and I split up due to perfectly friendly musical differences. He created his own, much respected hardcore fanzine called *Raising Hell*, covering the local anarchist squat scene with bands like the Scum Dribblers and Chumbawamba and anything from anywhere that sounded like missiles going through your ears. He really knew his stuff and a compilation book of *Raising Hell* has just been published.

I started to write more about the Three Johns, the Redskins, Sid Presley Experience and Serious Drinking, bands I either came across locally or knew from the John Peel show. As the bands featured became bigger I found people were more receptive to giving me 20p to fuck off and stop bothering them or actually seemed amused by my hyper sales patter. I would set off for the day with my blue-grey canvas RAF school bag covered in hand-drawn logos of the most unheard-of bands I could find and liked: the Human League, the Monochrome Set and local act the Sisters of Mercy. If I sold anywhere between sixteen and thirty fanzines that was a good night and I'd go home with my combat trouser pockets bulging with small change.

The introduction of the 20p piece was welcomed warmly by the seams of my pockets which were as thin as Tory lies. As each issue came out, almost totally written by myself, I'd print and sell more and more copies. There were no specific publication dates or deadlines, no one to lay it out but me. You know the 'cut', 'copy' and 'paste' buttons on your laptops and phones? That's what I actually did. Cut, copy and pasted bits of paper and handwritten and drawn headlines and photos sent by bands.

Interviewing was even more basic. After the Undertones played Bradford, Damian O'Neill and Mickey Bradley came out of the hall to talk to fans and a bunch of us interviewed them with no recording equipment. Someone had a paper bag and I ripped it open and just scribbled down their answers and then they both drew each other and the members of the band.

When Rik Mayall and Ben Elton appeared at City Varieties they were happy to do an interview with me in the dressing room. At that moment, meeting the guy who played Kevin Turvey was as exciting as meeting any musician, and this was before he, Vyvyan et al. burst into the nation's living rooms as part of the first student punk sitcom, *The Young Ones*. I just wanted to find out what these guys were like behind the performance. I had my own performance of sorts. My sales pitch.

'Do you want to buy a fanzine? *Attack on Bzag!* is hot, fast, freaked and funky, there's loads of great bands – Serious Drinking, the Three Johns, the Newtown Neurotics, the Sisters of Mercy. It's the best fanzine in Leeds, the UK, the world, and only 20p. It will get you drunk, make you attractive – yes, even you . . . I can just keep going like this or you can just give me the money to fuck off and have a fanzine into the bargain . . .'

Before the bands came on at the Tartan Bar at Leeds Uni I'd be standing before little groups of seated students, waving one of my fanzines around, smiling, ranting and rapping at high speed, trying to convince them they should give me 20p for a pile of papers I'd written, designed, printed and collated myself. One side of the room there'd be fledgling student groups like Age of Chance and the Wedding Present, on the other there'd be students John and Simon from *Nag Nag Nag* fanzine in Darlington and their flatmate Keir Starmer who all dressed like Echo & the Bunnymen and the Smiths.

At the bar there would be members of other smaller Leeds bands like Jeremy Dyson from Flowers for Agatha who'd go on to write *The League of Gentlemen*, or Rodney and Paul from the Cassandra Complex, and the mulleted anarcho-hippies Chumbawamba or my mates from my own band the Butter Cookies, all standing around with drinks in plastic pint glasses talking up dreams and ambitions and what they thought of whoever we were there to see. We were all glued together by the new information we received from the *NME* and the new sounds we heard on John Peel and we were queuing up to see and be part of the future.

Scattered around the gig were slightly more established members of local bands who actually made headway into the media, bands like the Sisters of Mercy, the March Violets or the Three Johns, talking to each other. There'd be people from the 1 in 12 club in Bradford, staff members from Jumbo Records, DJs from the Phono club and, surprisingly, a young economics teacher from school who had never taught me called Mr Gary Lovelace. He had a car and we realised if I could get us on the guest list to see Serious Drinking and the Higsons he could feasibly drive us anywhere on a school night. This was all well and good until the night his mate and I found him absolutely trashed in the corner of the Rock City having seemingly drunk half of Nottingham's alcohol allowance. In the end his mate drove home and I found Gary somewhere in the school the next day attempting to teach without throwing up.

There'd be people I didn't know too but who would go on to do great things in the future, like David Peace who wrote *The Damned Utd* and *Red-Riding* books, who'd tell me years later they'd bought my fanzine from me in some old club or other in Wakefield or Harehills. And many future bands too. At every gig there'd be a mixture of people I'd seen for years at gigs at Adam & Eve's, the Bierkeller, Brannigan's, the uni, the Astoria, Cinderella Rockerfella's, the poly and the Warehouse checking out Sonic Youth, the Men They Couldn't Hang, the Icicle Works, the Pastels, the Membranes, the Nightingales – whoever was coming through. The older bands would meet and play pool in the Faversham, but for me it wasn't a scene; I'd just come to recognise familiar faces who'd indulge me and buy my fanzine. And sometimes they'd give me a demo tape or a flyer for a forthcoming gig and the wheels of who we were and what we were doing turned.

In among all this would be the students who would either be intrigued and amused by this lippy kid with a bag of fanzines or just dismissive. But that didn't put me off, it just seemed like a challenge. Whatever reason they came up with not to buy one I would fire back faster and even more persuasively, trying to make them laugh or interested, and usually one of them would be won over and they'd give me the money. It was half performance selling, half protection racket. Buy one and I go.

I'd have to deliver this sales patter about twenty times at least to sell ten but I'd talk to every single person there because as I saw it everyone was a potential reader. Some left the fanzine on the bench they'd been sitting on but most took them away and the next time I had another out they'd gladly take it. As I started to throw tiny hand grenades into and get mentioned by the London music media they'd say they'd enjoyed the last one or they'd heard John Peel mention it or seen it mentioned in *Sounds* or *NME*. Some would already have bought it from Jumbo Records in town.

Time between gigs, however, seemed to last forever and I took to the British and Dutch underground fanzine scene with gusto. Postal sales started to fly in. The holy grail of fanzine promotion was to get your fanzine reviewed in a music paper or mentioned on John Peel; the basic aim was just to get mentioned in other fanzines. Serial fanzine buyers would send you 20p sellotaped to a letter and a stamped, self-addressed envelope, often with the stamps covered in soap so the post office franking mark could be wiped off and the envelope used again.

Fanzine editors sending copies to each other would include piles of home-made flyers and little thumbprint-sized change-of-address stickers. These were a forerunner to what would come to be known in mainstream magazines as blow-in cards – that litter that falls out when you open a magazine, if you still do. There was a whole cottage industry of fanzine editors all over the country doing this, some of them like John Robb of *Blackpool Rox* and the Membranes and Alan McGee of *Communication Blur* and Biff Bang Pow! were in bands, some of them promoted gigs in their own towns. I knew the names of areas all over the country without ever having been in them: Harlow, Spalding, Peckham, Greenock.

The fanzines largely looked the same, with headlines made of Letraset that would be transferred onto the layouts with a pen. The difference between them lay in the personalities of the editors, the tone of voice, the quality of the interviews. There were so many it really was a spider web of independent publishing spread across the country. And the names, although largely lifted from song titles, were great: *Idiot Strength*, *Noise Annoys*, *Blackpool Rox*, *Alphabet Soup*, *Furious Apache*, *The Legend!*, *Cool Notes*, *Slow Dazzle*, *Beaten to the Punch*, *Pack of Lies*, *Raygun*, *Love & Molotov Cocktails*, *Alternatives to Reality*, *Vague*.

It was a colourful, bright, angry, determined, passionate community of largely solo voices promoting local scenes and national bands. Our world was a million miles away from the weekly music press, a genuine underground. Hours were spent on bedroom floors or kitchen tables pasting together A4 sheets, typing out features and answering letters from readers and bands hoping to appear in our fanzines.

I spent much of my time trying to get *Bzag!* mentioned on Peel or Kid Jensen or get a letter printed in *Sounds* or *NME*, desperate to bridge the gap between where I was and where I wanted to be. I was sitting in my bedrooms at both my parents' houses in Headingley and Kirkstall, slowly passing through the last years of secondary school.

I noticed *Sounds* sometimes printed specialist charts like Reggae or Metal or Badges at the back of their paper alongside the main charts and the Alternative chart (independent sales). I sent one in for fanzines and put *Bzag!* at the top. It was a joke as much as anything, a cheeky attempt to see if they'd go for it. I just assumed they'd see I'd put my own at the top and disregard it but they printed it. I couldn't believe it. Semi-outraged postcards appeared in my letterbox from other editors but I was so young I could just hold my hands up, laugh and shrug my shoulders and say 'What?' It was like chalking or spraying the names of your gang or mates on a wall. After that there was no stopping me.

I just figured I'd have a go at anything. I wrote to the *NME* suggesting they interview me for their weekly Portrait of the Artist as a Consumer, and amazingly a guy called Paul Du Noyer wrote back and said 'Yes! Go on, then.' My dad took a photo of me in my cycling top in front of piles of folded but unsold fanzines, and they printed that too.

After four issues, one of the original editors, Andy, signed up for a YTS print scheme, which was the dole but they taught you a skill, and asked me if they could print the fanzine rather than just the boring local government leaflets. It meant the issues would be printed by 'offset litho'. I didn't know what this was but it sounded and looked so much better. Suddenly I was getting four pages on one A3 sheet that I could fold and staple in the middle, rather than single sheets printed on both sides stapled at the corner with a wrap-around cover. This sounds like a trivial development but the leap in quality was reflected in sales. Up until then every issue I printed went up a hundred on the print run but now, with artist Jon Langford of the Three Johns doing the covers, I could almost double the print run every time and they were selling so much better in record shops.

Getting the huge A3 parcels of printed sheets was a real bind, though, as I didn't have any cash for a van or a car or anything and my dad wouldn't take me over to the other side of Leeds to the Whinmoor estate to collect them, so I would do double trips on three buses to the other side of the city in one afternoon. My arms were like chicken wings but I carried the large A3 print runs like stacked wood under my chin, the edge of the paper cutting into my skin. This was the nearest I came to doing any actual physical work but I didn't care as it was about the only thing I gave a toss about, my only reason to exist, and it was starting to give me an opportunity to travel to new places, meet new people and get 20p off them.

As the fanzine started to look better it got more attention. One time I wrote something for another fanzine about the state of music and John Peel read the article out and said, 'Phew, this boy can write.' I was jumping up and down in my bedroom, I couldn't believe it. I hadn't expected it and was fucking delighted.

I knew from my friends in bands that if Peel liked you he would champion you. In their case he would play their singles and give them highly desirable sessions which would help them sell records, get gigs and even record contracts; in my case it sold me fanzines by post, and also helped when I was out at gigs selling by hand.

It's hard to explain to young people now who have any music they want instantly, but Peel really was a lighthouse in the dark for non-mainstream music fans, and if his beam occasionally caught you it made a significant difference. One review of the fanzine meant I'd get ten to twenty envelopes over the next week or so wanting to buy them. That was £4! Almost the cost of an album or, more importantly later, two days' worth of dole money which translated into crisp sandwiches.

Peel used to play tracks by the American comedian Eric Bogosian, and Sik O'War and I would be walking round quoting his stuff to each other. His show was so diverse, ranging from reggae bands like

Burning Spear to weird Scottish poet Ivor Cutler to noise merchants Einstürzende Neubauten to indie country act Helen and the Horns. For the second half of my teens he was a daily lifeline to a world beyond the frustrations of life in Leeds. All I really wanted to do back then was meet John Peel and find out anything I could about Hunter S. Thompson, both of whom seemed to have the greatest jobs going.

One time the Three Johns invited me to go to London with them in their van to record a John Peel session at Maida Vale studios where I was amazed you could get as much hot food as you wanted for a nominal 80p.

I wrote this information up for the next issue as a sidebar to an interview with a difference. Ben and I had taped a Peel show, written out typical fanzine questions and then ran his totally unconnected mid-song patter as the answers. Ben produced a bad drawing of Peel and we gave it a double-page spread. I don't know if it was funny to read but it made us laugh putting it together. Once we'd sent it to the John Peel office at Radio 1 his producer, John Walters, read out the guide to how to get a cheap meal at the BBC in mock outrage on the show they did together on Saturday teatimes.

All this self-promotion made the fanzine really well known on the scene. I didn't think it was particularly better than the others or anything; I just didn't have anything else to do whereas the others often had jobs or were students. The editors became a network of friends across the country, united by a world of stapling, bad layouts, dodgy spelling and enthusiasm for the bands we loved. My favourites were Peter Hooton and his gang in Liverpool at *The End*, Chris Donald at *Viz*, Miki and Emma from *Alphabet Soup*, and Richard Edwards at *Cool Notes* in London. Richard was twenty-six, which seemed ancient. He was a breakdancing chef who worked in the City and ran two fanzines: *Cool Notes* which featured the same sort of left-wing bands I liked, and a northern soul fanzine called *Out on the Floor*.

In the summer of '85 Richard recruited our mate Steve Lamacq, from Harlow fanzine *Pack of Lies*, and me into running a fanzine stall with him at Brockwell Park near Brixton where the Damned, the Fall, Spear of Destiny and Strawberry Switchblade were playing. It was a lovely sunny day and Richard had assembled piles of all the best fanzines in the country. To make sure we got people to the stall he gave me a megaphone. Naturally we sold loads of copies because people were constantly coming over to see who the lippy bastards with volume were. At one point the police came over but instead of getting us to shut up Steve and I convinced them to buy some fanzines and someone got a shot of us with them.

Something else significant happened at that gig. Swells (aka Seething Wells) showed up at our stall and asked me if I'd been there all day, and could I review the bands that had been on up to that point as he was late and the *NME* would kill him if he didn't have anything. I couldn't believe it; of course I could do the reviews. Back at Richard's flat I wrote my debut *NME* review on his manual typewriter. I hadn't specifically been down the front watching the gig so it was very much a review from the fanzine stall, but a week later it was published, a 150-word review with my name on it. A few weeks later I was sent a cheque for £5, enough to buy an album, but I couldn't stop rereading the review. I started to feel like things were changing.

At this time I'm finding musical connections like water finds a way. I've secured a job working on the singles counter at HMV so I can buy more records, ignoring the new rules about the Gallup machines we are supposed to enter sales codes for hit singles from Bananarama and Elton John on, instead keying in the code for the Redskins' latest single. I've got my own band, the Butter Cookies. I'm reading the music papers, and late on Fridays I'm going to the Phonographique subterranean club in the (Avid) Merrion Centre and 'Dancing with

Myself' to Gen X, Iggy's 'Passenger', all sorts of danceable punk rock and sweet New York noise from DJs Steve Elvidge and Claire. One night I'm speed-skating alone in my black and grey mohair jumper and Steve ambles over and says, 'You really are an extrovert.' The beauty of not being with anyone I knew at all was I could behave exactly how I wanted without worrying what people thought.

At school still, the first true sign the sixth form is different is in general studies when Joe 90, aka Mr Smith, the head of the school – who in the past has apologetically whacked me across the hands with a ruler for dicking about in a science class – explains how we will learn about British parliamentary politics by him selecting his own classroom cabinet.

'The first person I appoint is James Brown.' The class and I are amazed. 'I would rather have him on the inside than causing trouble for us on the outside. It's better to have some people pissing out of the tent than into it.'

Not only is a teacher swearing but at this point I realise he has said something really profound and that to get into the *NME* I should start pissing into it through their letters page. I set about firing off regular missives saying they are all old and don't know what's really going on in the music scene around the country, making sure I sign it 'Attack on Bzag!'.

And then I respond to a job ad and get an actual interview for a staff writer's job at *Sounds*. I had applied by sending them some reviews I'd done for the local political listings mag, *Leeds Other Paper* (the Fall, Depeche Mode), along with the best piece of writing from my fanzine – about the Jam – and some of the letters I'd had printed. When a woman rang my home one day when I was late for school to offer me the interview I thought it was a girl from school taking the piss. But it turned out to be real.

'How will I get there?'

'We'll pay for your train ticket.'

I couldn't believe it: I was seventeen and on my way to the *Sounds* office in Covent Garden to meet the editor, Geoff Barton. No one else could either. This was the moment when I was running out to play a school football match and the PE teacher McCreadie said, 'I hear you've got a job interview, Brown. Who the hell is going to employ you?' The idea of anyone employing a kid who couldn't sit still and shut up, who thought he knew it all, who was funny – or rude and obnoxious, depending on your point of view – was naturally a wonder to all normal people. But they clearly hadn't read the music press.

Despite all the noise I'd made in the world of fanzines and the letters pages of the music papers, I wasn't actually sure whether I could do this or not; it was a real *Billy Liar* moment. For a start, where would I live?

For most of the interview I couldn't actually hear much of what the editor was saying because the music in the office was so loud. Behind him he had a photo of the band who dressed like cavemen, Manowar, with a huge shire horse. It seemed so different to what I had imagined. He introduced me to Garry Bushell who was the big writer then, and he chatted to two guys called Sandy and Dave who both had suede two-tone Chelsea boots, and then he took me down to meet the editor-in-chief, Alan, who when Geoff introduced me and asked if he'd like to meet me, said he was on his way out.

I wasn't that gutted when I didn't get the job, because it was a good experience.

Back home I just carried on with my fanzine, blew up some cake with bangers and broke the sixth-form common room record player while trying to do some scratching like Malcolm McLaren and the World's Famous Supreme Team, and was commended by the head of sixth form, Mr Frost, for my choice of music when I DJ'd at the Christmas disco. With no revision or work done I got some of the worst scores in the history of mock A levels there but came top in general studies which was largely what I was learning from just watching *World in Action*.

The week the results were in I was lying on the sixth form common room sofa when I instinctively scissor-kicked a ball that had been lobbed to me into the ceiling. There was a huge bang and I was covered by a gentle snowfall of powdered glass from the tube light. As I sat there, the room was in total silence with people gawping at me and the head of sixth form came over and just looked at me with a mixture of amusement and caring dismay. Upstairs in his office we had the last teacher–pupil conversation I ever had, and I have to say his part in it was absolutely amazing.

When he said he believed I was bright enough to still get decent A level grades and go to university if I focused I explained I didn't really want to go to university. I was already spending a lot of time at universities across Yorkshire, seeing bands and selling my fanzine, and I would only really want to go to university to meet girls and play football, and I could probably do that anyway without wasting more years on another educational opportunity.

He saw I was being serious and just gave me a totally inspiring talk: 'OK, well if you leave here, go out into the world because you could achieve anything – you can pick tea in India, go to America, become a rock star, whatever you want.' And lots more like that. It was, I guess, based a bit on his experience in the sixties but it was a great moment. He believed in me despite me having been a distraction for the previous eighteen months. It was time to go but he was letting me know that could be a good thing. And with that I was off. Happy because it didn't feel like I'd failed; it just felt like I was being freed to do what I wanted to do. I wanted to get ... Oh no, we're not at that bit yet.

I travel round, decadence and pleasure towns

Berlin, Belfast, Amsterdam, 1984

Leaving school meant I was able to actually go out on the road for more than a night and I knew a few bands who were happy for me to tag along.

Leeds band the Three Johns were brilliant company and a great band. They were big John Peel favourites, released a few albums and singles and made the front page of the *NME* the same week I was in Portrait of the Artist as a Consumer. They played loads of miners' strike benefits with the Redskins and Billy Bragg and they were very much in demand. Musically they sat somewhere between the Mekons, Beefheart and the Sisters of Mercy, and guitarist Jon Langford had been in two of those bands. Alcoholically they sat somewhere between Peter O'Toole, Dylan Thomas and Keith Moon.

Along with vocalist Hyatt and bassist Brenny they were so funny to be around, very kind and encouraging, and they and their girlfriends pretty much treated me like their own kid, feeding me, picking me up off the floor at the front of the gig when my rolling around dancing was worrying them. Langford's girlfriend and co-Mekon Sally Timms even invited me over to their house specifically to meet Pete Shelley of Buzzcocks whose songs I loved. He was dressed in a brown V-neck Pringle-style jumper, small-squared M&S shirt and had a big beard, which was weird but hey, if the great punk romantic lyricist wanted to dress like a vicar, go for it. Most of all, though, the Three Johns took me out on the road with them and their biker-gang driver Baguley and soundman Tom Mekon.

Every day we would sit in a misted-up minibus drinking strong cider and listening to Hank Williams, Cajun musicians the Balfa Brothers and cult comedian Ted Chippington. It was great. Imagine going from lessons to that. As well as obvious local destinations we went further afield to London and toured Scotland. Travelling very late from Aberdeen because we'd stopped at a pub with a mynah bird for a long liquid lunch, we pulled up in traffic at one point and I de-misted the window to see we were surrounded by people in brightly coloured quilted clothing and goggles. I looked at the Merrydown cider bottle and looked outside again. It was like a hallucination. Not seeing anyone for hours and then people dressed totally wrong. Baguley said we were at the bottom of a dry ski slope resort. I didn't even know anyone skied in the UK.

Real hallucinations were at play in Amsterdam when Langy, worse for wear on their local produce, either walked or was pushed into one of the canals. He appeared in our room in tears of laughter, totally soaking, and then Brenny decided to sleep in the wardrobe. We made our way on to Sneek to appear at a small local festival supporting the Fall and the Ramones which was actually hit by a typhoon mid-gig. Mark E. was roaming around in a full-length black leather coat thinking he was the Red Baron and the Ramones were so good that when we went back to Amsterdam to support them there I stayed on for the final week of their gigs while the Johns went home. These tours were some of the best days I'd ever had and on top of that I was able to sell my own fanzines and another, *Get Sexy*, which I produced specifically for the band.

Serious Drinking were a band I heard on Peel and really liked, whose lyrics were largely about drinking, football and Sunday afternoon TV to watch while hung-over. They were probably the nearest template to what *loaded* would later become in one band. Their songs like 'Countdown to Bilko', 'Bobby Moore Is Innocent' and their cover of Wire's '12XU' were a familiar and well-loved part of a great live set. While I was still at school they were kind enough to invite me along to a tour of Ireland, both north and south.

After spending a few years thinking I knew about Northern Ireland, to actually go there, have a squaddie point a gun in your face as you drive round a corner and to go up and down the Falls Road and through both Derry and Armagh, was an eye opener. Belfast felt like an occupied territory. There were army helicopters hovering in and out of high barbed-wire police fortresses, armed road blocks in the country lanes on the border. It was a long way from just reading about it or watching *Panorama*. I didn't think I gained any greater understanding of what was happening there but it was obviously far more real than experiencing it through the media.

One of the band's singers, Eugene, went off on foot to find some relatives he had near the Falls Road and when he got there they were very concerned that he'd just wandered over with his English accent and crew cut. The security levels were high but less so at Coleraine University. We arrived there and were unloading the van when someone held the door open for a guy walking out from the student bar with a till. Only to be followed by alarmed bar staff about three minutes later. The support was one of the local bands who would tape the new songs from the chart rundown each week and learn the best new songs. That week they revealed 'Blue Jean' by David Bowie. It was a far more profitable affair being able to play the hits than have too many of your own songs an audience wouldn't know.

Another culture shock came in the south where the boys at the gigs would come up to us and ask if we had any condoms as they were illegal there and hard to get hold of. The gigs were riotous and great fun and the band were quite happy to have a finale with everyone on the stage. Serious Drinking were naturally made for Ireland where the name alone was a top draw. At Trinity uni in Dublin locals weren't allowed so they just smashed a massive plate-glass window and walked in. Great attitude.

Going to Berlin to meet Serious Drinking at the end of 1985 was about the most exciting thing I'd ever done at that point. I had a bag of fanzines, my camera, old woollen jumper, black combats, a coat, scarf, spare pants and thick socks and *The Great Shark Hunt* by Hunter S. Thompson, which I was consuming rapidly, and that was about it. I was so engrossed with the book at Gatwick that I forgot to get any German marks and when I arrived in Berlin with nothing but an address of the venue they were playing that night I really thought I was fucked. Eventually I found a small-change kiosk in departures and got a cab to the venue. I was about three hours early and a young Irish band were setting up, My Bloody Valentine. They were totally unknown then but happy to chat to me and they told me that it was their room at the KOB squat that we were moving into.

The squat was a huge old building, with wide staircases and a bar beneath where bands played. The Drinkers were going to play there a few times and a few other venues across the city. There was a big squat scene and we travelled around in beat-up old military vans, often taking the wrong turn down streets that were blocked off by the Wall.

The people who lived at the KOB were really pleased to have us there and amused to learn that what limited German we knew came from enemy soldiers in *Victor* war comics. One day we were rushing out to a gig and one stopped and shouted, 'Mein Gott, the Britischers are escaping!' Humour, ja!

It was a fairly rough and ready area we were staying in and a one-legged prostitute and her mate would work the pavement opposite, somehow managing not to slip on the blankets of snow that would intermittently fall.

Berlin was everything you might want it to be then – dark, crazy, full of character and characters. The Wall and the barbed wire across the rivers under the bridges gave it a really claustrophobic air; it was unlike any other city I'd been to before or since. I lived off tequila slammers and kebabs, neither of which I'd had before, and to be honest I haven't had so many since. It was relentless. On New Year's Eve the sky lit up with ferocious bangers being dropped from the Kreuzberg tenement flats.

The band had a friend there called Trevor who bootlegged concerts for a living, had an American Forces radio show, and did a fanzine called *Me and My Vacuum Cleaner*. He had a huge scar down his face – not a duelling scar but from a bottling, I think. He had perfected the art of being deliberately obnoxious but he was a great guide to the city. He took us to the Risiko bar which had a kid my age in Eastern European army uniform doing the door and Blixa Bargeld of the Bad Seeds and Einstürzende Neubauten behind the tiny bar. We bumped into Nick Cave on the way into the pictures one night, but the highlight of the few weeks I spent in the city was going behind the Berlin Wall which we did by underground railway.

Officially you were supposed to exchange twenty West marks for twenty East marks which was a terrible exchange rate – you were essentially paying to go into the country – but Trevor knew a black-market currency dealer and we went in with what our money was really worth, which meant we were extremely rich but with little to spend it on.

We had tea in a beautiful empty tea room and then dinner of venison in a high-end restaurant, full of Russian generals who didn't look at all happy to see a long table of scruffy punks drinking the finest wines and having a good time.

The East Berlin train stations had honesty ticket machines and great mosaics on the walls. Getting in and out was a serious business, though, and it was really sad when a German punk who had managed to escape the East came with us to give himself up on the way in as he'd been missing his family so much.

Looking back I wish I'd moved there but I had no money and no idea of how I might make a living. My friends were still studying back at home, and I barely looked old enough to drink in bars, never mind work in one. But they were eventful trips and they taught me the benefits of heavy drinking in unusual locations and how rewarding it was just to go to different places and meet people there.

Not long after this, Martin from Serious Drinking sent me a letter saying he'd bumped into Billy Bragg who wanted me to appear on the *Oxford Road Show* he was co-presenting on BBC2 and to call him. I couldn't quite believe it – actually going on television was a massive deal. It was the screen the world sat down and stared in at, the medium that shaped our culture more than anything. The idea of being on it, actually on it, sitting there talking about my fanzine, live, seemed unreal. I was spending most of my time watching the new station, Channel 4: Karen Grant and her family in *Brookside*, and *Boys from the Blackstuff, Hill Street Blues*. The *Oxford Road Show* was a good Friday night live music and chat show which usually just had musicians on. It was what I thought would be a once in a lifetime opportunity so of course I would go on. I spent more time worrying about which T-shirt to wear than what I might say. I figured I'd just come out with the same stuff I said when I sold the fanzines or wrote into the *NME* letters page.

I went to the BBC studio in Manchester, saw Billy, met the other guest Claire Short, looked round at the audience and crew staring at us, the business of TV moving around us. There was a rolling sense of trepidation, wondering how this would change my life, what it would mean, wondering what to say. Billy just asked me about my fanzine and politics, and after a few minutes my bit was over. You'd want to say it was all very simple because we were essentially just chatting but I was very aware thousands of people would be watching. It felt very strange how instant it all was. Then the cast and crew went to a student bar where I was buttonholed by a member of Manchester band Easterhouse who spent an hour talking at me about politics. I was in a slight state of shock and just wanted to hang out with my friends John and Sue who had come with me. After that it was gone, a fleeting flash of fame and no real way of gauging it.

The next day I went to Liverpool to see the Farm, Ted Chippington and John Peel DJ'ing and recording the event for his show on the *Royal Iris*, a ferry boat that went up and down the Mersey. I had a Travis Bickle Mohawk and my black and grey mohair jumper and combats. I was surrounded by young casuals in tennis gear all giving me the eye, asking my friend Peter Hooton, who was dressed like Sherlock Holmes, and the band's manager Kevin Sampson, who the fuck I was. It was a memorable gig and I was largely just relieved not to have been chinned or thrown overboard as the audience were threatening to do to Ted Chippington.

New journalism

La Honda, California, 1984

On the dole in the pre-Internet, high-unemployment world I existed in I was so culturally sand-banked I was thinking of reading my Biggles books again when my dad gave me *The Electric Kool-Aid Acid Test* by Tom Wolfe and I felt like I'd walked out of darkness into a fairground. The pace and quality of the writing and the energy and frontier-breaking subject of the book was like nothing I'd encountered before. Wolfe's exploding prose just filled my mind with possibility and Ken Kesey and his Merry Pranksters seemed to have had the best time fucking around in their bus and constantly pushing themselves further. I really liked Neal Cassady, the guy who drove the bus and juggled lump hammers.

When I told my dad how much I'd enjoyed the book, he gave me *The Great Shark Hunt*, a thick paperback with a black and white portrait bordered in yellow of a guy in a fedora with a patterned bandana, mirror shades and a cigarette in his mouth. It was a collection of long travel, political and cultural journalism pieces from *Rolling Stone* and other titles by Hunter S. Thompson. It was inspirational. The writing was less layered and psychedelic than Tom Wolfe but the intensity of the opinion and the variety of journalistic experience was magnetic. I read one description of him rowing his way into some Central American harbour with a portable typewriter in his bag, checked the dates, realised he wasn't too much older than me when he'd been doing this, and I experienced that same euphoric release felt by frustrated music fans when they encounter the Pistols for the first time, and realised, 'I can do this too. I want to do this.'

I was into politics, music, I hitched around the country and I loved reading and writing. It further ramped up my belief that I could become a journalist without any further education qualifications. Next I found Thompson's *Hell's Angels*, about his year embedded with the Californian outlaw motorcycle gang where he described the bikers coming over a hill like 'a burst of dirty thunder'. That line stayed with me forever. We used it for an *NME* cover line a few years on.

Discovering that Wolfe and Thompson crossed paths in these two books really excited me. I realised then these weren't just one-offs, they were a product of the culture they documented and added to. Writing about outlaws and corrupt politicians and graffiti artists and drag racers and men who juggled hammers and ran on speed and words and wheels and choppers and adrenaline. These two writers pulled me out of my malaise and changed my life. I told my friend Sally Timms my writing was going to be like Hunter S. Thompson and she just laughed. I was an eighteen-year-old kid with a curly quiff, shorts, no money and a bag of fanzines but I knew I'd made a connection that would help me get nearer to where and what I wanted to be.

My dad bought me *The New Journalism*, an anthology of writers working around the same principles that journalism can have the flair and properties of a novel to tell a story so long as the reporting is true. George Plimpton, Hunter S. Thompson and Tom Wolfe were all in there with many more. Plus an essay about the New Journalism genre. I'd never read anything like this, apart from *Down and Out in Paris and London*. And what also struck me was the diversity of subject matter. The idea that the form came before the subject, the reporting so vivid the writers could assume the roles of the subjects or retell the stories as if they'd been there themselves.

Thompson in particular seemed to break out of the story and fill it with his personal circumstances right down to the relationship he had with his motorbike, his typewriter, the music he listened to. I was enthralled by his poetic description of the pounding of keys on paper. His voice was as important to the story, how he filtered and explained it, as the actual events taking place. He became the story and it was a method that worked well for him. In the same way that Wolfe's writing exaggerated the possibility, hope and revolutionary self-belief of the youth of the late sixties, so Thompson grotesquely enlarged the features of the politicians and cops and Middle Americans he was encountering. In *Acid Test* Wolfe described the collective use and belief in LSD while Thompson drove us through *Fear and Loathing* with LSD as our windscreen.

These books were where I educated myself instead of going to university. What I could never have imagined was that ten years after discovering him, Hunter S. Thompson would be ringing the *loaded* office screaming with crazed delight at the mag. Or that I'd spend time in a classroom turned dressing room for a literary festival in Wales chatting with Wolfe, or that I'd actually have dinner with George Plimpton in the same room as Norman Mailer and he'd agree to write about playing football with Pelé for my early 2000s magazine *Jack*. I'd found something that complemented but also took me further than music, something that gave shape to my ambition, that created a template to channel that excitement I felt for music.

Everything counts

Hulme, Manchester, 1985

When I wasn't heading off somewhere to sell my fanzines the days dragged by. I really didn't like having to go down to the social security building behind the Marquis of Granby pub to get a hand-out from a government I hated, but it wasn't an option not to.

There weren't any jobs at all – I knew two people from school with them – and my parents didn't really have any money to support me. My dad, who I was living with in Kirkstall, wanted me on my way into the world.

Joining the lines of disgruntled, downbeat people with their own folded dole card, number and dedicated time to sign on was depressing; you could feel the fog of misery in there. I felt a sense of isolation, wondering: how do I get out of this? I felt inspired and euphoric down the front of Redskins gigs but back home, if there was no gig to go to, it just felt deadly dull and bleak.

It was a time when resentments and frustrations just layered up. My friends were still at school with subsidised lunches. When Mr Frost had told me to go to India to pick tea or become a rock star it was a brilliant, caring speech but I didn't even have enough cash to go to Elland Road, never mind the Himalayas. It's just impossible to explain this to the Internet generation, where so long as you can find Wi-Fi and a screen you can entertain or educate yourself in anything. The lack of a path forward was so stifling that in a way the dole was actually an acute inspiration because I was desperate to get away from it. Finally I got a call that changed things.

I was in my fanzine-cluttered bedroom in Kirkstall when my dad shouted, 'Romford Ron is on the phone.' Ronnie edited *Everything Counts* fanzine and freelanced for *Sounds*. Obviously he lived in Romford, but it was unusual to get a call from him as the fanzine network would communicate through letters. He had good news and I needed it.

'Tony Stewart, the ex-*NME* deputy editor, is the new editor of *Sounds*. He wants you to write for us.'

I'd written to him at the *NME* a few months before, insisting they should hire me to cover the new generation of bands coming through, but hadn't heard back. Now I was leaping around in excitement. I was more experienced now than when *Sounds* had interviewed me two years before when I was seventeen. Since then I'd had two reviews in the *NME* – including one of my own band that I was shocked they'd printed as I'd only sent it in on spec for a laugh – and various cheeky, insulting letters published and I'd been writing for the *Leeds Other Paper* and independent monthly music mags *Jamming!* and *ZigZag*. As far as I was concerned I knew what was right and wrong with the weekly music papers and I was ready to go.

I hitched down to London and met Tony in a massive open-plan office in Mornington Crescent, Camden. The first thing he did was pull out my letter: 'I kept this, it's great, I knew I was taking over at *Sounds*, that's why I didn't reply from *NME*. You'll get more chance here if you fancy it. How about writing some features?'

I was delighted and went straight off to Newcastle to interview Chris Donald of the hilarious *Viz Comic* which I'd been selling for him with *Bzag! Viz* was really making a name for itself and there was nothing else like it. After the interview Chris got his Subbuteo out, *Attack on Bzag!/Sounds* beat *Viz* decisively.

Tony ran my interview as a full page the following week and I couldn't believe how fast the turnaround was. I just stared at the feature for what seemed like hours. I really couldn't get over how

I could type something so long one week and it was in print the next, and then a cheque for £54 showed up at the end of the month. I hadn't had to lay it out or take it to the printer's, or collate and staple it and sell it.

Much as I loved being a fanzine editor, the turnaround speed had a real impact on me. Plus Tony had just given me an open brief to write about what I wanted. There seemed so little in Leeds at this point beyond the Johns, the Wedding Present and Age of Chance, who I was friendly with, so I decided to move to Manchester as there was an Irish girl I'd met at a gig and a bigger music scene there. Every Thursday I was heading over to see Diane and her mate Eileen at the band Big Flame's Wilde Club in Manchester. I'd have the last coach of the night to myself, the windows cold and wet to the touch, and nothing but the driver's dashboard to illuminate the journey across the dark Pennine hills with New Order's *Low Life* album on my Walkman. The songs called out to me with their utter brilliance.

I said goodbye to my mum and promised I'd send postcards from wherever I went, then packed my Dead Kennedys and James Brown 'Sex Machine' T-shirts, my dead man's leather jacket, Converse pumps and my records. My dad drove me over in his camper van to Alan from Big Flame's new house where I'd been offered a room, bought me a box of groceries from the Co-op for £12, and that was it. 'Good luck,' and he was off and I chucked my stuff on my bed and went straight off to William Kent Crescent in Hulme to meet Diane and get down to the Wilde Club. It was a great little night in a West Indian club beneath a flyover, where they were putting on great new live bands like That Petrol Emotion and the June Brides. On the decks *Debris* fanzine editor Dave Haslam and Big Flame members were playing Trouble Funk, Mantronix and Chuck Brown and the Soul Searchers instead of the Velvets, Killing Joke and Bauhaus that had been playing at the Phono in Leeds. It was different and opened my ears to a lot of music I hadn't heard before. At that point the only soul single I had was Womack & Womack's 'Love Wars'.

I spent a lot of time at Diane's in William Kent Crescent, on the infamous rundown brutalist estate in Hulme. Many of the flats were inhabited but boarded up and covered in graffiti, and the corridors and stairwells were full of needles, rubbish and stank of piss. The lifts, with little alcoves at knee height for coffins, were the only sanctuary from packs of wild dogs that roamed the estate; they'd jump up barking and growling in your face, which was utterly terrifying.

Manchester local bands were a step above the ones I'd seen in the pub scene in Leeds. Perhaps inspired by the success of Buzzcocks, the Smiths, the Fall and Factory acts, they had singles out, music press interviews, Peel sessions: Big Flame; the Inca Babies; the Weeds, whose frontman Andrew Berry cut New Order's and the Smiths' hair; the Bodines; World of Twist; Big Ed & His Rocking Rattlesnakes; Marc Riley and the Creepers; the Membranes – they all had their own distinctive style. There were many memorable gigs too: Big Audio Dynamite at the Haçienda, and the Primitives startlingly good at the International.

'What's the singer called?' I asked the merchandising man over the noise.

'Tracy.'

'What?'

'Tracy, Tracy!' he shouted.

In my review I mistook the repetition for her stage name and from then on she became known as Tracy Tracy in the music press.

I was never short of subject matter. At the Boardwalk, Slovenian noise merchants Laibach were supported by a woodsman in lederhosen chopping up a tree trunk. At the same venue the young Primal Scream delivered their West Coast, sixties-style pop in leather trousers and bowl cuts, with waves of attitude. I went backstage to see Bobby, who I'd met with the Mary Chain at his club Splash One in Glasgow, and he was sitting there signing a girl's tits in marker pen. This didn't happen with indie types like Yeah Yeah Noh. I liked the way he didn't give a fuck. People were really noticing the Scream's single 'Velocity Girl' about Edie Sedgwick. There were other bands taking note of this change of direction too – the Stone Roses were at that gig. They were like a Killing Joke-looking post punk band at the time. You'd see them and their mate Cressa taking the stage down at the International venue, which their manager owned. They'd had one big interview in *Sounds*, name-checking the Alarm as a band they liked, but they were probably more famous for their city-centre-wide graffiti campaign than their music. They'd sent me a demo but it didn't stand out and no one could envision what they'd become.

Anyway Manchester in 1985 wasn't a city where you had to travel far to find a genius or two. After five-a-side in Sale with Marc Riley he introduced me to his neighbours and former colleagues in the Fall, Craig Scanlon and Steve Hanley. They in turn introduced me to Mark Smith across my recording Walkman after a gig at the International. This Victorian street gang leader had the brain and tongue to dismiss fools and attract disciples. I liked Mark's music press interviews, singles and Peel sessions and I was fascinated by both him and the band, especially his screeching, mewling yelps and lyrics. Mark's charisma, bristling stage presence and fondness for less than obvious lyrical subjects meant there was so much you could write about him. Which I proceeded to do from close quarters for the next nine years.

The Fall had just delivered a total brooding masterpiece in *This Nation's Saving Grace*, but they weren't without humour. Craig told me he'd written what he thought was a great guitar part only for Mark to start shouting, 'Have you seen my new house?' over the top of it. He shook his head like he couldn't win. You could go wandering in the music of the Fall for days, the way Mark filtered lines from life, literature and history, and spun them back out into his own intriguing stories delivered with a driven beat or tense, isolated yelp, and here he was walking the streets of Manchester, boasting about his property.

The Fall and New Order and Tony Wilson and Factory Records gave the Manchester music scene a deserved self-confidence. Weirdly, the place you'd see Tony Wilson most wasn't the Haçienda but on TV at teatime co-hosting the local news with former *It's a Knockout* man Stuart Hall, who'd be covered in gold chains. They'd both be sitting there reporting a zebra crossing hit-and-run in Urmston, cockily implying something better awaited them later that night.

Apart from the pissing rain and the miserable bus drivers, Manchester appealed to me. I liked being surrounded by places I knew nothing about. My world had just got bigger and wetter. One day in Factory Records in leafy Didsbury I am interviewing Tony Wilson for *Sounds*. He is charming and inspiring, trashing the dreary offerings of everyday life, quoting Sid Vicious and Richard Branson, and introducing me to his Factory partners Alan Erasmus and Martin Hannett who looks like the scruffy, long-haired one from the Giles cartoons: 'This is James, he's the future of music journalism.' Which made me laugh.

The highlight of my eighteen months in Manchester was the Festival of the Tenth Summer, a Factory-produced celebration of the anniversary of punk. New Order, the Smiths, the Fall, Pete Shelley and OMD all played at the newly opened G-Mex centre. The Fall and the Smiths were both in great form between their best albums to date, Pete Shelley played his fine 'Homosapien' and 'Telephone Operator' electro pop, and New Order came on to 'Elegia' and closed with Ian McCulloch singing 'Ceremony' with them. Backstage was eye-opening decadence. I was sitting near Paul Morley and Adrian Thrills from the *NME*, when another writer Bruce Dessau got into a row with Bill Grundy, the TV host whose show the Pistols had sworn on, drinks were thrown and Grundy chased Bruce around a table with his walking stick. I chatted with Peter Shelley who remembered me from Sally Timms's kitchen, but when I asked him if he might get up onstage with Steve Diggle and Howard Devoto, who were both there, he just laughed and said, 'Fuck off!'

Sounds ran my review over a whole page. Mick Mercer, who had been mine and Romford Ron's editor at *ZigZag*, saw our names all over the place and predicted we were about to take over. Despite making great headway writing for *Sounds* I was still essentially a fanzine editor and the whole scene were getting more and more attention. It had developed so much momentum that in September 1985, as I turned twenty, the *NME* sent Swells to Leeds to interview me about it and commissioned Jon Langford to do a cover illustration of me. The opening line: 'James Brown is gangly, thoroughly obnoxious and rude.' The last line: '*Attack on Bzag!* has revolutionised the fanzine. James Brown is a self-opinionated, ignorant, semi-literate genius.'

What's your ego supposed to do with that?

In the end they ripped up a copy of *Bzag!* and created a montage with it for the cover image. 'FANZINE FEVER! *NME* sweats it out' read the cover line, mock fear, but we definitely were creating and documenting an underground that wasn't covered as extensively in the big weeklies. Their lack of coverage of it infuriated me. Each week I'd buy the *NME*, quickly scan to the writers who covered bands I liked like Neil Taylor, and then give up in exasperation at how little else there was in there I wanted to read. It was a paper I felt a real attachment to but it was seemingly losing its way. The fanzine was a real alternative press, consisting of hundreds of small-circulation publications. I was selling 3,000 copies an issue and there were many others doing likewise and a healthy community to read it and write about.

There was a network of promoters, record shops and fanzine editors all feeding the new bands into each other. Alan McGee had gone from putting flexi discs of the Pastels on the cover of *Communication Blur* to starting a record label, Creation, and running and promoting gigs under the name the Living Room.

In Hull, 'Swift Nick' Taylor was producing *New Youth* fanzine and running the Unity Club, a great venue that championed the fledgling Housemartins and promoted the left-wing miners' strike-supporting bands like the Neurotics, Johns and Redskins.

In Plymouth, record shop owner Jeff Barrett – who would go on to run Heavenly records – was promoting a bands' nightclub at Ziggy's. From Chris at *Slow Dazzle* in Greenock to Jeff in Devon, this was a nationwide scene. If you visited Nottingham for a gig you'd pop into Selectadisc Records; in York you went to Red Rhino; and you had Rough Trade, obviously, in London. All these places would sell our fanzines, and all the same bands were touring through the independently promoted clubs. On the radio, Lancashire had Steve Barker's *On the Wire* and Liverpool had Roger Hill, both championing new and interesting music.

Most cities had some semblance of this. And even though editors like The Legend!, John Robb and I would start to write for the music papers, the indie print momentum kept rolling, so that in January '87 Simon Reynolds dedicated a double-page spread to it in the *Melody Maker*. A dry but perceptive analyst of modern music, Reynolds wrote: 'When fanzines get good is when they abandon the pretext of providing information on new bands and get into ego-maniacal self-celebration. And what I'd compare the best fanzines to is rap – in both cases what you've got is a sort of theatrical megalomania and also a buzz . . . The rambling, aggressive self-regard of Bzag, Tom 'Vague', 'The Rox' . . . The cartoon pseudonyms echo the grand stage names of hip-hop and soul – James Brown, I ask you!'

Only it wasn't a stage name, it was real. And like the rest of the editors we were truly passionate about what we were all doing. It wasn't a hobby, it was a cause. It was an accurate and insightful article: 'Punk had endowed fanzine culture with a vague left-wing aura. But ... fanzine self-aggrandisement, lust for fame and schemes for world domination are not really socialist energies. The idea of DIY is actually uncomfortably close to the ideas of initiative and enterprise and self-help.'

All of this was spot on. When I joined the *NME* later that year I suggested to Alan Lewis we should hire Reynolds from the *Melody Maker* so his intellectualism would sit in stark contrast to but complement my own speed-writing. Alan ignored the suggestion, which was probably just as well because if he had they wouldn't have had the space for Stuart Maconie and the other future writing greats.

My fanzine was profitable every issue and allowed me to print more of the next. I hated Norman Tebbit but, like the rest of the community of independent creatives I knew, I was essentially getting on my bike. Not that he was right. We helped ourselves because there were literally no other opportunities. The aggression came from essentially being a child of Thatcher and Scargill. This was not a time for 'I ask you!' Or being vaguely left wing. It was a full-on left-wing response to economic hardship. The fanzine scene was essentially a cross-promoting and content-sharing front.

It was this fire that made it so easy for all of us to burn quickly through the mainstream once we'd been invited in. It was this fire that resulted in Oasis, Knebworth, *loaded*, XFM. But that was all a long, long way off.

I managed one more issue of *Attack on Bzag!* – the tenth, a collaboration with original influence Seething Wells, a glossy-covered combination of *Bzag!* and *Molotov Comics* designed by Mick Peek who would go on to do Man City's current badge. Swells was by now firmly established at *NME* and Mick and I and Marcus Georgiou, a writer from Bradford, did most of the zine. I put *National Lampoon's Animal House* star John Belushi on the cover after reading about his self-sabotaged, drug-crazed life and death as told by Bob Woodward in the biography *Wired*. I loved *The Blues Brothers* and *Animal House*. Most significantly, the last few issues of *Bzag!* featured pieces on Belushi, Hunter S. Thompson, drinking in Berlin and an appreciation of *Brookside*, a prototype of the *loaded* features mix to come eight years later.

Swells's most significant contribution was to literally rip the Shop Assistants out of my Japanese boombox, throw the tape across the room and shout, 'Listen to this!' It was a Def Jam/CBS promo tape of Beastie Boys yelling in high-pitched squeals over echoing bass and booming beats. My musical life changed right there and then.

Swells didn't want to write about them in our joint fanzine, though, not when he could be paid for it by the *NME*. By joining the music press we were abandoning the independent culture to promote the independent culture. You can only live on plates of peas for so long. I wanted excitement, and the excitement was no longer just being at the front of the stage slamming into someone else's sweat-soaked T-shirt, it was actually in getting published and paid too. Reaching loads of people and not just the fanzine buyers. I was changing from a fanzine writer to a music journalist and London was calling to the faraway towns. I was getting a lot of work and had met someone else I wanted to hang out with.

As I prepared to leave *Bzag!* and Manchester, designer Mick pulled me aside and said, 'Have you heard about this new band? I think they're signing to Factory, they wear all khaki and Perry Boys gear and I've heard they'll walk from one side of Manchester to the other just to get to a party where there's drugs. They're called Happy Mondays.'

East End boys

Mile End, London, 1986

After initially staying on and off with Serious Drinking in London at their place in Whitechapel, I brought my stuff down from Manchester and moved into an old four-storey, red-brick council block just down the Mile End Road from Whitechapel in Bow with an Evertonian from Blackpool called Tony. We made a bed for me out of two pallets we found on some waste ground by the flat and a new single mattress, and put it in a tiny room with a sideboard and Tony's tool kit in it.

The flat was unusual in that the bath was in the kitchen; it had a lid you'd lift up for a bath or pull down to keep pans on. You didn't want to wander in near-naked for a hot soak when there was sizzling bacon fat flying around. Tony had a mate called Paul who'd pop round and couldn't stand still. He'd bounce up to the door and ask us if we fancied going to the pub. Paul Whitehouse was a plasterer, 'up to his neck in it', *bosh bosh bosh*, earning *loadsamoney*. A couple of years later he'd turn this part of his life into a break-through character for Harry Enfield on *Saturday Live* and then in the nineties create and appear in *The Fast Show*. Nowadays he's much loved on TV for taking Bob Mortimer fishing.

Apart from enjoying the East End, by far the most important thing going on for me at this time was Tony Stewart teaching me how to write an actual feature rather than just a review that came across like a cavalry charge against mediocrity. I'd be going into the *Sounds* office by tube every day listening to 'Paninaro' by Pet Shop Boys and Cameo's 'Word Up' on my Walkman. When Age of Chance blew up with their hip-hop and the Test Department-inspired version of Prince's 'Kiss' started hurtling into the charts, Tony decided to put my interview with them on the cover. The only problem was, it was written in the ranting gibberish I was frequently submitting – sentences that didn't mean much but I thought sounded good. He called me over to his desk, rolled a fresh piece of paper into his typewriter and started rewriting the whole thing to weed out the incomprehensible stuff and expand on the salient points. I stood there for about fifty minutes as we went through it line by line. I wasn't exactly over the moon but I appreciated that at the end of it I was going to have my first cover story. It just didn't read like my fanzine writing.

So as not to lose the fanzine style completely I convinced Tony to print a bright-red underlay of Trouble Funk's 'Good to Go' sleeve beneath the singles reviews column. Once in newsprint you could hardly read it so he didn't take any more suggestions on layout from me after that. Likewise no one could get their head round it when I suggested they use 'This Is Shit' as the headline for a five-star review of a Three Johns album. I just figured it would attract attention. Weirdly, when I started doing things like that eight years later at *loaded*, people said it was genius and actually gave me awards for it.

As 1986 came to an end I had another distraction on the go: I was going to be in Mark E. Smith's play *Hey! Luciani* with performance artists Leigh Bowery and Lana Pellay, ballet star Michael Clark and the Fall themselves. I'd got to know Mark and his wife and musical collaborator Brix more after I'd interviewed and stayed with them one time at their semi-detached house in Prestwich. Brix had made the three of us American spare ribs and Mark had just served us speed. Mark spent the interview turning his little Dictaphone on and off, recording bits of our conversation and playing pre-recorded snippets from TV shows. On his wall he had a map of the world with a couple of Man

City Panini stickers on it. It was a normal semi-detached house, with a gunmetal grey German car in the drive, just like the houses I used to deliver papers to, only this one had Claus Castenskiold paintings on the wall.

I liked hanging out with Mark. He was funny, smart, spiky, but far less aggressive than he came across in interviews. He had a great laugh and he liked you making him laugh. He was interested in what happened in your life, how your family were. He'd always ask me how my mum was, knowing that sometimes she wasn't well.

Interviewing him about the play at his manager's house in St John's Wood, London, I just asked if I could be in it for a laugh. To my amazement he said yes. *Hey! Luciani* was based on the David Yallop book, *In God's Name*, in which he argued that Pope John Paul I had been murdered for his stance on Vatican corruption. Mark gave me the part of a Vatican Radio announcer and after just a few rehearsals we spent a month performing it every night down at the Riverside Studios in Hammersmith, where *TFI Friday* was later filmed and I would also see a preview screening of *Trainspotting*. I didn't have to do much, just sit behind a desk with a microphone on and either make announcements in English or mime Latin. Side stage, Mark gave me the megaphone he used at gigs, showed me the buttons to press to let out loud, electronic squeals and told me to use it to disrupt whoever was onstage.

He liked plotting a route of creative chaos and had soon tired of some of the real actors in the play wanting direction and structure. Michael Clark was a shooting star, bristling and confident, but also soft and interesting. I really liked him. He was the brilliantly talented *enfant terrible* of British ballet, and had make a huge splash by mixing top-quality dance routines to the Fall's music, with his troupe's arses hanging out of their tights. With Michael you could talk ballet, punk or football. Not many people could do that (not that I knew my tutus from two-twos). Performers Lana Pellay and Leigh Bowery were totally unpredictable, which appealed to Mark. He was happy for Leigh to do what he wanted and would encourage him to just run across the stage whenever he fancied it. Behind the scenes, out of his extravagant costumes, Leigh was just a calm, friendly Australian.

What the fuck is going on?

At the end of January '87 I made Pop Will Eat Itself single of the week, raved about Arthur Baker's Freeez track 'IOU', Mantronix and the Smiths. On a good week on the singles like this you'd get a great array of music to write about. It really was sheer luck. The week I had made Age of Chance's 'Kiss' single of the week, Dexys Midnight Runners released 'Because of You', a theme from a TV comedy I'd never seen. It was a beautiful song. Having to write about whatever was in front of me was opening my mind to the idea of being able to write about anything rather than just whatever I was into, which had been the way at the fanzine.

It didn't smooth my more impatient and dissatisfied edges though. Full-page interviews with the Fine Young Cannibals and the Bodines, whose records I liked, were just transcripts of rows accusing the FYC of being yuppies and the Bodines of having nothing to say. Fuck knows what they must have thought: Me: 'I'm only doing this interview because the editor asked me to.' Fine Young Cannibals: 'We're only doing it because our press officer, Eugene, said he'd get us Prince tickets.' Stalemate.

Chumbawamba, Marc Riley and the Wedding Present all got better treatment, and then Tony came up to me one day and asked me if I'd like to go to Holland with Pop Will Eat Itself for a cover story. Of course I did; I'd been championing them since I'd first met them tumbling out of the back of a van at a tiny festival in Halifax Piece Hall three months before. My mate Mike Stout, who did the publishing for indie bands, had seen them supporting Primal Scream and told me, 'You've got to see this band. They've long hair, but wear Breton shirts and sound like Buzzcocks, they're really good.' That night in Halifax they told me they didn't care where they got to career-wise – if someone was going to give them seventy quid and a load of beer to play they'd be there. Their songs were really well written, fast and poppy, and had unique comic titles. Now, a few singles later, proper music biz people were starting to notice them.

I was driven over to Holland by the band's press officer, Dave Harper, who did the press for Factory and the Primitives too and had previously been Morrissey's driver. I really enjoyed his company. I'd been abroad in the back of other bands' vans but always at my own limited expense. This time I was a guest. Harper's vintage Saab had just enough room in the boot for two crates of Grolsch which he bought with delight at local prices. He spent more time sorting that out than putting petrol in so we spent most of the time running on fumes.

The trip reminded me of the school football tour I'd gone on when I was thirteen playing against kids in Holland and Belgium – a lot of drinking, inappropriate behaviour and tremendous fun. The band didn't give a fuck about having a journalist along or what I was going to write about them. Like me, they were just amazed they were being paid to be out of the country. It was totally stupid high jinks and I had the time of my life.

In the tiny Fresian town of Sneek we were staying in a modest fifteen-room gaff with no staff, and the band went down so well at the gig that lead singer Clint announced there was a party at the hotel. The whole audience came back – about sixty people. At one point we were throwing potted plants down the stairs at each other, until a chef with a massive knife appeared and made everyone leave.

In Amsterdam it got even worse, or better depending on how you feel about young men behaving like big kids. Clint's opening line at the Paradiso, delivered with a massive friendly grin, was, 'Yo, Holland, you fucking stink!' A huge cheer of amusement went up, and as the band dived into their pacy love songs the Dutch just hit them with a barrage of half-filled plastic beer glasses. They could get away with this audacity because their music was really good. It was infectious, and having two singers helped keep the energy bouncing off the stage. There hadn't really been a band like this – a hybrid of the Ramones, Buzzcocks and AC/DC drawn by a comic-book artist. We ended the tour in a small Amsterdam club and the last sober thing I saw was the other band members lifting the smallest Poppie, up by his thighs so he could snort a line off the top of a high, black-tiled toilet divider. The climax was dancing to a megamix of the Cult's Rick Rubin-produced 'Wild Flower', Age of Chance's 'Kiss', Ciccone Youth's 'Into the Groovey', Madonna's 'Into the Groove' and, of course, the Beasties. It all felt like a new era of music. Everyone wanted to know about the Beasties but they were an ocean away. Weren't they?

Swiss monkeys, those funky monkeys

Montreux, 1987

It was May 1987 and Britain was weeks away from a general election. I'd heard the Beastie Boys were going to Switzerland to appear at a big TV music event so I decided to just go over unannounced and try and get an interview. I loved their huge pounding drums, the squeaky voices, the arrogance, the rhyming – it all sounded so different. It was the first time anything totally new had come along since the Mary Chain had exploded out of East Kilbride in a wall of feedback and black curly hair. As the Mary Chain had the Pistols' shock and awe and Velvets' feedback as their guiding lights, so the Beasties and producer Rick Rubin had mined heavy rock, rap and punk brattishness. I even found myself reading the infamous Led Zep book *Hammer of the Gods* because they mentioned it so much.

A music industry friend of a friend, John Reid, with a connection to the band's label Def Jam very helpfully told me which hotel they were staying in, who to ask for in their touring group, and said I could mention his name. So I bought a ticket to Switzerland for £85, which was all I had in the bank, and just jetted off and headed to the Hyatt.

To me it seemed the same as hitching to Liverpool to see the Redskins. I figured I'd just show up and say hello and ask the band if I could talk to them. When I got to the hotel there was some low-key security because of all the pop stars there for the music event, but I knew enough about blagging into places to just act as if I should be in there. When someone at reception asked my name and I replied

Mr J. Brown, they looked at a list and said, 'Yes, your colleagues are already here in the bar.' I was pretty confused by that, as the only colleague on his way was fellow *Sounds* writer Jack Barron who also took photos and had wanted to tag along.

I went down the huge stairs to the piano bar when I walked past the drummer from UB40, Jim Brown! Realising what had happened with the names at reception, I stopped and introduced myself.

The bar was full of instantly recognisable pop stars. It was like walking into the pages of *Smash Hits*. There was Depeche Mode, Junior Giscombe, the Thompson Twins, UB40, Eighth Wonder, the Georgia Satellites. Meanwhile, at the centre of it all, Spandau Ballet were running from one side of the bar to another, hurdling sofas in some sort of competitive bar room athletics. It was just bizarre and couldn't have been further from the world I'd been selling my fanzines in six months before.

Worrying about the depth of my pockets and the price of the drinks I went to the bar and asked the waiter if the Beastie Boys were about. I figured if I just sat there and waited for the Beasties to show up, they'd be mobbed, and conscious that I would only be able to get my air fare money back if I got an interview, I wandered off to explore the rest of the hotel and almost immediately bumped into Adam Yauch on the big staircase. I introduced myself, told him I worked for the English rock paper *Sounds*, that I'd just come out on my own and could I hang out with them for a story? He looked at me quite incredulously – with my suedehead and band T-shirt and RAF fanzines bag, I looked about seventeen years old. 'You've just come here to try and find us? No one from the record company is with you?' He said of course he knew *Sounds* from the punk coverage and then just turned and headed back up to the rooms and said, 'Come on, yes, I'll introduce you to the others, you can hang out with us.'

I spent the next day and a half with them through all the fun, chaos and exaggeration of the behaviour that was splashed all over the British tabloids while we were out there. The piece I wrote for *Sounds* was called 'Keep Taking the Tabloids' and was an account of what it was like being on the inside as the tabloid hacks and photographers peered in. There were three levels of Beastie behaviour: lively young guys enjoying being in the spotlight, having a great time arsing about (like throwing bread buns at photographers at a photo call); going up a notch and – encouraged by Def Jam label boss Russell Simmons – play-fighting or turning a car over; and then just being quieter and more intelligent than they let on in public.

Mike D was already very aware that some of their antics, like bringing a giant hydraulic dick onstage with them, were being picked up in different ways by different audiences across America, but they weren't about to go out and deal in subtleties. Just like the Poppies when I'd been to Holland with them, the Beasties were enjoying their own in-jokes, company and catchphrases and just having the time of their lives. All the other pop stars wanted to know about them; the tabloid hacks were desperate for any type of story (two even offered Jack and me a hotel room if Jack would give them some info on what they'd been saying to me). Yauch and Mike had been screaming 'coooooooooold medina' all day, unnerving their driver, amusing passers-by, and the tabloid reporters were desperate to know what it meant. Eventually Ad Rock – Adam Horowitz – was ordering a fuzzy navel cocktail (peach schnapps and orange juice) and asked the barman to 'fuzz it up a bit'. This, right there and then, became the cold medina. The tabloids had their story and described this lethal cocktail that was sending the young rap stars wild and would be yet another threat to the youth of the UK. Two years later Tone Loc would have a massive hit about a 'Funky Cold Medina' aphrodisiac cocktail, and cocktails called the cold medina are still served in bars today.

The Beasties had no real sense of what impact their reputation for bad behaviour had already had in the UK and they couldn't believe Tory MP Peter Bruinvels had actually asked in the House of Commons for them to be banned. When I asked them about the tabloids sniffing around they replied:

MCA: 'Are you allowed to curse in your magazine? They can all suck my dickhead. They can all sit on my dick . . .'

Mike D (mature, sober voice): 'I think basically, if I can interject here . . . they can all just twirl around on the head of my dick.'

They knew I wasn't going to stitch them up and were perfectly happy to drop the bragging and the front and just analyse what was going on around them. To me they were smart guys having fun and fucking about, plus they were the same age as me and they laughed a lot. I loved hanging out with them. I loved them for the music but also their apparent disregard for what people thought of their show, which was the living embodiment of John Belushi's Bluto scenes in *Animal House* – all beer, fun, drive and obnoxious confidence.

'The problem we had in America,' Mike explained, 'was that all the local papers would be putting us on the cover, writing about a show that didn't really exist and there's no way you can really live up to it. The kids are at our gigs because they like the records. I don't think they're going to take much notice of your tabloids.'

Before he left the interview Yauch turned and asked me, 'Hey James, are you going to hang out with us in London?'

Back in London Tony broke out of his weekly template of strong black and white photographs and red logo on the cover and commissioned a Simon Cooper illustration of the Beastie Boys with a plane crashing into the UK, all green with a yellow logo. The band were all over the tabloids, people were discussing them in Parliament, and the music world was alight with their *Licensed to Ill* album. I had the only real interview and feature so it was a genuine exclusive and the biggest selling issue of *Sounds* in years.

James meets the JAMs

Camden, 1987

In the first week of March I was walking up to the *Sounds* office from Warren Street tube when I saw the words 'SHAG! SHAG! SHAG!' and a logo saying 'The JAMs' on a huge billboard ad for *Today* newspaper featuring controversial religious Manchester police chief James Anderton, or 'God's Cop' as Happy Mondays would later call him. *Today* was the first colour tabloid, had brought to the newspaper world the modern technology that we now all use, and there'd been huge fights and riots with the unions and protesters over how it was introduced. The large 'shags' and JAMs big-block graffiti writing seemed to have been fly-posted over the middle of the ad.

When I got to the office there was a record mailer with a 12-inch white label inside, a handwritten letter in crazy capitals from a King Boy D, and a photo showing something similar to what I'd just seen on another billboard. Out of curiosity I took the 12-inch out and realised it only had grooves on one side. There was no writing on the centre of the record. I put it on and was blasted away by a song made up of samples of other people's work: MC5, the Beatles, Sam Fox. I'd never heard anything like it; it wasn't the odd spoken-word snippet, it was a whole sonic montage, and was startlingly brilliant.

No one else had ever written about them or seemingly heard of them so I decided to make 'All You Need Is Love' single of the week. This resulted in a row with the reviews editor about whether you could review a single that wasn't actually available to buy yet, until I pointed out that if I made it SOTW it would get some sort of distribution deal and then people would be able to buy it.

The review said, 'How have they produced a record more powerful than Lydon/Bambaataa's 'World Destruction' without laying a finger on a synthesiser or a guitar? THEFT! By stealing all the various beats, noises and sounds they've wanted and building it into their own stunning audio montage.' The whole review was full on and insistent that this was something new: 'the first single to capture the musical and social climate in Britain in 1987'.

The letter with the record claimed the band were three young rappers from Scotland and two lovers rock singers from London. I was genuinely excited, thinking this was the work of some kids my age. However, when I rang the number on the letter asking for King Boy D to arrange an interview, a child with a Home Counties accent answered. Nowadays, you'd just google all the info but there were no computers back then, never mind Internet.

The following week I wrote a really short news story based on the phone interview I eventually conducted: 'We were originally inspired to do it when we heard the Beastie Boys.'

'You cannot get more honest than that,' I wrote.

King Boy continued: 'Sorry, there's no information, we want as few people involved as possible when the shit hits the fan.'

It looked as if the legal situation meant the record would just stay underground but then a few weeks later a music PR told another *Sounds* writer that the JAMs were actually former Echo & the Bunnymen manager Bill Drummond and his mate Jimmy Cauty. There was a moment in the *Sounds* office in front of the editor's desk when we had a debate about how to proceed and I just said, 'Fuck it, it doesn't matter if they aren't kids, I've never heard of the bloke and the record is great, they're trying to do something different. We should put them on the cover!' And amazingly and to his credit, seeing I was frothing at the mouth, Tony Stewart went for it. Which is why he was a very good editor.

We were totally setting the agenda and were going to put two guys on the cover of a major music paper who didn't have a record deal. Well not one for the JAMs – Bill had recorded a very low selling acoustic album for Creation and Jimmy had actually been in some major-label pop band produced by Stock, Aitken and Waterman, but I didn't find that out till later. No wonder they'd done it in disguise. My own age and mainstream prejudice wouldn't have got me past their bio if it had been real, but I was totally taken by the track and thought it genuinely challenged the idea of creative ownership. The fact that respected documentary director Chris Atkins has just made a film, *Who Killed the KLF*, thirty-five years later suggests I was right. I had more belief in it than the band had.

Years later, when he came on my Soho Radio show, Jimmy told me the project was already over in 1987 as far as he was concerned and he had gone to New York where he was going to live. They didn't think the samples would be allowed in any way or form and it had just been an experiment. Then he said Bill called him and said, 'This kid in *Sounds* is absolutely raving about the single and it's really going off, you've got to come back.'

When I met them they looked as they still look today – Bill like he was going hiking and Jimmy like a skinny biker, nothing like young Scottish Beastie Boys-influenced rappers at all. I met them three times in total for the piece, including a straight interview in a *Sounds* meeting room and in Jimmy's basement studio in Stockwell. There they played me more music they'd made and told me they wanted to release a whole album like this. Afterwards we got on top of the 200-foot high tower blocks at the end of Jimmy's road and painted a massive JAMs logo on the lift head. It looked amazing staring north across London. That was the first of a few things like that I went along and did with them. Within hours of my first review coming out, the hundred copies they'd left with Rough Trade had sold out and no one could get hold of any more.

The cover story ran eight weeks later and cemented the idea that the Justified Ancients of Mu Mu and their KLF label were going to be around for a while. At that point they asked me if I'd manage them, because I saw more in what they were doing than anyone else. I didn't fancy that; I liked hanging out with them but I had other ambitions, and pretty soon they'd appear on the horizon.

'Maybe it's just time to frig about a little' – Joe Strummer

Nicaragua, 1987

I was sitting on the *Sounds* freelance desk one day when the phone went and a film PR called Toby Rose introduced himself. He asked if we would be interested in an interview with Joe Strummer around an Alex Cox spaghetti western he was appearing in called *Straight to Hell*. Strummer had been pretty quiet since his final, post-Mick Jones incarnation of the Clash had disbanded and I couldn't believe this opportunity. I told Toby if we could have it exclusively we would put it on the cover. I was a 21-year-old freelance writer, I was in no position to make such a claim but it just felt right and I walked over to Tony and said, 'I can get us a Strummer interview but it has to be the cover.' Tony, having worked at *NME* through the whole period of the Clash and knowing how good Joe looked and talked, agreed instantly. It was the first time I'd determined what should be on a music paper cover.

The sense of excitement was immense. I just felt like I had so much momentum; I was really prolific, writing loads of shorter pieces but now I was getting cover features too. Tony let me write five in seven weeks. Joe was to be the last.

I met Strummer at a pub called the Crown and Two Chairmen in Soho. There was a big crowd of film and media industry people outside drinking but Joe was able to get served without people mobbing him; for a moment the musical spotlight had moved elsewhere. Here was the great Clash frontman, sitting on the pavement opposite the pub with me, like it was the most normal thing in the world. At that exact moment my friends from Leeds, Age of Chance, walked down the opposite side of the road and saw us both and just did a massive double take, laughing in disbelief.

I was thrilled to be interviewing the man whose songs had accompanied me and my mates across the Pennines on a 36-mile long CND march a few years ago, but I wasn't in awe. It just felt natural talking to someone who'd inspired me and who I wanted to write a great feature about. Naturally I didn't shut up.

He seemed to like my youthful naivety and drive so he really opened up, at one point almost whispering, 'To be honest I wish we were still together today. It was a good band but the Clash fell to ego,' which ended up as the quote on the cover. I had never read or heard him discuss the end of the band before; it was only later I realised what an admission it was. He had a lot of humility. Fucking around with his mates making a film, wondering how to get a band together, being impressed by how lightly the Beasties were treating everything. There were no airs and graces, no rock star arrogance. He just talked to me like anyone else would have done, well better than other people actually.

He seemed a lovely guy. He was passionate about causes he believed in, he felt it was important to distinguish right from wrong, hated the Conservatives, thought democracy was a con, plus he'd written the lyrics to 'White Man in Hammersmith Palais'. The first time I'd heard it on John Peel that song had just shuddered through me – standing apart from most of the other very fine songs of the era. Years later we were drinking one night somewhere and he remembered this interview. 'James, you were the only person who interviewed me when no one else wanted to. I always remember that.' I was shocked; his low point was my highest. He was a great man and like so many others who got to meet him I really liked him. It was always a thrill to run into him, and friends I introduced to him still mention it decades on.

The exclusive interview ran on the cover in election week, a striking portrait by Peter Anderson in *Sounds*' definitive black and white style with red logo and type. It was my favourite-looking cover to date, and coming after the JAMs and the Beasties I was just in my element. We were making the other papers look poor. The same election week the *NME* had Kinnock on the cover, which tanked, sales-wise. They'd seen my flurry of covers and the diversity of music I covered – I was writing as much about dance and rap acts like Schoolly D, Kool Moe Dee, young London hip-hop act We Three Kings, Renegade Soundwave, Rhythm King Records and the brilliant debut LP from Public Enemy, as I was about pop and the new noise like the Poppies and the Gaye Bykers. The *NME* decided to do something about it.

Public *NME* number 1

Adrian Thrills, the features editor of the *NME* tapped me up coming out of a gig at the Astoria and said, 'We really like the work you're doing at *Sounds*, you should come and see the editor Ian Pye as we have a staff job going.' A few days later Swells called me to confirm it and to give me the editor's number.

I couldn't believe it. When you instinctively know you are right for something and then it presents itself it really is shocking and I was filled with trepidation. This was the moment where I suddenly wondered if I was all talk, if I had anything to back up that sense of frustration that I'd felt reading the *NME* five years before in my bedroom in Kirkstall.

For a while I felt like Billy Liar on the platform for London: should I or shouldn't I get on the train? Tony Stewart had given me my head and I was flying at *Sounds*. Whatever your politics, the Neil Kinnock *NME* cover had looked so wrong. More people wanted to read about the former Clash frontman than the Labour leader in a shirt and tie and the sales reflected that. I was writing about so many different things with such energy and freedom and there was a good feeling among the younger writers at *Sounds*. But this was the *NME*.

I went in to meet Ian Pye in his office in New Oxford Street in Holborn. He was a pretty affable, youngish guy and he just offered me the job there and then. Halfway through the chat *Sounds* photographer Jayne Houghton, who also did PR for bands, walked in to visit her friend Karen, the *NME* editor's secretary, and saw me through the glass in the door. We both looked really shocked.

I went away to think about it. The *NME* seemed really all over the place at the time – there was a graph on Ian's desk with a long, slow decreasing sales line which looked ominous. *Sounds* had momentum, my momentum that Tony had unleashed. But I also knew he knew what it was like to be on the *NME*; he'd been there for fifteen years when it was the world's number one weekly music paper.

Right then in 1987 the *NME* layout was often too stylised, and the content was off target and failing to connect with an audience, but it was still the *NME*. It mattered. A lot of the writers whose names I was familiar with from reading it – Adrian Thrills, Neil Taylor, Gavin Martin, Sean O'Hagan, Paolo Hewitt, Swells, Lucy O'Brien, Dele Fadele, Cath Carroll, David Quantick – were still around. These were the names I looked out for; the previous generation – Mat Snow, Andy Gill, Chris Bohn, Don Watson – had all gone. To me it felt like there were a lot of lesser, run-of-the-mill freelance reviewers there who didn't warrant the opportunity of the revered platform.

The staff writer job was a coveted position. I had wanted it since I was about eighteen when I'd started writing them letters and hoping they'd let the mouthy kid on the outside in. I'd spent endless Mondays in the newsagent's going through the *Guardian* Media section to see if there was an ad for a job there.

I'd watched Chris Dean of the Redskins, who I knew, and Swells make their way into the paper and then help light it up. I'd met Don Watson and Amrik Rai and Lucy O'Brien reviewing bands at gigs around Leeds and Sheffield. I was twenty-one, I lived in a squatted council flat in Peckham with my girlfriend Julie Jackson and her brother at the time. This would be my first ever full-time job.

I felt sick with the weight of the opportunity and excitement. I knew I could make the paper better. I'd been planning and projecting and scowling about it during my fanzine years. But now I could do something about it, the *NME* was actually going to give me a go at making it better. I didn't even have to do an interview or apply. I said yes and went to see Tony.

The *NME* within

New Oxford Street, summer 1987

Joining the *NME* was the best thing that ever happened to me. I had no concept of what would happen afterwards; I figured this would be the pinnacle of my life because it was all I'd wanted to do. Seven years later when I launched *loaded* I was able to lead that to become an award-winning, much-loved and innovative magazine mainly because of the excellent education in editing I received on the *NME*.

Whether you ever read music papers or not, I can assure you, getting paid to listen to music and write about it, to travel the world to watch concerts and interview people whose music you loved was absolutely amazing. Getting to do it on the best music paper in the world when you're twenty-one, unbeatable. It really was like wanting to play for whoever you support and making it. This was a staff writer's job and they offered me it. (Former editor Neil Spencer later described it to me as the centre forward position of music journalism.)

Not that it was really a job; lots of writing, yes, but it never felt like a job. There was virtually none of the bullshit of a normal job. IPC kept the *NME* at arm's length from most of their other magazines like *Women's Realm* and *Cage & Aviary Birds*. It was just an unruly editorial atmosphere and I think they were a little fearful of us. The office in New Oxford Street was a traffic jam of old metal desks, filing cabinets and shelves spilling over with brown 12-inch cardboard record mailers and demo tapes and a population of noisy, opinionated people. The record player was constantly on. And so were the writers.

Ever single member of staff had a lot to say and was unafraid to get on with it. In the middle of the office was the freelance island of desks crammed together which would usually be occupied by Swells or David Quantick and an array of visitors like Cath Carroll, Dele Fadele or Simon Witter. Swells was like the office dog, barking away all day about dogs' cocks, Jello Biafra and anything he thought would wind up individual members of staff. Most of us got used to it like you get used to road works, but one time C86 scene champion Neil Taylor just turned round and landed a full right hook on Swells, knocking him back, and a playground scuffle ensued. Swells would cut the legs off the toy sheep on Kiwi sub David Swift's desk, he'd turn all of Adrian Thrills's carefully placed wall posters upside down. He was insane.

News editor Terry Staunton, possibly the only trained journalist in the writers' area, was a cantankerous fucker who spent half the week chewing out his poor assistant Dennis and erupting into a fit of pique every time mail arrived to him with his name spelled incorrectly. The Celts Stuart Cosgrove and Gavin Martin were as dry as sandpaper and would gleefully wade into the heart of any discussion with a no-holds-barred attitude. Their Celtic soul brother Sean O'Hagan seemed very paranoid despite being one of the leading interviewers for the title. Senior editors Danny Kelly and Adrian Thrills spent a large part of the week discussing Spurs; reviews editor Alan Jackson was about the only normal person in the room and even he would be happy to raise his voice and hold his own, especially after a drink; and sat next to me was the Cappuccino Kid, Paolo Hewitt, often dressed in frayed white Levi's cut-offs, an Azzurri polo shirt and espadrilles like he'd just come back from Naples.

The subeditors and designers were in the next room along so they could actually turn the words we bashed out on broken old typewriters into a paper. Jo Isotta, Len Brown, Adrian Tierney-Jones, Bill Prince, Brendan Fitzgerald, Andy Fyfe and the others were very much the people who made our rhetoric presentable.

Editorially, the *NME* was almost unique in the way it managed to be a commercially successful mainstream title, a market leader, while often actually slagging off the music released by the people who provided most of the advertising revenue. Most record companies accepted this attitude because their other acts might well be getting a glowing recommendation, but some of the abuse dished out was really strong. When I joined there were still music legends who refused to talk to us because of interviews Paul Morley had done six years before.

So it had a unique position; it was respected and trusted and most acts wanted to be in it. From the moment I'd first read it as a teenager with a suedehead Ian Dury on the cover I'd found a connection. It felt like a place that was different to the rest of Britain, that had values at odds with what we were always being told to do at school. It was funny, confident, lived in its own world but was happy to let you in as a reader and be a part of it; in fact they assumed you were a part of it. I didn't want to just read it, I wanted to work there. I'd had some brief visits to the office to see Chris Dean, who I'd met on a march round Menwith Hill air force base when I was fifteen, and who was in a group called No Swastikas. They changed their name to the Redskins who I loved and followed round. After a few months he'd written a great diary of the youth Right to Work March and *NME* had not only put it on the cover but gave him a job as a subeditor. He laid out the Live pages, putting headlines at angles with screaming exclamation marks firing off the end. I'd pop in to see Chris at the *NME* offices in Carnaby Street if I was ever in London so I knew it was possible somehow to get in there. Apart from the first time I ever went, on a Saturday, and I was stunned to find the offices closed; I realised that they didn't lie around on the floor writing seven days a week like I did for my fanzine.

The *NME* approved of bigmouths, show-offs, drug fiends and know-it-alls – and that was just the staff; so long as they were great at writing and knew enough about why they liked or disliked a particular band or record to communicate it, they were in. In fact they didn't just approve of such scoundrels, they encouraged them. In many cases they were the very attributes uniting reader, writer and artist. Most places where people couldn't shut up they'd be asked to quiet down; at *NME* everyone joined in and made the situation even more enflamed. So long as it somehow influenced what was going into the paper that was fine.

As a young reader I really liked all this from afar, even if I didn't know who most of the older bands were and had no way of hearing them. If the new wave or 2 Tone bands I liked were in it I'd buy the *NME*, and if they were in *Sounds* I'd buy that instead. I was a promiscuous reader – *Sounds* was easier to read and had a tighter editorial line but *NME* had a character and humour and distinctive class about it. The conversation going on with the readers in the intros, the captions, the headlines, the cover lines were funny and knowing. While writing this book I called the editor who changed the *NME* from a trade paper to a genre-defining British music paper in the seventies, Nick Logan, and asked him where that confidence and wit in the blurbs/ intros and headlines and the speech bubbles on the photos came from and he simply replied, 'Monty Python!' Then added, 'Hiring very good writers with an authentic voice. Charlie Murray, Tony Tyler and Ian MacDonald filling Gasbag (the letters page) and the Next Week box, their sense of humour and using every opportunity we had to push decent music.'

When Nick subsequently started *Smash Hits* I was a first-generation reader, badge wearer and cutter-upper. After I'd finished reading interviews with PiL, the Jam, the Banshees, the Stranglers, Gary Numan, Blondie and so on I would get the scissors out and put the pictures, lyrics and covers on my wall. Original *Smash Hits* was a younger more colourful version of the *NME* – confident, chatty, inclusive – and it stayed great right through to its commercial peak. These were my education: reading *NME*, *Sounds* and *Smash Hits* and wanting to be a part of it. Seeing the freedom they had to say what they want, and to piss about as much as they wanted in the process of creating a magazine, while also getting to interview bands about their music. So you can see that's why I was kind of excited. I felt like I'd made it.

Five weeks after I arrived, the *NME* editor who had hired me was sacked. Ian was replaced by a guy called Alan Lewis who was apparently pissed off that the previous editor had been allowed to hire a new staff writer while he had been in discussions to take over. This gave me a momentary worry, as I was still on new employee probation, but I figured I was good enough to be there and I'd just show him what I could do; I felt I knew what was right for the paper. All I knew about him was he'd been editing IPC's pop mag *Number 1*. Before that he'd run a pub and in the distant past he'd launched *Kerrang!* and ran *Sounds* in its heyday. In fact when he arrived I realised he was the same editor-in-chief who was 'just heading out' when *Sounds* editor Geoff Barton had introduced me to him after the interview there when I was in the sixth form. Oh well, thank fuck he realised I was going to be of value to the paper because he ended up changing my life for good twice.

There was no doubting *NME* wasn't in an ideal place; companies usually only change editors with a ready replacement when the sales are carking it. Circulation had slipped down to the early 70,000s from a quarter of a million a week ten years before.

With a weak editor there were different factions at the paper, not at war or anything but slightly fractious, and the whole place wasn't pulling together in a cohesive direction. There were staff who wanted the *NME* to be very political, people who just wanted to cover indie bands, a clique of soul and hip-hop fans, people with very mature music tastes. I could see exactly where the space for me lay. The soul boys and girls around the paper would push for someone like stylish torch singer Carmel or a new American trend like shag dance music on the cover one week, and then the indie fans would push for ex-Shop Assistants group the Motorcycle Boy the next. These weren't strong covers collectively; it was a schizophrenic identity, and though the *NME* had traditionally been diverse in covering the stars of many genres, from Michael Jackson to the Birthday Party, as well as covering non-music ideas like politics, sport and film, they'd done it with a sort of unified voice.

In the late seventies and early eighties, in addition to all the music coverage, they'd had a weekly CND column and a pirate radio update. Later there were features on sprinter Carl Lewis, footballer Pat Nevin and film-makers like Coppola, Lynch and Scorsese. They made it all feel very *NME*. But now when they went big on something specific, like a thrash metal special one week, there'd be nothing similar inside the following week. Nothing to win any floating readers who'd picked it up the week before. The *NME* felt fractured.

And then it changed. Alan Lewis quickly established himself as a no nonsense, 'roll up your sleeves and get on with it' editor. He sat in the art room and the subs' room and worked on copy and layouts himself. In the same way I felt the need to splatter the grebo content like the PWEI and the Gaye Bykers all over the place to make a point of bringing some rough edges to the content, Alan was ruthless in his dismantling of the art department's design aesthetics. He started packing much more content into the title, running features on half-pages, three-quarter pages, and in one notable case he took a landscape photo, turned it on its side and run the feature over two columns at the back where previously a turn page would have been. Despite having originally been a soul writer himself he even squeezed a Barry White interview which had probably been 1,500 words into about 400 on what looked like a third of a page.

Looking back, I assume he was trying to clear the heavy backlog of content so he could start getting material in that he himself wanted, and he was demolishing any sense of graphic style to unsettle the art director who was pretty much at odds with how Alan believed a music paper should look. Features editor Adrian Thrills was being funny but not malicious when he started comparing Alan's design style to the plastering technique of Harry Enfield's Loadsamoney character. 'Have you seen the layout? *Bosh, bosh, bosh.*'

Taking over the *NME* at that point must have been like trying to walk into a room full of wasps, and after a few months of ups and downs some of the old guard were paid off and Alan could concentrate on the pages not personnel. He also gave me carte blanche to bring new writers in. Every week was like creating a new fanzine. Whereas I had to write *Attack on Bzag!* myself and it could take up to four months to create and sell an issue, here I was publishing twenty gig reviews a week. A magazine can only be as good as the people working for it, and editing the Live pages meant I could actually bring in some people I felt would improve them. When I took over the section, reviews editor Alan Jackson brought me over a massive pile of unopened envelopes and I set about going through the submissions pitched by hopeful writers. I'd sent the same sort of things in not long before so I figured there must be some people in there who could write, or maybe there were even reviews of good regional bands I hadn't come across.

Most of the submissions were poor but two or three really stood out. Barbara Ellen was one. I'd known Barbara at *ZigZag* where I'd once found her sitting on the floor throwing her clothes out of an opened suitcase looking for her typed-up articles. She was dramatic and goth-ish, with the pallor and physique of a drinking straw but she was a really talented and cutting writer who didn't fuck about at all. I immediately wrote back asking her to do more. Another opened envelope came from an FE teacher from Wigan called Stuart

Maconie, under the name Howling Studs Macoines, who'd written a very short but engaging review of Edwyn Collins at the International in Manchester on lined paper. I wrote back to Stuart and he quickly began sending regular dispatches from Wigan. Both could clearly write better than some of the existing freelance contributors.

A fanzine writer I knew recommended his friend Bob Shukman. He sent some reviews in under the name Bob Stanley, and not only could he write but he wasn't afraid to admit he liked mainstream pop, alongside his passions for vintage soul, 1970s European football teams and twee indie bands. It was quite unusual at the time to have that spread of interest. Bob was a real one-off; when Alan put Bomb the Bass with the great new club sound of 'Beat Dis' on the cover, Bob announced to the office that he intended to make a record like that, which drew sniggers from the older soul crowd. He didn't even look like a musician, never mind a pop star, more like a kid who'd fallen out of a Ladybird book, but appearances are deceptive and he was extremely forthright in his love of music and I liked him for that. When he did make his records he did pretty well with Saint Etienne, I thought. They're still making music and films today, and Andrew Weatherall's mix of their Neil Young cover 'Only Love Can Break Your Heart' is a defining song of the era.

The Live pages started to have a new set of names at the end of the reviews and pretty soon they were contributing across the paper. Where Stuart Maconie was eminently likeable and super versatile, Barbara had all the charm of a de-pinned hand grenade. She was essentially channelling the *NME*'s history of literary warfare as fought by Tony Parsons, Julie Burchill, Paul Morley, Antonella Black, Susan Williams/ Seething Wells. For those of us who'd grown up drawn to this full-on rudeness and bolshiness it was one of the best things about the *NME*.

Writer Jack Barron, who had joined from *Sounds*, walked in one day and said, 'I've just seen a band called Guns N' Roses at Hammersmith

Apollo and they are going to be absolutely massive.' Despite already playing one of the biggest venues in London, no one at *NME* had really heard of them and when Barbara interviewed the singer she slagged him to fuck. They then became the biggest heavy rock act in the world with an impressive debut album, and we didn't get another piece with Axl for years. Which also meant we were free to write whatever the fuck we wanted in the gossip column, like the time an associate of his manager claimed he'd had to go round his house because Axl had his piano stuck in his upstairs window and couldn't get it either in or out. Hollywood rock stars, eh? This didn't happen with Ned's Atomic Dustbin.

Sarah Champion was another really spiky young writer who started writing live reviews from Manchester for us after someone recommended her to me. Alan dragged the average age of the staff down even further by later hiring to the staff Helen Mead and Steve Lemacq, who I'd done the fanzine stall with.

Beyond the paper I had other issues to deal with, suddenly confronted by the amount of free booze available. In Soho and central London there are plenty of bars; I had an expense account, record company PRs were constantly buying us drinks, I pretty much had free access to booze every night and I was working in an office where there was plenty of speed around. Not too long after Alan and I had started I went out to interview Zodiac Mindwarp having taken far too much speed. The wrap had poured out onto the review room table which had a textured vinyl top and I had to snort it all out of the crevices. This wasn't typical behaviour but Bill Drummond (who was his A & R man at Warners) had told me Zodiac was a little put out with something I'd said about him in *Sounds* so I was just geeing myself up for a row. However, it turned out he was from Armley just across the Kirkstall valley from where I'd lived with my dad in my last years in Leeds and we got on really well. Too well.

We were absolutely steaming, knocking back the vodka, and listening to the tape back afterwards there's a moment when we left the room for the bogs and two people are caught on the still-recording Walkman saying, 'Those two are absolutely wasted.' It was only noon, we hit the pub after the interview, and then I went back to the office worse for wear and puked up all over the entrance to Alan's office where the *NME* editor's PA Karen Walter sat. Karen was a lovely woman but she wasn't too chuffed to have sick everywhere. Still, she helped sort me out. Alan just raised his eyebrows and suggested calling my girlfriend. I guess he'd seen worse at *Sounds* in the punk era. Writer Jane Solanas told me she'd once smashed the toilet sink up at *Sounds* and Alan had fixed it so she could keep writing there.

I was in a total mess. I punched Swells in the face so violently subeditor Adrian Tierney-Jones thought I'd been spiked. In reality I was still just a kid who threw up, threw a few punches and cried a fair bit after far too many hard spirits and sweet orange, not only because I seemed to just be able to keep drinking and drinking and drinking but I guess because of the ongoing news about my mum's on-off deteriorating mental health. Had my colleagues known about this constant worry they may have understood how touchy and punchy (verbally and physically) I was.

The night is high and the music's young

Stockholm, October 1987

They were probably relieved at the *NME* when I left the office for a few days and went to Sweden with the JAMs. Ostensibly the trip was to try and find Abba to talk them into dropping their rumoured law suit against Bill and Jimmy for sampling 'Dancing Queen'. Thirty-five years on they are making critically acclaimed films about this trip, largely based on the narrative I made up. It was a great adventure, though, one that helped cement the 'mythsterious' world of the future stars of trance and the charts, who go on to enthral, inspire and entertain a new generation of situationists.

The attitude of 'let's just go and do something apparently pointless and see what happens' also massively influenced my approach to many of the stories on *loaded*. The journey not the destination was the story, and having drenched myself in Hunter S. Thompson I realised the story – that drive to Stockholm especially – was an opportunity for embellishment, imagination and borderline recollection. Did what I write in the article happen? Bill seems to think so as he has since retold those stories on the radio.

However, if I'd written that the true highlight was Jimmy and me hanging out with some teenagers in a remote train station then going to look in a bra shop window while Bill was considering getting a plane back to deal with a problem with Zodiac Mindwarp at his job at a massive record company, it wouldn't have had quite the same impact.

But all the same, Jimmy drives Bill, photographer Lawrence Watson and me in Ford Timelord, his vintage black and white American police car with a massive speaker under the bonnet to give Abba a gold disc for the zero copies of *1987 (What the Fuck Is Going On?)* sold. They are brilliant company. Bill's life to some extent at this point is a performance; he's going somewhere he's not been before personally – music paper covers on the one hand, potential heavy litigation on the other – but he knows being the story defines the story. His performance is inspirational – Ken Kesey meets Ken Campbell. Jimmy is smart and dry and funny, and although he is less vocal about it than Bill we know he will always go further. He has, as they say in Daytona, the squeals to move the wheels. Driving across Sweden is nothing; he's driven America coast to coast more than once. And they look the part too, as I put it: 'This 6 foot 6 inch tall Scottish loony in his bottle green tweed plus fours, and his greasy, long-haired, non-designer rock 'n' roll tramp sidekick.'

On the boat over to Gothenburg Lawrence shot them frisbeeing records high off the stern and down into the ship's turbulent North Sea wake, we met a grizzled old boy who claimed he was the drummer in INXS, and Bill and Jimmy climbed onto the stage to do the JAMs' only live performance – a karaoke rendition of 'Dancing Queen' for which they were rewarded with a giant Toblerone.

Arriving on the far side of Sweden by car at 3 a.m. and realising there had never been anything more than a PO box to aim for, never mind the possibility of a nocturnal powwow with anyone vaguely Abba-ish, I suggest they give the gold disc to a lady of the night who vaguely resembles Agnetha in as much as she is a blonde woman. She looks confused but brightens up on receipt of a tenner, a framed gold disc and some albums, just for having her photo taken.

Gunning the Timelord hard back across 300 miles of the same land of crispbread and saunas to catch the same boat, we stop for a dawn shoot of a ritual burning of albums the JAMs cannot sell for legal reasons, get back on the road and Ford Timelord explodes. Relayed to a local town called Scar by a pick-up truck there is nothing to do;

Jimmy and I are very keen to do something, and Bill explains his theory that it is best to assess the possibilities of a situation and save your energy for another time when real excitement is on offer, rather than be disappointed when there isn't.

Thirty minutes later we are with the obligatory bored teenage kids who hang around travel stops in small towns, exploring the three-street town. Rockman Rock (aka Jimmy) and I are giggling in front of the bra shop. It's so pathetic we are almost in tears of laughter. In the morning I call the town's high school to explain two famous musicians are in Scar and could they come and perform for them, but perhaps unsurprisingly they say 'Nej.'

Towed once more to Gothenburg we head out into the city and with nowhere to stay we are taken home by a really friendly drunken Norwegian girl, whose parents are even more drunk but pleased to meet us at midnight. They are not celebrating anything but are actually devastated that their teenage son has been arrested and imprisoned that day for accidentally killing a horse while riding a motorbike. It's a really strange situation but they welcome us in and are happy to have the distraction. The dad strips off his shirt and dons my JAMs hat and leather jacket, his naked beer belly sticking out while he sings. Bill and Lawrence go to sleep on a floor, the family keep drinking and crying; Jimmy and I, still giggling like little kids, climb into the teenage kid's single bed and go to sleep.

Ford Timelord arrives back in Bow, east London where they drop me happy and smiling seventy-two hours after we left. No moose were accidentally run over as I suggested in my piece – it was an amalgamation of the family's horse problem and an old Woody Allen monologue about a hunter and a moose. And no farmer shot at us; Ford just couldn't do the miles – he was saving the energy for his future number one hit 'Doctorin' the Tardis'. The feature was a joy to write though. And one of only two times I ever scrambled the truth in the *NME*.

'There's these three DJs and I'd like to go to Ibiza with them' – Paolo Hewitt

New Oxford Street, 1987

At the heart of all this was the joy of getting to write about music every week. And all the while there were seven or eight other people doing exactly the same thing and just feeling very good about it. To bring a degree of democracy to how the paper was assembled Alan invited anyone who wanted to come to the weekly editorial meeting on a Tuesday at 11 a.m. Suddenly there were masses of freelancers and all the staff in a large horseshoe of chairs which Alan would go round one by one listening to ideas.

It would usually go:

Gavin: 'I'm going to Glasgow to interview Van Morrison.'

Terry: 'There's a new Elvis Costello album coming up so I'm looking to get hold of him.'

Me: 'I'm going to interview the Primitives.'

And then one week Paolo Hewitt sat there and explained he knew three soul DJs who were going to Ibiza to play some clubs there and a bit of a scene was supposed to be happening. Having been to Ibiza on holiday with my mum and sister when I was a kid I immediately started laughing because I figured he was just wanting to go on holiday. The whole room erupted with similar accusations. But he was right. That was the beginning of the new Balearic scene and acid house came out of those trips.

At another of these meetings early on, Alan announced we all had to do some HR questionnaires so he could get a sense of what everybody's non-writing work skills were. An HR woman called Jessamy came over from IPC to conduct the interviews. I got to sit in Alan's seat and asked her why we were really doing them. She replied, 'We want to find out who will make the editors of tomorrow.' To which I joked, 'This is the only time I'm likely to sit here.'

When the assessments of all the staff came back Alan announced them in his horseshoe meeting, thanking us for doing them, making a few mild jokes and reading various scores out without naming names. He finally said, 'According to the questionnaire, we apparently have one five-star guaranteed future editor in our midst. A natural born editor, it says.' All the senior staff were looking smug and firing into each other about which one of them it might be and then Alan added, 'He'll have to try not to vomit in the editor's office when it's his.' The room just went quiet and then there were howls of disbelief and outrage. It was like their worst nightmare. The mouthy, obnoxious, ageist kid just sat there laughing like I'd landed another golden ticket.

Alan set about rebuilding the paper. He took me off the Live pages and just told me to spend all week writing. I wrote cover stories on new acts like Renegade Soundwave, the Primitives, the Wonder Stuff, Nasty Rox, Derek B, the Mondays, Morrissey, the Pixies, the Cult, the Farm, Neneh Cherry, Sonic Youth, the Beasties, the Clash and many more. I'd go on to write fifty cover stories over the following four and a half years.

At Christmas the publisher asked the editors of *NME* and *Melody Maker* to present their Christmas covers together. Rival titles, same publishing company, and both Alan Lewis and Alan Jones pulled out their exclusives with U2. Lewis wasn't happy at all and come back and asked if anyone could come up with something special. I called Factory PR Dave Harper and asked if New Order would break their recent no-interviews policy. Bernard wouldn't, but they had 'Touched by the Hand of God' out and the others were happy but we'd have to get moving. Within a couple of days we were in Germany backstage dong the interview. 'Joy Division were four guys who used to get pissed a lot and then we were three guys who used to get pissed a lot,' explained Stephen.

'We're the success story of punk,' offered Hooky. Getting the cover was certainly a success all round.

A few months later Alan made me features editor when Adrian Thrills left to work at a record company. I was twenty-two. After he told me I bumped into my mate Harper, who was the only person I'd discussed the possibility of it happening with – he was representing New Order, the Mondays, Factory, the Primitives, the Sugarcubes and Pop Will Eat Itself at the time so we were seeing a lot of each other. He arrived out of a lift as I was walking out of Alan's office in a daze, waiting to explode with excitement. He saw me smiling and said, 'You got it! Oh, well done, James,' like John Le Mesurier. We jumped up and down and then I went into the review room and picture library and called my girlfriend Julie and my mum and dad. It felt like I was floating up in a balloon into a rarefied atmosphere.

Now we could really get going. From day one Alan had been intent on making the *NME* more commercially viable, selling more issues. He wanted more instantly recognisable cover stars delivered in an as *NME* a way as possible. He'd instructed us that if something went into the charts it had to appear in the front section, Thrills, at least so he could cover-line it, and he stopped worrying about what was cool or not. The most typical and extreme example was putting T'Pau on the cover, FFS, but his argument was that people wanted to read about music and this was a new band doing well.

To his credit there were other policies that made this seemingly mad mainstream-ism tolerable. Firstly he wanted the readers' favourite acts in again and again, so whether it was the JAMs/KLF, Public Enemy, the Wonder Stuff or Morrissey or the Smiths, he would just insist we found new angles all the time. It almost became a joke, but commercially it worked; it cemented the idea in the readers' minds that the *NME* would feature their favourite bands. When I interviewed Morrissey we ran it over three issues. He showed me his bootleg tape collection in his kitchen cupboard, we flirted about his rhododendron bushes, and then when it was published he sent me a postcard saying he never used the words 'my fans', but he had – it was there on the tape. I saw him again backstage after his debut solo show in Wolverhampton, in what looked like a throne. It was an astounding gig, the hall a riot of emotion.

In addition to all this we had interviews with other members of the Smiths, a piece about the Smiths' sleeves, a story about a Smiths convention, a Manchester Smiths tour, even Morrissey's hairdresser, Andrew Berry from the Weeds. Smiths Smiths Smiths. It was like the *NME* religion but it helped rebuild the sales.

The other thing Alan was very good at was recognising what trends were happening in music and being unafraid to leap on and cover them. After Paolo's initial mention of Pete Tong and the boys going to Ibiza, Balearic beats and acid house had exploded into Britain, and Alan ran covers and coverage from the off – from straight-up interviews with the likes of Todd Terry to more general scene and think pieces about the emergence of the rave culture and the police trying to stop it.

There was a week when Paul McCartney thought he had the front cover because interviewer and 1970s *NME* stalwart Roy Carr had promised it, and Alan happily replaced it with a cover feature about Krush's 'House Arrest', a British house track storming into the charts. You wouldn't even know who was making these singles; they weren't bands in the traditional sense, they were being created in studios by producers and then lead vocalists and keyboard players were performing on *TOTP*. But Alan understood that, just like when he built *Sounds* up through punk, these records were representative of the scene. He had in fact done the same thing back then, removing some rock legends from the cover and replacing them with the Damned.

He also trusted the young writers. When Steve Lemacq and I wanted to put the Psychedelic Furs on the cover Alan responded as he did to anything he associated with his earlier years in rock weekly publishing with the line, 'They've not done much lately.' It was typical of his pragmatism; he wouldn't belittle you, he'd just push back with that line but left it there for you to convince him. Same with Debbie Harry. In both cases they were artists who hadn't indeed done much lately but they had when we were young and the chance to promote them again was exciting to us. Obviously it was more pertinent putting new acts like the House of Love or Deee-Lite on the cover but there were moments for nostalgia for sure and it wasn't the much older editor driving that.

So I had been taking all this in – how to balance the cult, the commercial, the core audience, the new trends – and as features editor I set about commissioning covers to fit that pattern. Write about whoever we wanted but do it in a credible voice with authority and passion. Feature someone with a heritage and broad appeal like Elvis Costello or Kate Bush on the cover one week, and then the next a new act like the Charlatans or PJ Harvey, and then the third week an *NME* perennial like Morrissey, Pet Shop Boys or Public Enemy. After that someone fucking enormous like Def Leppard with a personality interviewer like Swells or someone with great access like U2 by O'Hagan or Gavin Martin. All the time making sure there was a healthy support cast that replicated this mix inside and could be credibly cover-lined.

Every week I'd give Alan a list of who we had signed up for the following week, who the cover would be, who would write it, who would photograph it and when it would be in. I kept him informed on bigger targets and also longer-term plans for the promotional period five months ahead when we'd cover-mount posters or postcards. And he really did leave it to me – writers would bring cover story proposals in and occasionally Alan or Danny Kelly might bring a cover in but it was my call to get that balance of features content right.

It was the basic dynamics of building and retaining a readership. Put things in they like and things they don't know they like yet, and if it's things they don't like make sure you do it in a way that engages them.

It was at this point that I realised one of the key factors needed for a front cover and the broader content of a mainstream magazine. It should attract the interest of the passer-by but also totally satisfy the knowledgeable regular reader. And there was an art to establishing that balance, usually by developing a writing team who shared a tone of voice and sense of humour. And as we recruited more writers like Andrew Collins, Roger Morton, Mandi James, Mary Anne Hobbs and Simon Williams there was this sense that we all had different tastes but there was common ground and we were all passionately going in the same direction.

Lemacq and Williams were like a little A & R team. I'd discovered and championed some bands that made it big but their whole drive in life was to find new talent at seed level. Which Steve did with Carter, Blur and Polly Harvey, whose tape I can remember him getting out and putting in the office stereo.

The challenge was getting the writing up to scratch. As Tony Stewart had done with me I had to sit with Steve and go through his reviews with a pen and help him go from *Pack of Lies* fanzine writer and straightforward news reporter to *NME* features writer. Simon came to me one time with a suggestion for doing the Stone Roses before they rose, and all I could think of was the post-punk Killing Joke-looking band I'd seen around Manchester. But he was ahead of the game, and after former Fall man turned radio plugger (and later DJ) Marc Riley called me and said, 'James, the Roses just played to 400 people at a benefit and totally blew the audience away. They've got Hooky producing them and they've really changed.' Then I realised Simon was right. Looking back I should have perhaps taken him with me when I managed to get IPC to pay for a helicopter into their Spike Island gig so we could get the traditional festival aerial shot. Swooping down under the railway bridge, we landed backstage only for security to rush up and ask if we had passes, which of course we did. We were from the *NME* – passes were normal. As was free entry.

Luckily the end of the eighties saw this brilliant upsurge of new music across the various genres, from the dance explosion which would see writers up all night to the club-influenced Manchester and Haçienda scene, the rise of the Midlands bands like the Poppies and the Wonder Stuff, the Camden and Bull & Gate indie scene with Carter USM and Half Man Half Biscuit, the grunge scene including Nirvana, Mudhoney and Tad. It meant we were never short of content in the office and it started going off in distant fields too. Not just raves but old hippie festivals came back to life.

'I think these people are going to destroy my company car' – Alan Lewis

Glastonbury, 1988

Glastonbury was like another world in the 1980s. Forget the music for the moment, it was sort of irrelevant. It was the event that pulled you in. The festival was where all the mad people went to be even madder, where the outsiders ruled like kings and the convoy counterculture roared around in huge converted army trucks. There were no Hunter wellies or recharging posts or fenced-off corporate lounges or decorated Winnebagos with product people giving away samples. At one point *NME* editor Alan Lewis's shiny IPC company car got caught in a huge crowd flowing quickly past after the main stage finished and it just looked so out of place, so corporate. The punters seemed to feel that way too as they streamed past, banging on the roof as we sat inside wondering if we were going to be dragged out and lynched by the mob.

It was a CND festival – that's what it was billed as – and the acts on the posters all had their names in equal-sized type. The first year I went, 1987, had a pretty cool line-up – Elvis Costello, Van Morrison, New Order, Trouble Funk, Hüsker Dü, the Woodentops and loads more – but I have no memory of any of them. My main memory was just a sense of how extraordinary the place was and how you could probably do anything here.

It was common knowledge that to get in you just showed up and walked through fields and down lanes until you got to a five-bar gate with a student on it and told them you were in a band. And they just let you in. I didn't have to do this when I was at the *NME* but I did later when I was managing a band called Fabulous.

In 1988, the *NME* sponsoring the beer cups and having a stall there with two showroom dummies in black branded T-shirts and caps and a pile of papers to sell or give away was the height of corporate involvement and stuck out a mile. While a mixture of editorial and advertising staff milled around the tent the true spirit of festival entrepreneurialism was lying on the floor five yards away. Two blokes had a salt shaker, a shot glass, a little breadboard with a handle and a bottle of tequila. Selling shots for a quid and making a fortune.

Wandering the fields was largely like being an extra in a scene from *Monty Python and the Holy Grail*. People pranced around on imaginary horses, openly talking to strangers, screaming with laughter; clothes were optional. Others wandered around believing they were Jesus, others just sat and stared and wondered why the stones in the healing field were making bagpipe sounds. The Catweazel look was massive, and this was the late eighties not the early seventies. I remember wandering through all this thinking how similar the big fairs of the Middle Ages must have been.

My hay fever was really fucked, and remembering my first experience of cocaine on a jaunt to Madrid with my old colleague Chris Roberts from *Sounds* to cover a Spanish band Duncan Dhu that Creation had some involvement with, I figured it might be a good idea to get some. I didn't have any desire to be some coked up music biz big-head or anything, I genuinely just wanted to stop sneezing. In those days you couldn't buy antihistamines over a shop counter you had to go to the doctor to get them. A friend, Roxanne, arranged to get me some after I asked her if she knew anyone in the bands who could sort it out. It took a while but she explained, 'They've got to go to Bristol for it,' which weirdly I believed. There wasn't a lot of coke swishing around in those days like there would be a few years later.

She didn't charge me anything for half a gram but as we were walking into the rudimentary artists' car park for her to hand it over, six souped-up black Land Rovers roared up to us and a load of commandos armed with machine guns and rifles and wearing bullet-proof vests jumped out. Roxanne and I just looked at each other in shock. They were clearly police but I'd never seen police like them in the UK – they were a SWAT or armed protection team, but I don't think anyone even knew the term SWAT then apart from geeky Howard in *Hill Street Blues*. I don't think I'd ever seen a machine gun before. Imagine the antiterrorist police you now see at airports suddenly appearing where the default look was Hawkwind's spring–summer season.

Thankfully their attention and guns were turned elsewhere and Roxanne went off to investigate while I dealt with my hay fever on a car bonnet. It turned out someone had made a credible coded threat to shoot Suzanne Vega. I didn't think her music was that bad; I liked 'Marlene on the Wall'. Very strange. Nowadays I guess they'd just anonymously tweet her.

It was the start of the boom in festivals that got bigger and bigger throughout my time in magazines. Vince Power was building up Reading with better bands, then launching the Fleadh and Phoenix which was fantastic. Then Madness reformed for Madstock where the moonstomping registered on the Richter scale. Then came V and Bestival and Creamfields and all the different opportunities to just go fucking eye-rolling insane in a field with few cops, lots of friends and constant live music. It became a vital part of the end of the century and of course at *NME* and later at *loaded* we were in the thick of it. If the working year was a schoolday, the festivals were very much

Filey, the Yorkshire Riviera, with my dad. Late 1960s.

My mum in our Simon Templar Volvo.

Left: I collated, stapled, folded and sold every one of these. Then rode to Ilkley and back.

Below: Pre-smartphone teenage selfie situation.

Left: Illustrated cover by Jon Langford

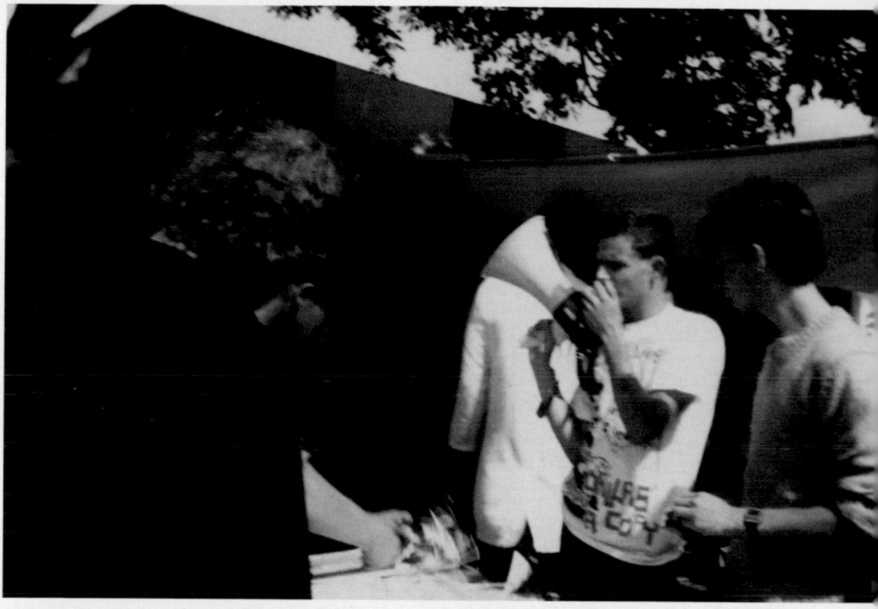

'Who will start me at 20p?'. Steve Lamacq and I selling fanzines in Brockwell Park, mid '80s.

loaded cover style in fanzine format.
Designed by Mick Peek

Interviewed for the *NME* cover.

With Mick Jones, Manhattan early '90s, about to go and see Strummer and the Pogues.
Photo by A J Barratt

Northern Death Cult. Meadowlands Arena dressing room with Ian Astbury.
Photo by Kevin Cummins

The JAMMs couldn't even keep the car going, never mind find Abba.
Photos by Lawrence Watson

Above: Hey Ho, Let's Go! Fabulous Ramones renditions with Keanu, Simon and Rob.

Left: Yauch's Laurel Canyon hideaway. The Beasties were so much fun to write about.
Photo by Derek Ridgers

Yes, Stuart Maconie and I modelling for *NME* and a TV doc seemed like a bad idea at the time too.
Photos by Peter Walsh

My late mentor, the much-loved Alan Lewis, *NME* editor, *loaded* publisher. 'Hang on, haven't we got an issue to get out?'

playtime. They were pretty much lawless in terms of what you could put inside yourself and how you could act out. I loved them.

Glastonbury undoubtedly became one of the highlights of the year but it hadn't taken me long to discover why all the staff writers were always going to America. Every week someone would be off enjoying the land of the free. Sometimes we went further. There were three bands that shaped my approach to what I would do later: Bill and Jimmy as the JAMs/KLF for pushing boundaries and defining and reshaping their own adventure; the Beasties in all their eighties brattishness and early-nineties musical glory, their grass-fuelled wild high jinks and prolonged ability to retain their childlike enthusiasm; and finally the full-on narcotic excess of the Mondays.

72-hour party people

Rio de Janeiro, 1990

Once the cocaine had arrived for the Happy Mondays no one saw too much of them in daylight. The sun was high and the sky was full of circling vultures. Up behind the Rio de Janeiro beachside hotel was what looked like a pretty village but turned out to be a favela slum with a million people living in it. On the driveway of our five-star hotel there were armed guards in bulging blazers and Ray-Bans. They spent a lot of time making sure the people who were allowed to break the law – the rock stars – didn't come into contact with those that weren't – the locals.

The bags of cocaine were huge. Walking round the hotel with huge cloudy white bags in their fists, the Mondays looked like a very well-dressed gang of glue sniffers. Someone had found a cheap Lacoste shop in a shopping centre and we'd gone and cleaned it out. I bought five shirts. Shaun Ryder bought twenty. Gaz, the drummer, ten. We'd found round-necked vintage Brazilian national football shirts for sale on Copacabana Beach; Bez wore one for the *NME* cover shoot. That's all the entourage had to spend any money on – drugs and shirts; if you consider how many shirts they bought you can imagine how much they'd invested in cocaine.

The two guys from the entourage who had gone to get the cocaine were no shrinking violets but had come back in a state of disbelief. 'There were two Polish guys in the room and they just had a block of cocaine the size of a television set. A block this big. They just took a big knife and scraped a load off for us. I don't think either of them have been outside that flat since they got here, they were both totally white.'

Some time later I was sat by the swimming pool of the enormous luxury hotel and I asked Shaun Ryder's cousin, Muzza, who was his sideman, where the singer was. Muzza finished his margarita, wiped the froth from his mouth and replied, 'The Devil is in his coffin and he won't be out till sundown.'

And that was that.

I was asking for a guy from New York with tight curly black hair, a camera round his neck. 'Hi my name's Bob Gruen, I photographed the Pistols – in fact Sid Vicious once nearly killed me with a knife for my boots. Can you introduce me to Happy Mondays?' Unfortunately for Bob, for the first time this week, X, as Shaun was known to his gang, was asleep.

Bez, a man who runs to no one's clock but his own, wasn't quite so keen to get his head down. We lay on the loungers watching the vultures circling way up in the sky. 'I want to do that.'

'What?'

'Go up there with them. You can jump off that mountain over there and get up there with those guys.'

I looked at the vultures and then at Bez, then down the bay to the cliff at a much lower altitude than he was referring to, from where hang gliders were launching.

'Bez, those blokes up there are vultures, the blokes with hang gliders are down there over the beach.'

'I don't care, I wanna be up there with them. Look how high they are.'

The pure block cocaine and the biggest rock gig in the world wasn't enough. Bez wanted to go higher.

The decision for the *NME* to accompany Happy Mondays to Rock in Rio was a quick one. A week before they were due to go, photographer

Kevin Cummins had said, 'The Mondays are off to Brazil.' I called the publicist and said we would put them on the cover if we could go. I was twenty-four, features editor of the *NME* and that was my call to make.

When I'd first interviewed them three years before, around their debut album, they were extremely paranoid and kept bitching at each other because one of them had chosen a pub where the only other customer appeared, to them, to be an off-duty copper. Their debut album *Twenty Four Hour Party People* on Factory records sounded like no one else that had gone before. And on top of all that they had a skeletal dancer with an Easter Island look and huge windmilling, marching-puppet dance. The singer Shaun was a mix of shy elf and street thief. If Bob Dylan had worked in a factory in Lancashire he might have sounded and written like Shaun. The first time I'd actually sat down with them in their dressing room at Manchester University Shaun had to be cajoled into confessing to us that he'd spent the previous night on a roof watching two women having sex through a skylight. You just didn't get this type of conversation with the Soup Dragons. Back then no one could have predicted they'd be on their way to play to a massive audience in Brazil.

The local newspaper had announced: 'Happy Mondays to Bring 10,000 Ecstasy tablets'. This was news to the entourage. The band didn't even manage to get their equipment into Rio in time for their opening slot on the Saturday night of the world's biggest concert so the suggestion they were importing 10,000 Es was wishful thinking. It did, however, have an interesting effect.

We were queuing for customs across the way from Bananarama and Andrew Ridgeley – who was rejoining George Michael for a one-off Wham! reunion which was being reported as Andrew's pension top-up. So it was perhaps a surprise to the real pop stars in Rio airport when the fifteen-strong gang of young northerners were asked by an official to step out of the queue and through a side door. There were a lot of nervous strip-search gags being cracked but we were guided through a couple of corridors and out to a bus. That was it. No customs, no passports, no baggage. I had a visa but no need to show it, made no official entry to Brazil; technically we weren't even there.

Like many tourists we had gone to meet the Great Train Robber, Ronnie Biggs. Ronnie and Shaun had their picture taken for the *Sun*, and we all gave Ronnie fifty dollars to have a BBQ by his pool. I went and sat inside in the shade in his small house for a while, where there were photos of family and friends in Brazil and Britain stuck up on his kitchen wall. To be honest, it didn't look like Ronnie was living the high life. In fact spending your life a million miles from home under a hot sun working in the tourist trade where everyone asks you about a one-off job that you didn't have too much to do with and went wrong and ruined your life thirty years ago, looked like a drag to me.

On the way back from Ronnie's, Shaun went into great detail about his heroin use to the showbiz reporter from the *Sun*, Piers Morgan, who just kept reassuring Shaun he wouldn't stitch him up. These were very strange times; bands like the Mondays had never been featured in the tabloids before. When they had – the Beasties, the Pistols – they'd been hounded as dangerous degenerates. But strangely, given the band were degenerates, Piers kept his word and when the interview came out it was like every other Mondays piece – drugs, partying but no mention of heroin or crime.

At the BBQ I got chatting to an Irishman in flip-flops and cut-offs. He looked like any other shirtless ex-pat with a beer in his hand, but he promised to hook the band up with a local supplier. Someone said, 'Hey come and look at Tim's car.' The guy in the flip-flops was driving the sort of vintage car Stirling Moss used to race, with numbered stickers on the bonnet and everything. In fact it was exactly the sort of car Stirling Moss had driven, the fifties equivalent of an F1 car, worth a fortune.

He explained how he earned a living. His business formula involved fishing fleets from North and South America swapping cargo: the Miami boats brought fish and money; the Brazilian boats brought cocaine. Years later he was arrested on a trawler off Spain with the biggest amount of cocaine ever intercepted in European waters. He was jailed for fifteen years.

That night we went out in Copacabana to a nightclub called Help, and to be honest you needed it if you wanted to hang out there too long. Everyone was either involved with Rock in Rio or a prostitute. It was like the United Nations of prostitution and roadies. I didn't like the place at all. Not long before leaving London a friend of my then girlfriend's had died of HIV, and just before I left Britain I'd read that Rio had one of the highest AIDS rates in the civilised world. At this point they were also stressing it could be transferred by saliva as well as unprotected sex.

The festival security were very nervous about any of us leaving the club unaccompanied, and with reason. That afternoon a giant British showbiz photographer had been mugged for his money belt on Copacabana beach by little kids with a butcher's knife. After a while Rowetta from the Mondays and I said, 'Fuck this' and headed back to the hotel. Our paranoia was just easing off a little as we came through the rocky passage that linked this part of the city to our bay, when the cab slowed down in front of a silhouetted row of armed men blocking the pass with assault rifles.

Rowetta and I looked at each other and just wondered, 'What the fuck is going on? Surely it can't be Terry Waite time?'

Rowetta started telling the driver she was the backing singer with Happy Mondays on Factory. I didn't think this was going to have too much pull with the men with guns.

When you think about getting mugged you don't think of blokes with machine guns. We were out of the frying pan and into the firing range. After some lengthy discussion in Portuguese between the driver and a gunman it emerged they were 'night security', making sure the poor didn't come down from the mountain and go for the rich. That's what Rock in Rio was like – they didn't just guard the hotel, they guarded the whole bay.

Next day was showtime but the Mondays' equipment hadn't shown up. In a move that can best be described as a stroke of genius someone pointed out that if the gear arrived two hours before the headliners finished then the band didn't mind going on last. I should just point here that the acts included Guns N' Roses, George Michael, A-ha and Prince. Weirdly it was agreed this was a good idea. Happy Mondays would go on last – after the headliners at the Maracanã stadium. To over 150,000 people.

The backstage bars in the football stadium's hospitality lounges were full of furry animatronic models. I didn't want to spend the entire evening with a five-foot long anteater so I used my AAA stage pass and wandered out to watch Deee-Lite play. I climbed up the rigging to stage height, which was about twenty feet off the ground, and just sat there as Lady Miss Kier, the Queen of New York, posed and pouted around this massive stage in her harlequin one-piece. Their multimedia guy was walking round with a video camera and projecting shots of the audience onto the big screens behind him. This was state-of-the-art stuff back then. Or it was until he forgot about the zoom turned on on his camera and he just walked straight off the front of the stage and dropped twenty-odd-feet into a crumpled mess. Groove was in A & E after that.

It wouldn't be the last I saw of Deee-Lite. They were so good I set up an interview. Like Kraftwerk before them the band were genuinely interested in what technology would allow them to do – musically, visually and socially. They spent time explaining to me a new form of communication called the Web that would soon be accessible via portable computers.

'So what you're saying is someone could sit on a mountain in Africa with a computer and communicate with someone in Manhattan instantly?'

And they looked at me and replied in unison 'Yes!'

I thought they were insane. That was the first time I heard of the Internet or email – it was 1990, and no one had heard of it. And they were right, they knew what was coming; it was just a pity they hadn't had the foresight to warn their bandmate about the lip of the stage.

Backstage at Rock in Rio, as well as the animatronic anteaters there was a very clear rock 'n' roll class system. Everything was about having more – the darkest sunglasses, the biggest security. The Mondays didn't have any of this; they had one security guard from east London and two mates from Manchester. But it didn't stop the group coming into contact with the giant egos sailing through the area. George Michael's entourage insisted that *no one* was allowed to be in the artists' corridor when George went to the stage. Our party sat in the dressing room and giggled.

So the Mondays somehow managed to stay on the bill, be bumped to the next night and go on after headliners A-ha, to 150,000 people. The opening song from up high on the Maracanã stage was greeted with confusion. The billed concert had finished after A-ha but suddenly a new band appeared. Many concertgoers were drifting away but well over two thirds, 100,000, were happy to have more. Until the set started up. Bez started moving to the music but when the audience realised they didn't know the songs they started throwing plastic bags of rubbish at the band. It was like a riot in a tip. The stage started to fill up with what looked like a load of old takeaway bags.

I was on the edge of the stage watching this barrage of rubbish bombs and after a few numbers the heavens opened and more people headed for the doors and home, but the people at the front of the crowd who were into it started thrashing round even more. Everyone assumed the band would walk off but they just pulled their hooded tops and jackets up and carried on in the rainstorm, they didn't even stop playing. This elicited a massive roar and suddenly the bag bombs ended. The Mondays had won the Brazilian audience over. There was no more 'us and them', just music. The band played just like they had every time I'd seen them, unfazed by the crowd's initial aggression. It was their show, and they were playing for themselves, not the crowd.

My name is James and I am funky

Prince's party, Rio, 2 a.m.

After the show we went to Prince's party where a massive security guy with a line in genuine diplomacy said, 'Now Happy Mondays, Prince likes your music and welcomes you to his party as American labelmates, but let's make sure we all have a good time.'

No one had any intention of fucking up Prince's personal party and as we filed in we were each given what looked like a lottery ticket. It turned out to be a novel idea for speeding up bar service. Every time you ordered a drink, they just clipped your ticket off in the appropriate square and you paid your bill at the end of the night.

In the middle of the main room there was a giant statue of a horse, and a balcony above the dance floor was made out of the front of a boat. This was Prince's VIP area. There was hardly anyone at the party except Lisa Stansfield. Shaun's dad used to be a stand-up comedian on the working men's club circuit when Lisa Stansfield was a child entertainer so old friendships were rekindled.

Uninterested in the Saturday night line-ups in Rochdale's WMCs circa 1974 I began chatting to a very attractive and tall Brazilian woman who lived in New York. I asked her to dance and she said she'd like to but 'Hang on a minute,' and she walked over and cleared it with this old-looking fella who looked like an Italian Mafia hit man. He took one look at me, nodded his approval and we were away to the empty dance floor. I looked about sixteen years old in my shorts and Lacoste polo shirt and the chaperone obviously figured there was no worry there.

No one was paying any attention to the dance floor and for the first song we were the only two on it. Then we were joined by another couple and we were doing that four-sided group dance that happens on empty dance floors at functions when strangers or friends group together. There was me, this very tall, good-looking Brazilian woman, a small guy in stack heels and a powder-purple suit and his date. I looked at him and realised it was Prince. He'd been up on his boat balcony waiting for someone to break the ice and start dancing and the moment we had he wanted in.

We stayed like that for the next few songs – a little private enclave – until people realised who was making the moves and the dance floor filled up, at which point Prince just left but my friend and I kept on moving.

That was the ultimate trip. It was one of my most memorable moments at *NME*.

Most of the writers had their moments though. Mike Scott from the Waterboys told Stuart Bailie he was the person whose opinion he was thinking about all the way through recording an album. Swells's career, which was dwindling on the paper, totally changed when he delivered an unlikely masterpiece based on playing tennis with *Tubular Bells* star Mike Oldfield in which he ran the whole piece full of *thwock!*s as Oldfield batted the ball and answers back. It was funny and just set him off on a great run of pop interviews with people whose star had faded – Gary Numan, Ozzy Osbourne – or who were deeply unfashionable, like Phil Collins. This elevated him to doing heavy rock cover stories like Def Leppard. It saved his career; that was his moment: THWOCK!

Stuart Maconie's came right at the start of his *NME* career when I rang him to see if he wanted to go to Canada to do INXS. They hadn't broken at the time and the record company had taken loads of ads so Alan was being encouraged to feature them. No one on the staff fancied it so we decided to offer Stuart his first feature interview. I left the message for him at the FE college he taught at in Skelmersdale and he later told me when the school secretary walked into the class and said, 'Stuart, a James Brown from the *New Musical Express* has just called to see if you can go to Canada on Thursday to interview INXS,' the whole classroom cheered for him.

My non-musical moment was just one line. I was in the bar at the Stone Roses gig in Alexandra Palace and I heard someone say in a Keith Richards-style drawl, 'So where's this James Brown everyone's talking about?' And I turned round and said, 'I'm here, why?' And it was Nick Kent, the great *NME* rock 'n' roll writer from the 1970s. I liked that, and a few years later he put me and a mate up when we hotfooted it to Paris for the weekend.

As news editor, Terry Staunton had the opportunity to run the most stories and photos at the very start of the paper and he was permanently courted by record companies. He'd think nothing of leaving at lunchtime to fly or take the train to Glasgow to review Texas or the Voice of the Beehive or someone. 'Why do I go all the way there for one night?' He explained, 'Because I get to drink for free all the way up, I'm then treated to an amazing meal, more booze, then a great gig which I can review on the way home next day. I get to sleep in a hotel bed far nicer than my bloody flat and most of all I get to spend a day away from all you bastards.'

They also showered him with even more freebies than the rest of us. Most of us were walking round with New Order or Pogues T-shirts but one time I stopped Terry and asked him exactly how much freebie gear he had on. 'Swing Out Sister Ray-Bans, Springsteen jacket, Blue Aeroplanes denim shirt, House of Pain pants, and dead man's cowboy boots bought for me by a PR in Hollywood.'

'OK, what about your socks?'

He kicked up his legs – in Steve Earle promotional jeans – to reveal familiar-looking red towelling numbers and said, 'Virgin Airlines.'

That was the luxury end of the job; at the sharp end was, well, the sharp end. We were gathered round the light box working on the cover one day when photographer Ed Sirrs and Steve Lemacq walked in with shots of Richie Edwards from the Manics with '4 Real' carved into his arm and blood everywhere. Half the staff were disgusted but I thought it was a great statement. Bev in the subs' room was really put out by my reaction, but knowing Ritchie I just knew he meant everything he said about being in a band and believing in everything he did. Political comedian Mark Thomas was in the office at the time recording a documentary and captured the whole discussion which the Manics later ran as a full track on the back of a single.

Ritchie made his ultimate statement and removed himself from the vice of pain and expectation he must have been caught between a few years later. Some people believed in the purity of rock 'n' roll self-destruction as a statement, and for others it just fed into intense mental health problems. He was a lovely guy and, in my experience, very sweet to hang around with.

My own adventures with bands spread from Moscow to Los Angeles via Leeds, Warrington and London's Chinatown. America was amazing – actually going to the States to a party at REM's house, to be appallingly and unnecessarily rude to Sonic Youth and then chat about the Jam with Gibby from Butthole Surfers in New York; to play football with the Cult and Sex Pistols in Coldwater Canyon in Los Angeles; to watch the Pixies play in a school hall south of San Francisco and then watch Kim Deal considering ordering congealed blood in a Vietnamese restaurant; to bump into Lloyd Cole in a pool hall in New York where he'd relocated, broken-hearted, and end up turning it into a cover story about a very good album; to see Joey Ramone walk into a bar on the Bowery in the early hours and be a little bit star-struck; to be trampled underfoot by teenage Public Enemy fans trying to get to Flavor Flav who'd jumped down off the stage in San Diego; to drive round LA with Rick Rubin in his Corvette listening to classic rock and pop stations where he took his production inspiration from. That was just America – a huge, thrilling country that gave us rock 'n' roll and rap. Those journeys on the road and in the cities are worth a book in themselves.

To Russia with Pop Will Eat Itself, where we were all too immature to see the importance of us being there to be a part of the start of glasnost, Richard from the band looking at the clothes the gig-goers were wearing and saying they looked like when you'd have to be awkwardly dressed for your auntie's wedding, where food and colour were virtually nonexistent, and then to return a few years later with Band of Holy Joy and find Lithuania far looser and wilder than the parent state.

In Leeds I interviewed the Charlatans as they were breaking, box fresh and ready to take on the world. They'd sent a single in for review which was the big surprise of that week and I began relentlessly championing them, thinking they would definitely make it, Tim being an instant star and Rob and the band writing tunes and lyrics that stay with you from the off. For their first gig in London they brought a coachload of fifty fans from home who danced and sang the whole gig through, which left the A & R men gawping from the bar and fighting for their signature.

There were other upstarts coming through. The Wonder Stuff wrote spikily titled instant hits; from the first time I saw them they were already too big for the venues they were playing. Miles was so gobby and so many of the staff liked the band (one of us married one of them) that they featured often.

To London's Soho to find Mick Jones of the Clash and Big Audio Dynamite resplendent in his Stüssy gear, smiling, happy with the music he was writing and illuminating with film and audio samples, as inspired by the rise of house as he'd been when the Clash first discovered rap in America. One night I sat in Mick's flat with his young daughter staring in disbelief as a giggling spliff-sucking Mick played a video of a very, very early Clash interview from German TV he'd recently been sent. He couldn't believe how audacious and arrogant and big-headed he was; she couldn't believe the hair and the clothes. He was lovely company always and the BAD II material was missed by many whose attention was turned elsewhere.

Then there were weird moments, like interviewing Kiefer Sutherland in a suite at the Savoy where I caught a glimpse of a press room with a century's worth of black and white headshots of the most famous and legendary actors to have passed through the hotel. Kiefer was promoting the cowboy film *Young Guns* which was as sanitised as a Tiffany video but he mistook my question about whether he really thought cowboys were like that, for asking if they really existed. And then compared them to our own knights in shining armour as examples of our respective pasts.

The time I met Donny Osmond on a later visit to the Swiss music TV festival where I'd doorstepped the Beasties. This time I was there to enjoy the pleasure of interviewing Chuck D. I just bumped into Osmond and was chatting to him. His new single was pretty well delivered in a 'George Michael meets Prince' sort of way and I was uncharacteristically nice and considerate, and wrote a piece about the realisation that rather than being a 'Soldier of Love' as his single proclaimed, he'd grown up as a prisoner of fame. I've just read it again now – it's an unusually compassionate piece. Anyway the week after it came out he rang the office *five* days in a row to thank me, and each time I was genuinely out and on returning Alan Jackson would announce, 'James, Donny rang again.' I had no idea why he was so keen to thank me but maybe no one had every quite worked out what his life had really been like before. It was a departure for me, being nice and being thanked.

Chuck I interviewed in London, in Switzerland, just north of the Mexican border and in New York. Public Enemy were undoubtedly the children of the Clash, Gil Scott-Heron, the Black Panthers, Chester Himes and Def Jam. PE were an amazing act and Chuck was the smartest man I'd put my Walkman in front of. Interviewing him one time on the front row of rehearsals at *Saturday Night Live* a blond chap came to a podium and impersonated George W. Bush. Chuck looked at me and asked, 'Do you know who Dana is? He's very funny.' *Wayne's World* hadn't broken then or maybe I just didn't recognise him without the suburban metal gear.

Stalking Hunter S. Thompson via his transatlantic flight schedule was a shot of adrenaline which involved research that now would be impossible without hacking, and illegal too. Having spent a number of years scouring the index of every sixties and seventies counterculture book of journalism and politics or anything *Rolling Stone*-related I was transfixed with the man, loved his work, was hooked on the speed-charged energy of the way he wrote but was frustrated there was so little new output. *We had no Internet then!*

The weekend before he was due to land in Scotland I discovered he was booked to talk at the Edinburgh Book Festival. Ralph Steadman had mentioned it during a vox pop about John Lennon we'd approached him for. Claiming his quote had been lost I called him on the Monday and managed to get Hunter's estimated time of arrival in both London and Edinburgh, and by calling round the airlines and airports I was able to work out which flights he was on. When I then asked the airlines whether a passenger of his name was booked on both, because I had to meet him, they amazingly both confirmed he was.

Spending my own money, I booked onto the first row of the same flight to Scotland and got down to the airport departure lounge with an eye on the transit line. There was no one who looked like Hunter there so I had time to go over my plan. I intended to tell him I'd been sent by the publisher to carry his bags. He'd be too fucked to know any wiser and then on arrival in Edinburgh I would clearly be accepted as being with him and ushered along into the vehicles provided and to the festival.

Despite being shown his name on the passenger list he never appeared and I went on ahead to the event myself, hoping he might just be late. There I met and introduced myself to Steadman who was furious his former partner in devilment hadn't arrived – Hunter had called to admit he had missed his flights and wasn't coming. He was even more pissed off that the subs had chopped both of his quotes about Lennon from the vox pop.

Alan Lewis loved a combination of names and faces in conversation for the *NME*: the Darling Buds, the House of Love and the Wonder Stuff as new acts of the year; Joe Strummer and Roddy Frame discussing Amnesty International; Lenny Kravitz and Slash on rocking out; Peter Hooton of the Farm, Paul Heaton of the Beautiful South and Peter Hook of New Order reviewing the year's singles . . . Maconie to the hotel receptionist where the latter took place, when Hooky was late: 'Shortly a man is going to arrive looking like a U-boat captain. Please send him up.' They did.

In pursuit of the ultimate combination we hit upon the idea of getting Mark E. Smith, Shane MacGowan and Nick Cave together. I was friends with Mark, Sean O'Hagan knew Shane and photographer Bleddyn Butcher was close to Nick so we each asked each of them and they all said yes.

Mark always stayed in touch, occasionally sent me a few gifts, like John Waters's book *Crackpot* and a large wrap of speed in a Sky Saxon album sleeve. He'd sometimes crash at my house in Camberwell; he was there when his marriage to Brix collapsed, and took delight in finding phone numbers of journalists in my address book, ringing them up in the middle of the night, pretending to threaten them and then ringing off before he broke down into his cackling laugh. If I asked, he was happy to write something for the *NME*. It didn't surprise me he was up for this, as he and Nick had known each other for a long time and he knew Shane was both a talent and well read.

Despite this he still came to the table in his fieriest form, teasing Nick for getting clean from drugs and drink, and baiting Shane like the dressing-room bully he could be. We met at some semi-gothic pub near Millwall – I'd previously interviewed the Mary Chain there for the cover. There was a small stage with a house band's instruments plugged in and a spotlight. The room was full of weird junk and a huge old stage coach but the real colour was taking place around the table. Sean and I would frame questions but once they got going they were off.

It's a remarkable encounter and conversation, Nick slightly reserved, speaking when needed, Shane holding his own and being exceptionally honest about his performance, and Mark doubling back almost in consecutive sentences between being a pure provocateur and revealing something more candid about his songwriting and world view. There was enough respect and experience for none of them to truly take offence when Mark was prodding them.

At the end they climbed onto the stage unbidden and began jamming with a drum kit, small keyboard and a home-made percussion instrument which was actually a broomstick covered in metal beer bottle tops. There were just a handful of us there to see Mark E. Smith, Shane MacGowan and Nick Cave perform together but I taped it. I've never listened back to it; maybe I'll get it out one day.

With the pub so dark and Bleddyn not sure if he had the light for a cover shot we headed back to my flat in Camberwell, a large, bright three-bedroom affair that belonged to my girlfriend's brother. The drink and speed flowed. Bleddyn shot them grouped against the wall. Julie, Bleddyn and Nick sat in the kitchen and had a cup of tea and talked about Australia while Mark, Shane, Sean and I were in the living room shouting a lot. When it peaked and they left, Shane took my copy of Nick's book *When the Ass Saw the Angel* and Mark stayed over – not that he slept.

It was a momentous night, the most intense triple-header we did. And it was one of the great covers and days at the *NME*.

Always have a beatbox in your dressing room

New York, 1991

Night-time in New York, two years on, and I'm sitting in the Mayflower hotel in the early hours and Carl from the Farm is saying, 'Look if the Clash get back together and Paul doesn't fancy it, can I play the bass?' In any pub this would be a fantasy conversation but Mick Jones and Joe Strummer are sitting right here, a small group of us all half on and off the bed and on the floor in this darkened room. They laugh and the rest of us pile in with what we'd like to do if such an opportunity arrived.

It's the night after my twenty-sixth birthday and I'm in Manhattan with Mick's BAD II who are supported by the Farm in a disco club in the Meatpacking District. Uptown in a West Side theatre, Strummer is fronting for the Pogues on the tour Shane didn't make. Joe's on earlier so Mick and I and a few of his crew go to watch him fill Shane's shoes. I sit next to Sean Lennon in the theatre. It's a fine performance, Strummer the perfect stand-in. Delivering the songs in his own style, which complements them perfectly. Raw, passionate, authentic. It would be a great gig, regardless, but watching it with Mick makes you feel like your parents are back together.

After the BAD II set we are in the dressing room and the Stüssy guys walk in and dump a pile of new clobber onto the floor. The younger guys grab the swag but Joe is sliding a tape into a new-found ghetto blaster. As his mixtape blasts out he turns to me and says, 'We always had this with the Clash, James, everywhere. It's a rule, always have a beatbox in the dressing room.' It's a fantastic rule and I carry it with me into my next magazine.

It's not all rocking, as folk duo Mulligan and O'Hare might almost say. A music PR, Ted Cummings, took me down to the Albany Empire in Deptford to see a comedy night he said was like no other he'd ever seen. He was right. The *Big Night Out* with Vic Reeves and Bob Mortimer was just amazing – a long, rambling, funny – always funny – and often very strange show, but I loved it. The whole audience knew they were watching something special. I went again, Sunday after Sunday as their residency progressed but that first night I went straight back stage, wanting to meet and interview them both. I felt a kinship – Vic had come on to the Human League's *Travelogue*.

I went down to Greenwich to their writing studio which they rented from Jools Holland. Derek Ridgers took photos, and along with a profile of an extremely dry, pint-sized comic Jerry Sadowitz had taken me to see in an audience of six, Jack Dee, we ran the feature over a spread called 'Far from the Manning Crowd'.

A week later, Jonathan Ross, who already knew Vic and Bob and had been at the shows, called me and said, 'Is Jack Dee really like Dave Allen and as good as Vic and Bob?'

'Yes.'

'Right, I'm standing in for Wogan next week. I'm going to get him on the show.'

Both acts were catapulted by the *NME* into an orbit they rightly still occupy today. Vic and Bob in particular became regulars in the title, appearing twice on the cover in my time there, including a tour story when I ended up stomping in Novelty Island each night in front of a thousand people or more. And in Liverpool virtually the whole crowd at Liverpool University gathered outside when they saw them in the second-floor classroom that was their dressing room. What followed was effectively a second set – a call and response session of 'You wouldn't let it lie', and so on.

As exiled Northerners we got on very well. I loved hanging out with them, they approached life and performance with all the energy and imagination of schoolkids for whom everyday rules of logic and common sense don't apply. They were as funny off as on stage. Bob loved music and Middlesbrough FC, Jim loved hanging out with his old mates – the Darlo mafia – playing 1970s rock albums by the likes of Free. And between us we drank and drank so much. Jim had a fine-wine cellar I had the freedom of and Bob would happily bring a plastic bag of cans into London's swisher media drinking dens. They seemed like some of my mates back home in Leeds. And I was very lucky to be in close attendance as they became successful. They asked me to co-edit their spin-off book, and a couple of years later I'd move into Vic's notoriously lopsided flat (one side was one foot higher than the other). It's great to see them thirty years on, more popular than ever.

When Alan Lewis left *NME* after three and a half years, promoted to publisher to launch *Uncut*, *Vox*, *Muzik* and others, the cocksure firebrand in me was disappointed they didn't even interview me for his job. I was promoted to the role of assistant editor which meant I no longer commissioned the covers; in many way it felt like a demotion in terms of what I actually had to do each week. I also split up with my girlfriend, Julie. I started to feel pretty restless, and with reason.

Things weren't any better at home. My mum climbed out of the Velux window on the roof of her three-bedroom terrace in Leeds and jumped to the street below; she somehow walked away with broken ribs. But the previous three years had been a case of finding out she'd been back in hospital only by realising she hadn't answered my calls for a few days. The background unspoken pressure just built and built. Some days I'd come out of this amazing job, having been biting and narky with my colleagues after finding my mum was in High Royds again, and gone and sat in Julie's car with her on the South Bank in tears. I didn't really know any way to deal with what was going on beyond talking to her and drinking heavily.

The *NME* was part of a music business where not only were you allowed or encouraged to drink, but it was seen as a badge of honour. I'd come home to the flat topless, with my jacket pockets full of puke, tears in my eyes, distraught. Once I got into my stride drinking it wasn't about how many drinks I could have, it was just a sense of there was no stopping. Numbers never mattered; it was just like drinking from a running tap.

One night in Soho a street dealer and I had a few words and he pulled a knife, and instead of backing off I just lunged at him. He shat it and ran, shocked, but I went on to the bar I was going to and sat between Stephen and Gillian from New Order in tears. There was so much filling up inside me, and instead of getting it out I was topping it up till I overflowed with emotion, vodka, wine and tequila.

I look back on it and now think if I'd spoken to Len Brown, Adrian Thrills, Alan Jackson, Karen Walter or production editor Jo Isotta or one of the adults who hadn't slipped into the rock 'n' roll journalist caricatures many of us had – they'd have helped me. But there felt like no way through the force field, in or out, that I had placed around myself. I was a wound-up, angry, driven young boy. Sub Bill Prince once said to me near the end of my time on the paper that I'd had too much too young, and he was right. Amid my rapid success I didn't have the maturity or understanding to navigate a way between my deeply disturbed personal feelings and my desire to make my contribution to the *NME*. The publishing and social schedules kept me going, the alcohol numbed my feelings, there was no room or opportunity for the quiet chats in soft furnished rooms I gladly encountered later in my life.

It was perhaps inevitable that somehow it would break. The job had meant so much to me that in a funny way it was easy to walk away. Weller had done it, Lydon had done it. It was what you did. I didn't really think or worry about where I would go, just that I didn't feel I was contributing as intensely as I had previously been able to, so I realised someone else should have a go.

When I found myself with nothing to do each week, a senior position with no actual production requirements, I just started to write again. I went on the road round Ireland for the first Manics *NME* cover – 'Punk Rears Its Ugly Head'. They were a brilliant shot in the arm. A reality check. A flashback to where I'd come from. Swells had told me, when he'd discovered them, that they were like my fanzine *Attack on Bzag!* and had been readers. They certainly reminded me of myself when I was seventeen, and in their pitiful tour bus they were accusing me of selling out. It didn't hurt or anything but it resonated. I was twenty-five and I already thought that was too old to be an *NME* writer.

I went on tour with Pet Shop Boys, which was utterly exhilarating – the humour, the ambition of their art-inspired stage shows and their thundering disco pop breaking across the skies over the Prague venue. I sat with them as Neil put on his anti-ageing cream. I knew I wanted to leave the *NME* and would in a few months, and as ever I was looking for solutions in the conversations with the people who made music that made me happy and excited. They all produced magic really, had the ability to affect your emotions. That's what you need from music, which is why I'd get so irate at things I considered bland. Neil told me I was the most intelligent music journalist he'd met. And he'd been one. I told him he should get out more often; it was something I intended to do myself. I wrote my resignation letter within the last column of copy about Pet Shop Boys but only one reader – Momus, a singer-songwriter signed to Creation – wrote to me and asked me if that was what it was.

I interviewed Bobby Gillespie for a great Primals *NME* cover for the launch of *Screamadelica*. My last as a staff member, I think. Opening paragraph: 'Imagine an LP that can hold its own alongside *Let It Bleed*, that burns at its own boundaries.' Gillespie was another person who believed in some sort of rock 'n' roll purity. In possibility and magic. Whose drug-framed creativity was fuelled with the need to make music as great as that of the artists he adored. Primal Scream were about to tour America with Electronic. They'd contacted Phil Spector to produce a Christmas single. He'd declined but they didn't need him – they had Andy Weatherall and *Screamadelica* was burning brightly.

And then that was it. I said I'd still write for the paper but I needed to get some space and freedom. I gave the £80 they raised for me in a whip-round to the Terrence Higgins Trust. People Julie and I knew were dying, and it seemed better than buying myself a new Walkman.

I'd learned so much from Alan Lewis and I'd had a brilliant time. We had put on 50,000 sales a week, from 75,000 when I'd joined in the summer of '87 to 125,000 when I left at the end of 1991. A phenomenal sales increase. It was intense, but the only thing I could learn possibly by staying was patience. I didn't know it then but bigger things lay ahead for me. For now I wanted some different action. And I was gone.

Intermission

By the end of my time at the *NME* I was permanently wound up. The production process and the constant demand to have an opinion on all music meant my antennae were – as the Beasties sang on 'Sounds of Science' – 'constantly on'. It was really intense, magnified by my drinking and the pressure of not knowing if my mum was well or not. I was the most tetchy, narky little shitbag going.

Yet by the time I started *loaded* eighteen months later I was riding a bike round the office, laughing, waving a golf club around and having a much happier time altogether. What happened in between was a personal rewilding scheme. I basically had a lot of stress-free fun. None of the regimented employee bullshit that went on in the wider corporation *NME* was a part of. Lots of reconnection with the world of small gigs and venues I'd experienced before *NME* and *Sounds*. No deadlines but masses of grass and great music listened to. Lots of hanging out with Vic and Bob, who were becoming very famous very fast. I moved in to Jim (Vic)'s flat in Greenwich and regularly laid waste to his wine cellar in his new house. One night Rowland Rivron and I deliberately locked ourselves in with a corkscrew. Absolutely loads of high jinks and loud noise managing a bunch of mates, the punk band Fabulous. That's a story for another time but the chaos and fun of doing something totally unconnected to a career really helped me to chill the fuck out.

Some people enjoy this sense of freedom at college before full-time employment; for me it was the other way round. After the high life and power at *NME* I was now enjoying my time on the lowest possible rung of the music business ladder, travelling in freezing, shitty vans again, recording in tiny studios the size of bus shelters. The most notable change was how unstructured my life was, the only constant the music I was loving again. I would get up, stick on *3 Feet High and Rising* by De La Soul, *The Stone Roses*, the Beasties' *Paul's Boutique*, the soundtrack to *The Harder They Come*, Curtis Mayfield's *Superfly*, recently released *Screamadelica*, Love's *Forever Changes* or BAD II's *The Globe*, work out what had happened the night before and decide what I was going to do that day.

I liked those albums I was playing on repeat because *The Globe*, *Screamadelica* and *Paul's Boutique* in particular had very different sounds created under a brilliantly diverse array of influences. I liked how experimental and unfinished they felt, how the band were trying something different but weren't sure where it was going to take them, with no regard for what anyone else beyond their inner creative circle cared about. I felt a bit like that as a person – I didn't really know what I was doing; I was just enjoying feeling free.

I loved going to some of the new clubs in Soho: Tongue Kung Fu, Smashing, Magik, Carwash, Ultra Vixens. By 1992 even *The Hitman and Her* were playing house music on TV to blokes in black trousers and open-collared white shirts, and girls in spangled dresses. Balearic super clubs had superstar DJs, and the mainstream was plundering the underground for the latest beats. In Soho, though, something very curious and different was going on. People were again looking backwards for something new. Club runners were turning to the sixties and seventies for punk, funk, rare groove, hippy, heavy rock, new wave, flute music and psychedelic blues. And mixing it all together. It felt colourful and exciting and fun. You had no sense of what decade it was at all.

In Carwash they were playing full-on superfly New York disco, Kinky Gerlinky was a drag queen extravaganza. And Tongue Kung Fu,

Smashing and Magik? Well, it was just another world. No one seemed to give a fuck who was coming into the clubs because they were invariably in venues you had to have some curiosity to discover. Quiet nights at escort bars, forgotten dens above Chinese restaurants. There was lots of dancing and loads of different drugs but it felt different to Ibiza and the high street. There was a total disregard for anything going on anywhere else but the club runners' minds. Selfishly brilliant, all three felt like children's parties for adults with great music.

For a little while I was close friends with a strange, boyish girl called Louise, who would purr when she spoke and who took me to all of these clubs. She was the singer in a French-inspired pop group called Un Homme et Une Femme and I'd lie around on her bed in Mornington Crescent listening to her favourites Serge Gainsbourg and Curtis Mayfield, and she had these great mixtapes she'd make with glitter on them. They had felt like *Paul's Boutique*, the smashing together of genres and rare songs you wouldn't expect to live together, and after I'd played him one of her tapes I took Mike D round to her flat to meet her one time but as was the case in those pre-mobile times, she wasn't in.

At Tongue Kung Fu, in a basement in Covent Garden, I was dancing with Sue from EMI Records who I was out on a date with. I looked down at my feet and we were dancing in an inflatable paddling pool full of water and plastic cups. The club was full of stuff the guys running it had found in the street – there were coffee stirrers scattered everywhere, inflatable globes, a full bath and shower unit. You'd be dancing and laughing and thinking, 'What the fuck is going on?'

Magik took place every Saturday at Wilde's, up above a shop in Gerrard Street, Chinatown. There was never a big queue and I didn't remember anyone ever asking for money to come in, but inside was busy, the music one long, rumbling, danceable groove. Onstage Louise's band or Subjagger would be playing, and when it got too hot and crushed I'd head out the fire escape at the back to chat with the guys who became Kula Shaker and Tony Horkins and Magik main man Adil, who would take the mixology of the club and have a number one hit in the charts by blending the Pearl and Dean cinema advertising jingle with Led Zep's 'Whole Lotta Love'.

Smashing was my favourite club and would later be the first club reviewed in the launch issue of *loaded*. They played Bowie, Lou Reed, Blondie, the Regents, Martha and the Muffins and other lesser new wave and glam one-offs, film soundtracks and kids' TV themes. All in all it was like a youth club disco with amazing music and brilliant, rotating kitsch venues. Eventually when pop stars started showing up it became a very well-known club and people would queue for ages to get into it in Regent Street, but at the beginning, in keeping with the original rave scene, you'd ring one of the four club runners to find out where it would be each week. And you'd go down and join in a big circle and dance to the *Bugsy Malone* theme. Right there and then, freed from worry, these felt like the best times in my life.

In Soho one night I met Keanu Reeves in a bar when I was out with Murphy Williams from *Vogue* and invited him to come down to Smashing. They couldn't believe it when we walked in and I never had to pay to get in again. He was in London for something to do with Coppola's Dracula film and he had his mate Rob with him. Together they had a band called Dog Star and he was so down to earth and fun and up for anything. He thought nothing of driving round in the boot of Fabulous's psychedelic Maxi, and he came down to rehearsals where we jammed and hung out and generally had a very good time. We got on so well he invited me to come out and see him in LA which I did with a little camera and made a tiny film for Janet Street-Porter's *DEF II* show. During that trip we were hanging out at his sister's house just below the Hollywood sign and he said, 'James, tomorrow I'm going out riding classic motorbikes with Sofia Coppola. Do you want to come?'

And I thought about how that would be really great, and while I knew how to drive a car without a licence I hadn't ridden a bike since I was fifteen. Even then I'd gone so fast I'd come off, and there was actually a good chance I'd fly off one of the Hollywood Hills and crash into someone's house like Iggy had in the book *Wonderland Avenue*. And so I reluctantly turned the offer down and came back to England and immediately booked driving lessons.

Midway through 1992 Leeds won the league for first time since I was eight and it felt like the first time I could totally and utterly be happy, joy overshadowing the devastation I'm about to come on to. At G-Mex, U2, Kraftwerk, Public Enemy and BAD II played an astounding anti-nuclear benefit gig beneath dangling, twisting Trabants, and backstage there were as many footballers as there were rock legends. Kenny Dalglish, Lee Chapman, Graham Souness, Ian Rush, John Barnes, Mark Hughes, Kevin Moran and many more. And Bono's mates were in abundance – one table alone looked like a *Q* magazine front cover, with Peter Gabriel, ex-Velvet Undergound members and Chrissie Hynde all chatting.

The moment of the night came when someone shouted, 'Look, there's Lou Reed' and Pete Wylie from Wah! replied, 'Never mind that, there's Peter Reid!' And the collected horde of members of the Mondays and Inspirals and Northside and Roses and their mates and myself all gathered round to hear the Everton legend's tales of great times on and off the pitch. It felt like a significant moment – football and music combined. As New Order and England had been in Italy two years before.

This period between *NME* and *loaded* was so important to me because by the end of it I was determined to find a way to continue that sort of lifestyle, one where I had masses of fun, but was actually paid for it. I wanted fun to be my job. It opened my mind up to what *loaded* could be in terms of attitude. Along the way I'd be wrongly arrested for the very serious heist of a *Roger Rabbit* vending device (as the charge sheet called it), be saved from a cliff edge death by brambles, invent a sandwich, go a week without washing for a *Sunday Times* story, release a herd of shopping trolleys, ride down a motorway on top of a van, drink a lot of Courvoisier, eat a little too much acid, go to Vegas with U2 – in general go wherever I thought there might be some excitement.

If I needed any money I could flog some records or maybe write an article for someone. I wrote about diving off a balcony at a Cult gig high on grass, about badly dressed icons, and about the return of smack in the music biz – all for the *Sunday Times*. And for *Arena* I wrote about men who got so pissed they urinate anywhere, men who treat their cars like a shed, and so on. Basically guys who weren't the archetypal alpha male, people a little rough around the edges. I pitched articles to magazines about Vic and Bob and Denis Leary, the travel element of my trip to Brazil with the Mondays, skydiving in Nevada, and tattoo artist Mark Mahoney who I met in LA with the Cult, but people didn't want to publish this sort of thing – there really were very few places to write about being a young man. Which was annoying me, and would have an influence on what happened later in the year. But first something even more impactful happened.

Pressure drop

Tower Bridge, London, 1992

On the second of March 1992 my dad called to tell me my mum had been found dead in her house over the weekend. She'd apparently taken an overdose of pills. There was no note and a blood-stain on the kitchen wall suggested she may have had some sort of panic attack.

I stopped listening to the details while he was still talking and walked over and put 'Pressure Drop' by the Maytals on from *The Harder They Come*. My emotions were racing and I just felt like I was slipping into a daze, but for a moment I was feeling there was a sense of pressure dropping. 'OK, she's done it now, so she won't be trying again and she won't be in pain any more and I won't be getting calls saying she's in hospital again.'

But they were fleeting moments, looking for a positive. I was just stunned. Even now I can't remember anything else from that day apart from knowing I had to go home. Everything else I was conscious of just ebbed away. I thought about getting the train but just couldn't face sitting in one surrounded by people while crying so I went to the airport knowing it would save time on the journey and the plane would be almost empty.

My dad and sister met me at Leeds Bradford airport and we just hugged and cried. It had been a long painful journey for us, and most of all my mum, but it was over. It was so hard to fathom that the ill side of her had won; she was a really nice, caring person when she was well, which was the majority of the time. The Friday before she died we'd chatted for quite a long time on the phone as we did every week and the only thing she said that later made me pause to consider if she had in any way been planning the overdose was that, apropos of nothing, she'd suggested I go for a walk by the river, as if offering a solution to something that hadn't yet happened.

At her house I had to go through her papers and talk to the authorities with my granny who had found her, and we had to work out how to bury our mother and daughter. Five minutes after arriving in her kitchen the phone went – a friend ringing to confirm a night out – and all I could say was, 'She won't be coming, she's died.' I didn't know what else or how else to say it. All I knew was everything was going to be new and devastatingly painful now.

Back in London I went to Paul Smith and bought a ridiculously expensive suit for the funeral as if that would make some sort of difference. We cremated her at the cemetery near school. As the coffin disappeared into the furnace a butterfly flew in through the open door and down the aisle. I had felt sick for most of the day but that moment lifted me; it felt like her spirit was flying away, something alive to be able to hold on to. I've no memory of who was there – I guess just relatives and her friends – but my old head of sixth form Mr Frost who'd given me the great send-off talk came over and spoke to me briefly. His family had lived near my mum and I appreciated he'd come. She'd died on the 29th, the extra leap year day, which meant that, going forward, there'd be only one year in four to actually remember her anniversary. The other 29th Febs disappeared as surely as she had done.

My gran, sister and I went to the police station to deal with the death certificate. My gran went frequently – she wanted mum's death to be recorded as 'by misadventure'. They couldn't really decide what it was so in the end they went with that.

Her death was such an abrupt and shocking experience, there were things I couldn't get my head round at all. On the day of the funeral I'd stayed at my gran's and woke to find a missing button had been sewn on my shirt cuff. I was really thrown by that. It never occurred to me that my gran had done it; I wondered if my mum had or if it was magic or something. I'm not sure my own grasp on reality was very strong right then.

I didn't feel any anger and I'm not sure I even felt pure despair because that suggests a lack of understanding. I understood she'd wanted to stop what was happening in her mind. And if she had managed to do that then I was OK with that; you can't be responsible for managing other family members' long-standing mental and emotional states. What I was struggling to come to terms with was the effect it was having on me. Certainly nothing mattered any more. I didn't have a girlfriend or a proper job at the time, just some occasional freelancing and knocking about with the band, so it wasn't as if I had any boundaries or structure to break out of or stay within. But inside I just thought, fuck it, as if I'd been unchained from whatever might be expected of me anywhere.

My friends Mary Anne Hobbs and her husband Miles from the Wonder Stuff came and collected me from Leeds. Before we left we went to a night match at Elland Road where Leeds had just signed two young South African players, Lucas Radebe and Phil Masinga. During the game Masinga was fouled and as he lay on the floor a little boy behind us asked his dad what had happened. His dad replied, in broad Yorkshire, 'Dunno son, praps his bin bitten bah a tahger.' I can remember how surreal that comment was but little else about the immediate aftermath of mum's funeral.

Coming back to London felt like coming out of hospital. I was so raw. We went to see John Shuttleworth perform in Crouch End and I just sat there with tears streaming down my face. Back on the balcony of their flat the comedian Sean Hughes put his arm round me and tried to kiss me, which was weird. I don't know if he was just trying to cheer me up but I had to ask Bob Mortimer what that was about and he couldn't fathom it either. I was a broken boy but I wasn't about to let any old comedian kiss me. Maybe Jim or Bob, but no one else.

There was no grief-counselling service I was aware of, no Internet to research anything. I couldn't find any books about coping with suicide. Friends and former colleagues sent me cards of condolence but I never even acknowledged them – I only just found them researching this book. My friend Harper's wife Nikki gave me a photocopy of an article from *Marie Claire* about how a woman who'd lost all five of her immediate family members to cancer coped with it. But there was nothing to explain the basic disconnect that it was better for my mum to take her life in that moment of mental meltdown than be able to ride it out and be with her family.

I never considered her death selfish, as those who haven't experienced it sometimes say – more an overall state of devastation that she'd gone and I'd lost the good bits, the important bits, the maternal relationship; they'd all been ended by the paranoid psychosis that tormented her. I was still a boy really. I'd had success and travelled a bit, I had IPC Magazines' Best Young Journalist Award, but I'd just turned twenty-six, was single, drifting a little. With Fabulous I was enjoying a sense of recklessness. I didn't have the maturity, support or emotional experience to deal with my mum's death in a constructive way so I just upped my drinking and drug taking.

I was in bed with my friend Miranda at Jim's house after I'd collapsed and she was really worried as she lay awake listening to my heart racing. The next morning Jim said in disbelief, 'You drank five bottles of wine last night. I was on the red, you finished five bottles of Chablis.' That felt fine, I wasn't even badly hung-over.

I thought a great place to be at this point would be G-Son studio with the Beasties in Los Angeles with its basketball hoop, halfpipe and, most importantly, Mike D's fine 'government grass'. Which is where I headed off to. First stop San Francisco, to write one of my favourite ever pieces about them around the launch of *Check Your Head*. Jeff Barrett of Heavenly Records said 'the best thing you've ever written', and years later hip-hop writer Angus Batey wrote that it was more a reflection of my state of mind than where the band were at.

But much of it was true – I did sleep in my boxers under a drinks table in a meeting room in a hotel Mike called a 'New Wave Prison Cell', and I did emerge to ask the Beastie Boys all the weird questions they'd had sent in from MTV territories around the world, like what was their opinion of Christopher Columbus? And if I somehow dived into the world of the spoken-word samples the Beasties had used on the album and the stories they liked to tell about people selling parrot shit to smoke and suggested they were real, does that really matter?

I spent a lot of '92 visiting LA, running wild in the canyons, driving cars without a licence, playing football with the Cult, with whom I'd been on the best American tour I'd ever experienced. Knocking about with U2, the Farm, Keanu and Rob, my mates Martyn Atkins, Brandy, Meredith, Sean Renet, Rodney Biggenheimer and Chris Carter, Andy Delaney and *NME* writer Jane Garcia, living off grass, tuna melts and lots of margaritas.

Fabulous didn't have any songwriting ability and I didn't have any managerial experience, but we were loud, confrontational and eye-catching, so we were well matched. And together we managed to have a brilliant time for a year, starting in a council block in Elephant and Castle and ending in a Bel Air restaurant with legendary music moguls Seymour Stein and Lenny Waronker of Warner Bros. In between we toured a lot, appeared on TV, featured in *Q*, the *Face*, *Gay Times* and a porn mag for women, mastered the art of stealing sausages from service station hot plates, and hung out with Andrew Loog Oldham, Peter Waterman and Malcolm McLaren. In showing me there was a less uptight way of living it was an education of sorts. And it readied me for what was coming next. A magazine like there'd never been before.

Part 2

Chocolate and the charlie party

'I know exactly what you *loaded* boys are like. You want to lie in bed with a beautiful woman, eating crisps and watching *Match of the Day*.'

Paula Yates (she was right)

'This magazine is so good it should be banned.'

John Lydon of the Sex Pistols calls the office

'Birmingham fertility clinic blames *loaded* generation for sperm shortage'

Broadsheet newspaper headline, autumn 1997

Laurel Canyon calling

Los Angeles, 1992

The Farm were pretty successful in the States. They'd had a top 10 hit and their manager Kevin Sampson, a mate and a Fabs fan, arranged for Fabulous singer Simon and I to go to LA to meet legendary A & R man Seymour Stein (Blondie, Talking Heads, Madonna, Ramones), who had seen us featured on music TV show *Rapido*. Unfortunately singer Simon hadn't brought the recent demo we'd recorded because he didn't think it was good enough and we were late for the Bel Air dinner with the heads of Sire and Warners because we'd been at Beastie Boy Mike D's Silver Lake home throwing lemons at each other over the swimming pool. As the manager I should have had the demo in my hands myself when we left the UK. We were just idiots arsing about and Mike had the government grass – weed he said he was getting from government labs – which blitzed everything else into oblivion.

At the dinner we drank $4,000 of wine, Simon froze and didn't speak, Kevin had to pick up the tab. After watching Lenny Waronker sing Sex Pistols songs, Seymour said he wasn't interested. It felt like we'd been so close. We'd gone back to the Mondrian really annoyed and I'd thrown chairs off the pool deck into the service road in frustration. Drunk and wound up, an unprofessional manager with a band with more charisma than talent. I hung over the balcony and thought, 'I've been having a great laugh, I need to have this lifestyle but get paid doing something I'm good at.' I'd been the features editor of the *NME* aged twenty-two. That's all I was good at.

Back in London, the same phone on which I'd heard Eric Cantona had left Leeds and mum had died rang, but this was better news. Alan Lewis was wondering if I would come in for a chat. The *NME* editor's job was available again. As I was enjoying my life I said I thought they should go with an internal candidate. He called back two weeks later and persuaded me to come in. My mum had once told me she believed I'd be *NME* editor by the time I was twenty-five. I'd just turned twenty-six. It felt like fate. Alan was very keen, he thought it was the chance I deserved. So I went with her words in mind.

It turned out I was down to the last two without even interviewing. During the interview, after we'd talked extensively about the *NME*, they asked me if I would like to do my own magazine if they didn't give me the job. I said yes. I'm not sure what my interview was like but I was still disturbed about my mum's recent suicide and I was living a pretty drug-riddled, carefree life. Even in my own apparent state of advanced relaxation I probably came across as very intense.

Alan rang me a week later and I could immediately hear the disappointment in his voice. He had wanted to give me the job but the suits didn't trust me – they thought I was too young, aggressive and unmanageable. They still remembered me throwing my pass in a security guard's face, wandering round the canteen with my ripped-up Ramones-style jeans, spitting champagne at the *Melody Maker* at the awards night. They'd forgotten the 50,000 sales Alan and our team had put on when I was features editor and instead they went for a safe pair of hands. Would I like to start my own magazine instead? It was less risky for them and an opportunity for me. I said yes.

I went back in to see them with a one-sided sheet of paper. Two hundred and fifty words. That was all. Almost everything *loaded* became was on that piece of paper, apart from girls and fashion. My idea was for a magazine like *Arena* but edited by Hunter S. Thompson. It would feature young, up-and-coming entertainers, musicians, comedians and sports stars, as well as icons who were knackered and past it with great stories to tell. It would create generational tension. It would have a lot of attitude. A lot of music and football and nightclubs and drinking. I was describing my life in a magazine. With nothing to lose, they went for it.

I was shown to a room no bigger than a parking space next to where the IPC bins were. The last project to have foundered in there was a news magazine for teenagers. There was a friendly, dyslexic designer, Phil, who listened to Radio 2 all day, and just masses of old layouts and scrap paper. I was on a few hundred quid a week. There were no windows in the room, the office was impossible to find. Somewhere Spinal Tap were wandering around down there.

Back in LA I was having lunch with Adam Horovitz and his girl-friend Ione Skye and her mum in a healthy place called Houmous or something. Adam and Ione were just about to move into their own home together and vacate Ione's mum's pool house and all three of them said, 'Why don't you come and live in it, James?' What an offer. It was sunny, there was a pool house, a nice woman my mum's age inviting me to stay. Friends in the best band going. They'd just started *Grand Royal* mag and maybe I could help them with that.

I was mulling it over when I walked into a rock 'n' roll merchan-dise and record shop – laminates and backstage passes and decorated leather jackets for sale – and saw a guy I'd grown up watching present a cool BBC2 music show which at that time looked like a very good thing to do, and now he was working in a shop like I'd done when I was seventeen. And in a moment I glimpsed what you might cruelly call the scrapheap of Hollywood dreams and decided maybe I should give this chance to do my own mag a go and then if it works I'd be in a better place to come back and get a job and a life here. So I left the lovely people of Laurel Canyon behind and went back to the shitty little IPC development room with more dustbins than windows and just got on with it.

Fifty ways to leave your liver

Anonymous office, South Bank, London, 1992

My first thought was that I'd better do something to help my mate who paid the $4,000 wine bill so the first idea I wrote down was 'Bald Footballers by Kevin Sampson' and I went up King's Reach Tower to *Shoot* magazine to find a photo of early seventies players Terry Hennessey or Bobby Charlton. The *Shoot* photo library was a goldmine of memories from a time when football was on TV once a week and we learned about players from football cards. I wrote down 'Football Nostalgia'.

I started writing lists of people I wanted in the magazine. I'd had an idea previously for a book of drinking stories called '50 Ways To Leave Your Liver'. Alcohol was my life – I was interested in it, slightly. So I wrote down the famous drunks I liked: Hunter Thompson, Jeffrey Bernard, Charles Bukowski, Brian Clough, George Best, Alex Higgins, Paul Calf, Withnail, and the list just continued from there. A long list of people I never got to read about in magazines who my mates and I would talk about.

The list expanded into the bands I'd liked at the *NME* but who had stopped functioning: Happy Mondays, Stone Roses, New Order. The New Order audience were the people I thought would read this magazine – gig-going lads who would chant like football fans and happily sing along to Bernard's lyrics. Them and the guys I went to football with. Alan picked up on a story I told him about how I went to Elland Road with a bloke who was fast-tracking into the police graduate scheme (he eventually became the head of the anti-terrorism squad in the north), another who was a trainee barrister (youngest judge in Britain) and a third who was a very small-time pot dealer. He later wrote, 'The guy in the dock or the guy defending him', explaining how the mag would be for everyman. I wanted it to be for my mates I played football with, the (Northern) Exiles.

The lists went on: heroes from my childhood Paul Weller, the Sex Pistols, John Belushi, Michael Caine. Films I loved: *Withnail and I*, *Performance*, *Get Carter*, *Quadrophenia*, *Animal House*, *The Italian Job*. Music and films about being boys and men. *Animal House* in particular: 'You guys are on double secret probation.' I'd never been a student. *Animal House* made it seem far more exciting than it felt living among them in Leeds 6. So I had a framework and a load of ideas but I needed a proper designer and I needed other people to help put it together.

I called in a guy called Tim Southwell who had done some reviews at the *NME* and was working for the free secretarial recruitment mag *Ms London* and freelancing for *Smash Hits*. He had written about the week I'd spent hanging round with Keanu Reeves and Fabulous in London a while back. He was tremendously enthusiastic about things, like me he supported Leeds United and liked the Jam – both those attributes meant to me he'd be smack bang in the middle of the intended audience. He didn't really care about what was cool, he just had masses and masses of energy.

We started to put new pages together on a variety of subjects. While the Beastie Boys had been on hiatus, Yauch had been off doing something called snowboarding, surfing on snow. He'd shown me his board in his cottage in Lookout Canyon, LA, and given me a phial of liquid acid he had left over from the trip. No one was doing this snowboarding thing in the UK – in fact it was pretty much unheard of – so we found some photos of an early snowboarding pro mid-air off the side of a mountain from American mag *Men's Journal*, which I had a pile of, mocked up a layout with an irreverent, lively headline and the spread looked ace.

We both agreed we wanted Weller in the magazine. We had a page from New York magazine *Details* about some massive slippers called Matri-Mines that soldiers could wear in minefields to stop them getting blown up. These were the mags we had for reference: *Details*, *Men's Journal* and a young British skate mag called *Phat* which I mainly noticed because it had these new type of images called 'screen grabs' that Alan and I realised would allow us to capture exact moments from films and videos we wanted to cover. There was also an Australian book I'd read called *He Died with a Felafel in His Hand* which was just tales about young guys living together. It really captured the extremes of stupidity men could reach when under one roof. The total opposite of how magazines suggested we were supposed to be.

After Tim's enthusiasm I needed more humour. I called in a friend called Mick Bunnage who I knew through a cartoonist from Leicester called Alan Jenkins who'd drawn a brilliant and popular cartoon in *Attack on Bzag!* called *Tricky Problems for Rockstars*. Mick was also a cartoonist for trade magazines for dentists but he kept that quiet (and his dad had drawn the *Whizzer and Chips* logo). He also occasionally wrote funny pieces for *Arena* which seemed a bit out of place tucked away in the back somewhere. He wrote a definitive piece about 'Essex man', Rod Stewart and the Beverly Hills of Essex. Mick was quiet but very droll. He mentioned covering Rod, *The Sweeney* and *Minder*, and also suggested we have an agony uncle giving out bad advice and a table charting celebrity bad behaviour called Platinum Rogues. This would be illustrated by an array of what we now know as emojis but back then were little drawings of underpants and pints of Guinness.

I had a Hawaiian-shirted GP in Wapping who liked to be called Dr Mike. He was already having to regularly deal with the physical effects of my self-destructive alcoholic lifestyle so I asked him if he would do a proper medical column with advice for young guys. He declined. Bunnage and I mixed the two ideas and Mick's bad advice guy became Dr Mick, our back page anchor – a cross between Michael Winner and a morally questionable Peter Cook character.

I remembered a photo of French football executive Claude Bez which we had once used in the *NME* as a joke about Bez from the Mondays – in it he had a comb-over, a massive moustache and was cradling a revolver. I went back to the *Shoot* archive and found it. Claude Bez became Dr Mick. I was spending a lot of time in the *Shoot* photo library with Duncan who ran it. I figured if the mag didn't go anywhere I'd at least lift some old Leeds pics no one had ever used.

I gave the mag project the working title of the *Right Stuff* after my favourite book. We never intended to use it; it was just good to concentrate on the content and not the title. The fashion content was terrible – just a photo of a suede jacket that belonged to a young, then-unknown comedian I'd met called Mark Lamarr. I wasn't bothered about having fashion in the mag but Alan had said it would be a good source of advertising revenue. When I was best man at former *NME* features editor Adrian Thrills's wedding I met a Scottish woman called Gillian McVey who did press for Paul Smith. I explained my problem with having no decent fashion shots and she sorted it instantly. She told me to hire Beth Summers, a former fashion editor at *i-D*. And then she took me in to meet Paul at the newly launched PS jeans shop. 'This is James, he's going to start a magazine for the guys he goes to football and gigs with.' Paul suggested we use a shoot they'd done for a rebooted workwear line they were doing called R. Newbold. Paul and Gillian became very supportive and helpful. They understood what I wanted to do. The fashion looked right now.

I saw a really funny cricketer on *Question of Sport* who was talking about how he spent a lot of time helping his dad out as a roofer. His name was Phil Tufnell. He didn't seem like other cricketers – he was much livelier and didn't seem to know how to behave. There weren't any photos of Phil so I called a kid called Michael Holden who had interviewed Fabulous for a fanzine. He was a terrible interviewer, waffling on in a spaghetti junction of ideas and theory but the article he'd written had been really good. We photographed him in whites holding a cricket ball and said it was Phil Tufnell. This was how far away we were from anything. Some of these people and subjects had never been covered. We were faking photographs of famous people, people who had never been photographed other than in action.

We were producing pasted-together dummies with U2 on the cover – I had just been with them on the return-to-form Achtung Baby and Zooropa world tours for the *Sunday Times* magazine. Another *Right Stuff* dummy cover had their support act Stereo MCs, as the Mondays, Roses and New Order had all gone underground or broken up for a while. Another had a great shot of Denis Leary, a young American comedian I was getting to know and going to see whenever he came over to London, smoking. It was a great shot from *Details* magazine and we would much later use this as a real cover. In terms of age group *Details* was the only thing I came across that seemed close to what I wanted to do but it was still presented like a mini-*Esquire*, a cosmopolitan New York magazine about how to better yourself – only through the arts and music, as well as fashion. Their annual music edition was excellent though.

We were putting these dummies into focus groups led by a guy who looked like the singer from Hothouse Flowers – a lecturer type with long dark hair, soft floral shirts and a waistcoat. He was politely soliciting the opinion of blokes who read motorbike mags, music mags, *Shoot*, *Viz* – people who were recruited because they'd accepted £15 and a sandwich when stopped and offered it outside a newsagent's. They didn't seem like the guys I knew who went to clubs. Some blokes were clearly just there for the cash and a bite to eat.

The research process was so painful that, at times, the food was the highlight for Tim and me too. We stood with Alan behind a one-way glass partition, watching. He was taking notes; Tim and I were examining grapes stuffed with brie. This was in Oldham, and we'd never encountered anything like it before. People were just sitting round slagging off what we'd been doing. When we weren't scoffing the catering we were swearing at the glass and genuinely being held back from going in and fighting the blokes.

I followed one wanker in a cycling top under a suit jacket into the bogs intending to have a go at him. He was leading the group's conversation rather than letting everyone have a say and in doing so was fucking up our chance of a job. He didn't really care about what we were doing, he was just trying to dominate the conversation and destroying any chance of actual discussion about the pros and cons of the proposed magazine. In the bogs he had no idea I had anything to do with his freebie night out, it was a totally neutral experience for him, but it was killing us behind the glass. I realised I needed to calm down. Alan had asked me not to go to Texas to interview the Black Crowes for the *Sunday Times* mag so I could anonymously watch people taking my potential future apart.

It wasn't looking good; they didn't understand what we wanted to do. The layouts weren't helping us at all, as they didn't have a look that reflected the energy and humour we wanted. The final feedback was presented in the head of research's room at IPC. There was a whiteboard with two lists of words either side of a white line. Top left, GOOD; top right, BAD. First line, GOOD: 'This is like the really interesting bloke in the pub who always has the best stories.' BAD: 'This guy is really fucking irritating and thinks he knows it all.' I don't remember the rest of the words. It was a fine line; I recognised both descriptions in myself.

Now we were put in a holding pattern, supposedly developing more editorial, but we were as ready to go as we would ever be really; I felt it would come together better live. Some of my mates started hanging about the development room – Rob Wheeler who had the Medicine Bar, the UK's first club bar with battered sofas and decks. David Donald, an A & R scout who discovered Fairground Attraction. Some of the Fabulous boys would pop in.

We moved to a larger room with no window. At this point we were so far down the pecking order at IPC that we shared a fax machine with the *Amateur Gardener* classified ad department. Seriously, I'd be writing to U2's press officer asking for pictures with 'Am Gard Class Ads' in dot matrix across the top of the fax.

With the project under review at IPC we were mainly practising our putting with one of those office golf holes that fired the ball back at you if you got it in. Tim was writing phrases for *Smash Hits* stickers, I was writing pieces for the *Sunday Times*. I wrote a piece about a new football boot called the Blades for *Arena* which also mentioned a new boot in development by an ex-Liverpool player called Craig Johnson: the Predator. *Arena* stuck it away at the back in a single column. This was what we were up against – no one really gave a fuck about everyday male culture. Even as a simple design piece with a photo of the Predator or Blades prototypes it warranted a picture spread. *Arena* founder Nick Logan would acknowledge this years later. *Loaded* was able to happen because the London-centric fashion and style magazines had nothing to do with the rest of the country or indeed the vast majority of the male population; their low sales figures and lack of cultural impact reflected this. They barely featured new bands or football, or nightclubs that weren't in central London.

I had so many different influences on what I wanted in the mag and how it should be. After my mum died I didn't have the high output and creative motivation I'd had at *NME*, couldn't get going, just wanted to either excite or numb myself, didn't write for a while and then publishers 4th Estate sent me three books that really inspired me and would come to influence *loaded*: *Joe Bob Goes to the Drive-In* – consisting of spoof redneck movie reviews, with films judged by the number of breasts exposed and heads that rolled; *Road Fever* by Tim Cahill – adventure journalism about driving the length of the Americas in record time; *Rivethead* – an account of the decline of Michigan's car industry and the city around it by Ben Hamper, an associate of *Mother Jones* editor Michael Moore. All three came in the same envelope, all were passionately written. The first two became a big tonal influence on *loaded*; the third reflected a lot of my political opinions.

I watched two young guys holding court on Channel 4's *The Big Breakfast*. They were really cocky and funny and totally confident but I didn't know who they were. When I got into the office Tim Southwell told me they were Robbie and Mark from Take That. *Smash Hits* loved them; they were on their way to being massive. I later had a photo of Robbie and the American cover of one of my favourite music books, *Dance with the Devil* about the Stones, pinned to the wall by my desk – that was the spread of blokes we were aiming at. From populist, funny and lively, to legendary, talented and infamous.

Meanwhile Alan was up in King's Reach Tower with a pen and some Tippex changing the percentage approval results of the research groups. He only told me this years later, but thank fuck he did. It was late 1993. He came in to see me and said, 'Listen, I need a mood board about as big as this whiteboard with quotes from women's magazines IPC and other big companies publish. They're worried about what the tone of voice might be and any sexual content so I need to show them what's already out there in the women's mass market sector.'

We got to work with a pile of magazines, scissors and photocopier blowing the quotes up and turning them into a collage of headlines and pull quotes. In the middle I pasted a massive headline from *More* or *Just 17*: 'How to give a blow job!' It was weird because we had no intention of writing any articles like this or indeed having any sexual content in the magazine.

We'd been waiting for months to get a yes or no, and we weren't improving the dummy in any way. Alan went away and presented the research results he'd altered to the board and explained my idea in full. He showed them the mood board and explained how they'd market the mag in other IPC mags and how it would be a very low-risk investment. One of the IPC board said, 'That's all very interesting, Alan, thank you.' He had made them a lot of money rebuilding the *NME*, they trusted him, but he wasn't sure if we'd done enough. The director referred Alan back to the sexual mood board. 'One last question, Alan. What's a blow job?'

Then he gave him one and we got the green light.

Away baby, let's go

South Bank, London, December 1993

Once our light turned green there was an avalanche of live journalistic activity, things I'd had in rotation in my head, things that had become apparent through development and research. Attitudes and ideas I'd written on the first piece of paper I'd presented: 'Up and coming and dangerous, knackered and past it, great stories. Generational tension.'

After almost eighteen months in development it just felt absolutely great to be let off the leash and Tim and I just went into overdrive, constantly amazed and thrilled by the opportunity we now had. First up it needed a name, staff, an art director and a logo. And we needed a dummy to help the music and football title ad teams sell ads. We had about twelve weeks to go but given that we used to produce a whole *NME* in a week it didn't faze me; if anything it certainly made me more focused, as I knew we'd get staff and ideas. The design was the only issue we were yet to resolve.

For the magazine name we threw masses of potential titles down until we had thirty which we filtered down to four: *Flip*, *Rogue*, *loaded* and the *Right Stuff*, and then put back into research. The 'ask the audience' style graph came back with three little blocks and one massive tower of approval.

So that was that, the magazine was going to be called *loaded*. It had multiple meanings, which was good: loaded gun; loaded rich; and in America loaded meant drunk. But obviously and most importantly for us, it was the name of the single that changed Primal Scream's career from music paper favourites to proper cultural game changers, introduced by the Weatherall-sourced sample:

'Just what is it that you want to do?
'We wanna be free, we wanna be free to do what we wanna do. And we wanna get loaded. And we wanna have a good time. And that's what we're gonna do. We're gonna have a good time. We're gonna have a party! Away baby, let's go!'

The quote fitted what the magazine was going to be about perfectly. With this name we produced the sales dummy with thirty-two pages of sample images and articles: footballers in trouble with the law, adrenaline sports, music, film, humour, clubbing, girls. Paul Calf was on the cover at the top of the list of our alco-heroes, the logo was lower case and yellow on a purple background. It looked rough, garish and a bit different.

Editorially it was of no importance to us; I always knew it would be better live. One of our future staff who was keen to get involved told us that the editor of *Smash Hits*, where he worked, actually gathered his staff together, held it up and said, 'This is the worst magazine dummy I've ever seen.' Within nine months the same bloke would be desperately chasing into the market editing *For Him* magazine.

My feeling was we would either sell 10,000 or 100,000. IPC set the target of 30,000 and a break-even point of three years.

We gave Mick (writer), Beth (fashion) and Michael (editorial assistant) the same three-month contracts we were now on, and put an ad in the Media *Guardian* and one on the IPC staff noticeboard. I wanted people with character and a bit of real-life experience, a sense of humour, personalities. I was interviewing applicants with some very basic questions to see how they would react: 'Who do you support?'; 'Have you got a girlfriend? If so has she got any mates?'; 'Have you got any drugs?' The responses were exceedingly helpful and told me a lot about them as people – I could see whether they were any good editorially or not because of the examples of their work.

The ones Alan and I liked sort of felt like frontiersmen – they had a slight air of desperation, and were very keen. Production editor Christian Smyth had been between jobs since he'd left the *Big Issue* distraught that a vendor he'd befriended had hanged himself. He was pretty friendly and together so we signed him up. We picked up a Scottish picture editor, Robbie, who was a mate of *NME* photographer Martyn Goodacre. I asked a loud, funny, cockney character Reece who always seemed pretty well dressed when he worked on the door of the Love Ranch nightclub if he fancied assisting Beth in fashion. And Alan and I interviewed a guy called Martin Deeson who was doing the late shift subbing the *TV Times*. He had a blond loaf of a fringe, a massive grin, was very personable and confident enough to come wearing a bright-red denim jacket. He'd written an article about bars in New York and another about breaking up with the mother of his child after family counselling. He had a good turn of phrase, so he was in as subeditor and writer.

With seven weeks till the print deadline we were almost ready to go live and as Martin left his office Alan and I felt pretty good about where we were. We were discussing how to launch without a proper art editor, just freelancers, when the phone went. I picked it up and it was a guy called Steve Reid on the phone calling from the design department at *Select* magazine asking about the new mag. I pointed out *Select* had just run a full page taking the piss out of the idea, a fake front cover of a mag for blokes. He replied, 'Yeah I laid that out but while I was doing it I thought it was actually a really good idea.' He came over right there and then with a mini portfolio and loads of great opening spreads and covers. *Select* had been doing really well since half the *NME* writers I'd worked with had gone over there.

We did a deal with Steve, didn't tell him IPC was only definitely putting us on the payroll for twelve weeks, and he resigned the next day. He also said he had a mate called Jon Link who designed record sleeves for Erasure who he'd like to be his number two. Steve came back two days later with a brilliant long-lost but just-released Bauhaus lower-case font called Archetype Bayer and said we should use it in neon orange, which virtually no one did. It was the last and most valuable piece of the jigsaw.

Something I absolutely wanted in the magazine was a sense of attitude, cockiness and a hunt for fun. As far back as October 1992 when Tim had first joined me on the project we'd had an amazing night out in Barcelona when Leeds had beaten Stuttgart at the Camp Nou at a replayed European game. We'd wandered round the city looking at great architecture with a fireman and a plumber we'd met, then I'd blagged us all into a club by convincing them we were the Farm. The way football could give you such a great time but also appeal to people regardless of their jobs really struck me, and I said to Tim, 'This feeling tonight is what our magazine should be like.'

A less colourful influence was Prime Minister John Major, a grey man who referred to pubs as 'wayside inns', who had just said young men in Britain were in danger of becoming a generation of 'yobs and slobs'. That really rankled with me and I wrote down the line, 'Get fit or get fucked up but for fuck's sake do something.' That really was my attitude for the mag.

Alan wanted to subtitle *loaded* 'The Hedonist's Handbook' but Mick and I had both mentioned the concept of men who should know better. I was thinking about what people had repeatedly said to me about my life, and he was alluding to the sort of famous male he wanted to write about. So I wrote down the self-deprecating line, 'For Men Who

Should Know Better', and Steve fitted it in nicely between the upper stalks of the 'l' and first 'd' in the *loaded* logo.

As the magazine was announced, industry people who'd never really done anything started slagging the concept off. Staff on *NME* started calling it 'Folded' and actually wrote a letter to IPC to complain their profits were being used to fund its development. (These presumably being the profits Alan and I and others had put on in that 50,000 sales increase between '87 and '92 – they'd not done much, sales wise, since then.) The editor of men's fashion trade mag *For Him* laughed and said his title had nothing to worry about as his writers were 'past masters at humour' – the evidence on the page and the lack of sales suggested otherwise. Only the editor of *GQ*, an American guy called VerMeulen, had anything positive to say about it when he told the London *Evening Standard*, 'I don't mind a magazine for lads into music and football so long as they aren't sick on my sofa.'

The general consensus in the trade papers was that men wouldn't read a mainstream lifestyle magazine in the same way women did, only specialist publications. I used to do all the multiple choice sex and relationship quizzes in my girlfriends' magazines so I figured that was bollocks. If women could create magazines men would read I was pretty confident men could too. It was just that no one had had the vision or confidence or backing to do it before. We couldn't give a fuck what the industry thought. I was still in grass-smoking, Fabulous management mode, happily riding my bike round the office waving a golf club about, feeling extremely happy. The energy in the latest development office (we had a window now but it had bars over it) was really electric and a few more of my mates had started popping in now that it wasn't a secret project any more.

The opportunity to edit a magazine again just felt fantastic. I knew I could make it anything I wanted and had decided I would go about it in a way influenced by my time fucking around in vans and on hilltops with Fabulous and inspired by the new journalism writers I'd leapt on in my late teens. They'd written about the American counter-culture in the late sixties and early seventies when it was changing so much and I knew there was so much going on in Britain right then.

I had three rules that I'd picked up and that I kept telling people:

Always have a beatbox in your dressing room.
Know the limits of a situation.
Be the story.

With the advice of Joe Strummer, Bill Drummond and Hunter S. Thompson ringing in our ears it was always going to be different. The challenge now was to get the magazine onto the shelves so people could buy it.

I had read about Neil Bogart's Casablanca Records, the big disco label, and how the coke dealer would arrive at the end of the week meeting and just plonk all the orders out in front of all the staff. Billy Bragg's manager Peter Jenner had told me Hawkwind were always popular because they sorted their fans out from the back of the van, and Creation were the most popular indie label and were awash in narcotics. All these struck me as an interesting way to go about things and I made sure that we would have as many competitions giving away beer as possible. A magazine with free alcohol and easy access for whatever stimulants the staff wanted seemed like a winner.

It was now just a matter of filling the first issue. I knew I wanted to have great images all over the mag because I wanted the readers to know they were in the right place. I understood the importance of iconic images in terms of inspiration rather than just decoration. No one had seen those images we unearthed of Michael Caine in *Get Carter* and *The Italian Job* for decades. It was publishing them in *loaded* that put them in the window once high street print shops started up a few years later. To me they represented a combination of realism and fantasy, a fairly-tale greatness. *The Italian Job* was like a young men's Disney film – a bright, colourful, singalong with memorable scenes, quotable lines, car chases and fantastic scenery. That's where I placed *loaded*; it was for boys who wanted to retain the fun of childhood – the colour, the adventure, the desire not to lose the early green shoots of possibility while progressing through life. Very early on, Paul Smith said to me, 'Be child-like not child-ish,' and that was a blurred path we stumbled down.

Amazingly we produced the first issue live over the same four-week schedule as all future issues would be. Who starts a business in real time?

For the front cover we wanted Weller, as the Jam had meant everything to both Tim and me growing up and I sent Sean O'Hagan off to interview him. Sean had previously written a piece in *Arena* using the phrase 'new lads' to describe his, Paolo and Stuart Cosgrove's lively night-time behaviour at the *NME*. Politically correct socialists by day but crazed music and football fans by night, dancing on top of cars pissed, getting thrown off airplanes on the way to Scotland games and looking for women. It was a light-hearted admission but the press took to it as the successor to 'new man'. None of these labels meant anything – we were all just young men.

Steve Pyke shot Weller wearing a sporran and he looked really good but then IPC suddenly got worried that the readers of *NME* and *Melody Maker* might think it was a new music magazine and not buy them that week. So they asked us to change it. We decided to switch to Eric Cantona who we'd loved at Leeds United when we won the league two years before. Even though he'd left for Man U, his upturned collar attitude, affected mystery and supreme ability captivated the football world. He was an enigma, and had rarely been photographed. These were the days before individual sponsorship and branding deals descended on footballers, and the only shots we could find of Eric out of his kit were one of him in double denim hitchhiking, one in a cream suit on a catwalk and one at a bar with his agent. They were so terrible we couldn't put them on the cover, and as we didn't have an interview we put him inside and asked a guy who had interviewed him a few times at press conferences for the Man U programme to stitch all his own quotes together. Years later I'd get to meet and hang out with Eric at a memorial party for Joe Strummer, which was a great night apart from my red mate Bucky getting Eric in a headlock and trying to kiss him.

Gary Oldman had just had a pretty twisted cop thriller called *Romeo Is Bleeding* out so we brought an interview in from an agency and I wrote a page on why I liked him and what he meant to us. From *The Firm* to *Sid and Nancy* he'd been in loads of films that young men liked and he had an attitude that fit what we wanted to do perfectly. There were always loads of good photographs of film stars so Gary Oldman would be on the cover. When the title went live it was supported by festival-size billboard fly posters of his face on the cover and he was shocked when he saw them while coming into London from Heathrow. He had his agent send us a fax thanking us.

A mate of ours at *NME*, Iestyn George, told us about a black American teenage golf prodigy called Tiger Woods he'd read a tiny 'news in brief' story about. He sounded perfect, and after finding his agent Tim called his family home and his dad said he was in the shower then off to school but Tim should call back later that day. Which he did, and that was our non-football sports content, the first British interview with the man who became the greatest golfer ever, and then we got to take our own shots too when a photographer I'd worked with at the *NME* happened to be in the area where Tiger lived.

Alan found a *Rolling Stone* interview with Beavis and Butthead; Tim wrote a piece about skydiving; Deeson wrote a piece about the joys of hotel sex; Emma Forest wrote a piece saying MP Stephen Milligan was more rock 'n' roll than Kurt Cobain because Milligan had died in some auto-erotic asphyxiation game whereas Kurt had taken an OD in Rome but hadn't managed it – blunt to say the least. We had a travel piece by a guy called Trevor Ward which involved his fear a woman he'd dated in South America had been eaten by a shark. We found some really striking but strange photos of Italian football team Sampdoria managed by Sven-Göran Eriksson and featuring David Platt, Ruud Gullit, Roberto Mancini and Attilio Lombardo all dressed as fighter pilots around a fighter jet. They appeared in a brilliant Italian magazine called *King* but had been taken for a charity arranged by a guy with a clothes shop. Tim interviewed both the guy and David Platt. It was an uncanny discovery but as with Tiger it gave us something totally new.

I wrote a piece about my favourite film, *Withnail and I*, which had kind of disappeared after being released in early '87. It had a real cult following among my friends and we would quote lines from it even though it wasn't on anywhere. No one had ever reported this *Withnail* appreciation scene so I got hold of director Bruce Robinson and told him about it and he agreed to an interview. This covered off our cult film requirement and made for a great cover line: 'Withnail You Terrible Cult'. Momentum around the film built and two years later they rereleased it.

We needed a main cover line and, wanting to focus on the fact we had sizeable pieces on each of our potential cover stars, I thought a lot about what the three of them had in common. Ultimately they just struck me as being regular guys made good. A footballer, a musician, a film star. Guys we'd have liked to hang out with. Then, based on the old Leeds United chant 'Super Leeds', I just put each of their names on the layout and wrote 'Super Lads' underneath. Little did I know how contentious this word would become decades later; to me it just meant lads, like lads and lasses. Boys I'd grown up with in Yorkshire, where 'aye, lad' just meant 'yes'. It was how my dad and his brothers still spoke to each other. It had no connotations beyond that at all.

On the advertising front they sold quite a few pages. Most of ads were music-related, and Creation Records, believing in us more than IPC management, booked a year's adverts for the Primals, Heavy Stereo and a new band called Oasis.

Two young guys called Tyler Brûlé and Zed Nelson came in, a writer/photographer team, and they wanted to do some reportage for us. An opportunity to go on a survival course for journalists in combat zones had already come up so they went off and did that, but they were also dead set on going to a gun bazaar in Pakistan and writing about Médecins Sans Frontières in Afghanistan. Which they did with commissions from us and *SKY* magazine.

A week later Tim picked up the phone, went very quiet and serious and finally put it down and said, 'Blimey, Tyler's been shot by the Moulin Rouge!'

I looked at him just wondering what the fuck he was on about. 'The Moulin Rouge is a strip club in Paris.'

'Ah, no – the Khmer Rouge.'

'No, wrong decade, wrong country. Do you mean the Mujahedeen?'

'That's them!'

Tyler had been very badly shot up and was in a really serious condition. Soon as he was back convalescing in a UK hospital Tim went off to see him and quite sweetly took him a bag of fruit and some magazines. Zed came in and told us how terrible the incident had been, how they'd been in a car that came under deliberate fire and there'd been blood pumping out of Tyler's arms. Zed said he thought the combat journalism course had probably save Tyler's life. He said neither of them was going to write about that part of the trip yet but that as he'd been to the gun market in Pakistan and had photos he would write it up. Thankfully Tyler recovered and went on to have a brilliant media career, launching *Wallpaper* and *Monocle* magazines. Zed became a regular *loaded* photographer and contributor.

You'd think the serious action stopped there but it didn't. At the last minute Mick's 'Rod Update' spread, full of the former Faces frontman's life of high jinks was rejected by the lawyers as some of the clippings Mick had based it on had been subject to huge lawsuits. We had two days to go and two pages to fill. Alan pointed out we didn't really have many fit women in so we called photographer John Stoddart who sent over some pretty sexy portraits of an aspiring actress called Elizabeth Hurley in a negligee, and we just whacked them in.

We were done. It was 6.30 p.m., Friday, 8 April 1994 and the issue had been sent to the printer. We had to move out of our final development office and into a real-live, newly built one above *Marie Claire* in a four-storey building away from the main IPC tower. Everyone went to the pub and the office was totally empty but for me dancing around to Blur's 'Boys and Girls' which had just come out. I was absolutely delighted. Totally thrilled, spilling over with excitement. The issue looked great.

I was about to tip my whole desk into a packing crate when the phone went. I could hardly hear it above the music blasting out. It was a journalist from the *Daily Express* who had been put through because no one was picking up any of the phones in the music papers. 'Had we heard Kurt Cobain was dead?' She wasn't sure but they were hearing rumours from Seattle and wanted to check. I hadn't but I walked down to the pub, past all the *NME* and *Melody Maker* writers laughing and drinking away, quietly whispered to Tim that he needed to come outside urgently and we went back to the office to verify it.

Tim got through to the police and coroner in Seattle and they confirmed it was true. There were still police and medical officers at the scene. This was before the Internet; there was no instant information. It was pretty strange sitting there in a totally empty office with this information that such an iconic singer had died and no one else knew. Shocking, in fact. I called Alan and he called the printers and they pulled Emma's article about Cobain and Milligan and repeated the 'next issue' page.

We didn't have any down time to spend between putting the issue to bed and it coming out because given we only had a twelve-week window of employment before IPC decided to proceed or can the mag, we'd both arranged trips away. Tim went off to do something dangerous in the sky somewhere and I went to Barbados the next day to interview the real Phil Tufnell playing for England in Barbados and then planned to head straight off to LA to interview the Beasties. If *loaded* didn't take off we could at least say we'd hit the ground running and had our money's worth from the IPC travel department.

As it was, luck was on our side, as it seemed to be so often. By creating and pursuing stories ourselves instead of just following PR lines we were defining our own landscape and often things started to come really good. In Bridgetown, Tuffers not only took wickets but also a catch – by his own admission he was shit at catching – and England beat the Windies for the first time on the island in over thirty years. The photos by Derek Ridgers of Phil and the England Barmy Army fans and the interview really caught the mood of young men enjoying themselves. Phil was a great guy; he genuinely loved cricket but didn't seem to take anything too seriously. I had a huge grass spliff on the go in the England camp, only hiding it away once the England vicar, Wingers Dingers (as Tuffers called him) wandered up to say hello.

So Tuffers would be my second *loaded* feature and the Beastie Boys in LA would be my third. I had a great week with the Beasties and Derek Ridgers shot a huge posse of them and their friends up at Griffith Observatory and then it was home on the day the magazine was to be on sale.

I arrived at Heathrow so excited and went straight to the newsagent's at arrivals and just started to feel sick. *Loaded* wasn't anywhere to be seen. I always felt that if IPC distributed it right it would work; they could be pretty slow and bureaucratic as a company so I just didn't know whether they could get it together. It really looked like they hadn't. The retailer didn't know what I was talking about but suggested trying departures. I went there and it was the same thing: nothing on the shelves or by the tills, no *loaded* anywhere. I just felt crushed, all my expectation and euphoria was slipping away as I left the large open-plan newsagent's. Then as I'd actually left the premises a glimpse of neon orange behind me caught my eye. Really bright. I looked back and there was a whole stand facing the airport entrance. Sixteen *loaded* front covers. It looked amazing and I just stood there in disbelief then went and bought a copy. The rest of the team back in the office had already had early print-run issues but this was the first time I had. I was laughing all the way back into London.

Immediately the *Sun* started calling us to try and buy the Hurley photos. They rang and rang over and over again; they called John Stoddart, the photographer, and he didn't want to sell either. Then, within a couple of weeks, she showed up at her boyfriend's film premiere in a dress held together by safety pins. The film was *Four Weddings and a Funeral*, the tabs had as many shots as they could print of her and life for Hugh and Liz was never the same again.

Parklife came out; then a few months later, *The Fast Show* ('Which is nice', 'Brilliant!' 'Scorchio!'); *Pulp Fiction*; and then, within a year, *Trainspotting*. In September Oasis's *Definitely Maybe* went to number one in the album charts in the first week of release. Two weeks later Oasis gatecrashed my birthday party with my old *NME* colleague Paolo Hewitt. After a few too many drinks a girl came up to me and said, 'Those lads have nicked my handbag,' to which I replied, 'They've just had their first number one album, I think they're past the handbag nicking stage now.' The *loaded* world was just erupting. In 1994 our world and the world itself had changed.

But before then we had a second and a third issue to do. About a week after we'd gone on sale an IPC post boy huffed and puffed his way into the office and dumped a solid grey postbag overflowing with postcards and letters, and then another showed up and did the same. 'We've been looking for you all over IPC, no one knew where you were or what your office number was. There's another one of these downstairs, the mail's been pouring in.'

It was like the scenes on the *Blue Peter* Christmas appeal. There were hundreds and hundreds, well over a thousand letters of appreciation and requests for subscriptions, 'I've never read anything like this, it's the best mag ever,' was the common tone. Some just sent postcards with lines like '*loaded* is brilliant!' We were shocked.

Then the sales figures came in. It had sold over 60,000 copies. Again we were amazed. IPC gave us full-time contracts and everything. *Loaded* instantly became subject to masses of media attention. But more importantly, the readers loved it and the sales were stepping up issue by issue.

Setting off for a late spring holiday Alan Lewis left a slightly nervous and carefully detailed memo telling me what I needed to look out for. Reading it back twenty-eight years on it essentially reads like: I've given you the keys to the house – please don't fuck it up. A sense of wary trust. It went on, referring to Andy MacDuff, the group publisher of music and sport titles at *NME*: 'Don't forget the publishers' meeting at 2.30 in Andy's office on Monday. Given the sales figures (of the first two issues) the mood should be euphoric but Andy may comment on the editorial page costs.'

He suggested asking for a PA for the project, and some suggestions for autumn cover promotions: 'I think we should do another sex supplement (different angles of course) and definitely a fashion one of some sort.

'SCHEDULE: for god's sake make sure the issue stays on schedule. We got away with it on issue two by the great good luck of finding a second printer with spare capacity. Running so wildly adrift makes us look sloppy and unprofessional. Failing to meet the on-sale date is the ultimate sin in publishing.'

'LEGAL: make sure that Christian sends *all* the pages to the legal department. In particular the drugs story and Mick's Platinum Rogues, which is a potential minefield.'

He went on to suggest a feature on the Simpsons' 1,000th episode which was about to air. And that we should commission another feature from the brilliant and quite unique Jon Ronson who I'd recruited when I met him on a train on the way to do research the autumn before. And 'another Action Man piece from Tim'. The memo continued, encouraging me to highlight the amazing luck we seemed to be having in covering people like Liz Hurley just before they became famous or topical.

'AND FINALLY . . . SEX!: Don't be fazed by negative feedback from politically correct journalists; we're not producing *loaded* for peer-group approval. I'm sure that (apart from its general brilliance) the reason the second issue is going well is because of the sex supplement. Sex sells, and we shouldn't lose our nerve. Fuck 'em if they can't take a joke.'

I had scribbled out 'joke' and written 'bloke' in pencil.

Within a year the *loaded* luck was still flying, the magazine became market leader, I won the Periodical Publications Association's Editor of the Year and *loaded* the Magazine of the Year, the first of many awards to come. The luck held, the sales grew and the magazine came to life with a powerful bond between reader and editorial staff. They had plenty of reasons to like it.

I didn't get where I am today . . .

Spring 1994

Once we'd been given the go ahead I had to set about building or finding some staple regulars for *loaded*. The men we had talked to in focus groups all wanted to read about people who had made a lot of money so I created a very simple Q & A for entrepreneurs and business people called My Brilliant Career – the high-roller questionnaire. Would business people want to tell us what the first money they ever earned was and how much they had on them now?

The first one was an easy win, Chris Donald from *Viz*, who had made a fortune out of strips about violent vicars and boys with explosive backsides. My favourites from those we ran were the less obvious ones like Russian-looking American Victor Kiam who had been famous when I was younger for advertising his own shavers on TV with the phrase 'I was so impressed I bought the company'. In the pre-Internet days it was sometimes a bit of a hunt to track these people down – you couldn't use Google or LinkedIn. When someone uttered the line, 'I didn't get where I am today by . . .' in the office one day I realised we should feature the businessman whose catchphrase it was. CJ, the boss of Sunshine Desserts in David Nobbs's brilliant sitcom *The Fall and Rise of Reginald Perrin*. I wrote to their creator to see if he could get CJ to do it. David Nobbs didn't get where he was today without recognising a good opportunity and agreed to write it for £200. Many years later I'd call David back to come and script-edit a BBC sitcom project written by Mitchell and Webb about my time 'adrift in a sea of women' at Condé Nast Publications.

A lot of these high-roller questionnaires were just sent out as a fixed list of questions with gaps for the answers to be written in by hand. I didn't expect the targeted high rollers had too much time on their hands but I did think they probably liked telling their stories of how they made it and figured that requesting short answers would be an attractive workload for them.

Film director turned brilliantly obnoxious restaurant critic Michael Winner, who was largely the basis for Dr Mick, our back-page 'aggro uncle' and a regular in the Platinum Rogues chart, knocked back the idea of a written exchange and invited me out to his famous 58-bedroom mansion in Holland Park, next door to Jimmy Page's even more impressive gaff. I found Winner sitting ready and waiting behind his desk with his own tape recorder rolling with the intention of making sure he had a true record of the conversation. This didn't bother me at all but when I started to ask the questions he turned to his side and began staring out of the window and answering airily like a pompous regional Roman governor, thinking he was plucking genius from the air.

I was bollocksed if I was going to talk to his profile so I decided to bring out the best question immediately: 'What would you think if you met yourself at a party?'

He stopped, turned and looked at me and said, 'That is a very good question,' and from then on we had eye contact for the rest of the interview. At the end we talked about when he'd been a music journalist and he congratulated me on how well *loaded* was going and asked me what I wanted to do next. I told him I wanted to produce a play of *Withnail and I* in the West End and he instantly replied, 'Well come and see me when you do and I will invest £50,000.'

There were other regular sections that would become reader and writer favourites like the Greatest Living Englishman and Great Moments in Life. Jon Wilde was one of the key figures in *loaded*'s original architecture – not that he ever claimed any responsibility for it – inventing must-read sections and writing astounding interviews. I'd known him since *Jamming!* and *Sounds* and it was Jon who Mark E. Smith had called from my phone book to amusingly abuse at two in the morning.

With the Greatest Living Englishman and Great Moments in Life his intention was to celebrate the great men we loved who were often overlooked, and moments of public and personal brilliance. The first GLE was Dave the Barman at the Winchester Club in *Minder*, written by a guy called Pete Campbell I'd once met in Berlin, and the first GMIL Wilde wrote was when a crowd of kids in parkas mobbed Ronnie Radford when he'd scored an unexpected screamer for lowly Hereford, knocking Newcastle out of the FA Cup in 1973. Both sections were written tributes to the sort of late-night drunken discussions we spent ages having ourselves. That invariably would start, 'Do you remember . . .'

Both columns became pillars of the magazine, perfect examples of how we were different from other magazines. They allowed us to celebrate people and events we loved when there was no topical reason to do so. Peter Cook's tribute was published by pure coincidence a couple of days before he died, which was perceived to be a super-fast and respectful ironic tribute. Sid James wasn't even English, but he was heralded as a GLE, albeit with some scribbling out and alterations in the title.

Great Moments in Life covered film, sport, music, life – Keith Richards dealing with a stage invader by 'chopping the mother down' with his guitar, scraping together a fish finger sandwich from the back of the freezer after the pub – which was actually submitted on spec by a reader. In these sections we began to realise the magazine should reflect the way our lives were, rather than some artificial concept that was put out by upmarket magazines or newspapers.

Heeeeyyyyyyyy, Bruce!!!!!

Cannes, May 1994

One defining early story typified the sort of luck we created for ourselves that helped us gather editorial momentum and increased our cast-iron self-belief. After reviewing a theme park ride and a mass wine tasting to great effect in the first issues, our new staff writer/subeditor Martin Deeson walked into my office with an idea for his third story and said, 'I think I should go to the Cannes Film Festival. There'll be loads of film stars kicking about and I can interview them. It starts this week.' It was a great idea and unsurprisingly he was brimming with enthusiasm for the trip, given that a few weeks before he'd been subbing the listings at the *TV Times*.

His enthusiasm was crushed, however, when he came back two hours later and told me that as we'd only had one issue out and no one in Cannes had heard of the magazine he couldn't get press accreditation or a decent place to stay, so there wasn't any point going. On the contrary, thinking about the fun I'd had writing about the JAMs for *NME* when we had no chance of meeting Abba, to me this seemed like a great opportunity to define our outsider status and increase the likelihood of adventure, and I told him he must go as 'a pauper in paradise'. Representing the same lack of access a reader would have seemed like a totally different perspective you never read. So with a weird mix of reluctance and appreciation he called the IPC company travel agent and with my former *NME* photographer colleague Derek Ridgers in tow they set off for Cannes.

Twenty-four hours later I got a call from the departure gate to Caen. Now Cannes is the jewel of the Riviera, full of splendid hotels and film stars, very much in the South of France, whereas Caen is an industrial port that saw a lot of artillery action in the Second World War, very much on the north-east coast of France.

'I thought that was just how they must spell it in France,' Deeson explained when I asked him if he hadn't noticed the difference on the ticket. To be fair to Martin and Derek, it wasn't their fault, the travel agent had misheard him, and as the festival had already started I suggested he immediately try and find a private jet or a helicopter and I'd insist to IPC it was vital.

Whenever I visited New York for the *NME* I was always getting a chopper from JFK into Manhattan and convincing Alan he had to sign it off as my plane was late and I would have missed the gig otherwise, so I thought it was time to test the expenses account for *loaded*. I felt it would cheer the guys up, but years later Martin told me the suggestion totally threw him. 'One minute you wanted me to stay in a hovel on the outskirt of Cannes, the next you were offering to pay for a helicopter.' It was important to keep the guys ambitious and on their toes without just being sucked into the PR industry but that didn't mean I wanted them reporting on Cannes from Caen.

Anyway they couldn't find one so they had to come back to London and start again. It was a sign of things to come. They went to Cannes and despite pretending to be a film producer Martin couldn't get anywhere or anything. I guess the town was already full of bullshitters with the same story but better credentials. Thankfully Derek was able to photograph the crowds round the topless aspiring actresses on the beach – it had worked for Bardot and was still seen by some as a possible first step on the ladder to fame, stalkers, a tiny dog in a handbag and a fragrance deal.

With his calm, unruffled to the point of boredom nature, extreme height and gnarled looks – Chewbacca hair, Bukowski face – Derek was in fact an exceptionally talented man and had always been very adept at attracting attention and finding interesting people on our trips to California. Sure enough, he was able to get a great shot of Clint Eastwood in the back of a limo driving past a wall of fans and photographers that totally summed up the approach I wanted to the article. We ended up using it on the opening spread.

Martin was having less luck. After four days of marching up and down the Croisette very much on the outside of proceedings – too far outside – he did exactly what any sane person would do, and thinking he was going to be sacked on his return decided to get drunk. Martin was a very affable character, something that had drawn Alan and me to him when we first met him, and he would soon prove you could send him anywhere and he'd make friends. He had a big, shit-eating grin, a loaf of blond hair and looked like Billy Bunter played by Arnold Schwarzenegger. He had a sort of corrupted charisma that people liked. I always thought that in times gone by he'd have done well as a raddled British representative in some far-off, sun-kissed dead-end of the Commonwealth where all he had to do was shake hands, grin and drink.

Totally out on his arse in baggy shorts and an alcohol-stained, body-hugging green camouflage T-shirt with an amber neon lightning strike down the front, he found himself getting shitfaced at a very nice hotel bar with a kindly looking Jewish businessman who asked him why he seemed so down. Martin explained the outlook of the new magazine, what he was doing there, how badly he was doing it and how he thought he was going to lose his cushy number on this great new mag.

If ever there was a true guardian angel moment this was it. The man turned out to be Lloyd Kaufman, the head of Troma Films. At that point *loaded* was probably the only mainstream magazine in the world that would give his film productions the time of day. If you've never seen a Troma film they were the most deliberately trashy contemporary movies around. With titles like *The Toxic Avenger* and *Class of Nuke 'Em High*, they were a deliberately rancid take on the American dream that weren't so much straight to video release as straight to off-licence video basket release. They were loved by comic books fans and John Waters and Russ Meyer heads, and naturally Deeson knew of them.

Lloyd listened to Martin's plight and, recognising a kindred spirit, whipped out a heavy gold-embossed party invite and said, 'I'm sick of this town, I'm heading back to the States. There's an industry party going on upstairs, take my ticket.'

Martin couldn't believe his luck. He thanked the departing Lloyd, waved his way past security with the ticket and jumped into the elevator. It was only as he arrived at his floor that he saw the ticket was the Miramax client party. As the door pinged open, everyone was looking at the apparition before them and the first person he saw was Bruce Willis. Martin boldly stepped forward shouting 'BRUCE!' like they were old friends. Bruce, not knowing who the hell he was, but bowled over by his very 'artistic' look, assumed he was someone hot, new and cutting edge and returned the greeting 'HEYYYY!' and Martin was in!

He'd made it from the pavement to the penthouse and the suite was rammed with famous faces. He had his story. Eventually, without the appropriate insider chat and interior designer names to drop, they realised he was just a blagger and like Flounder at Delta Tau Chi in *Animal House* they steered him out to the balcony with arms full of drink and food to the only other unknown guy they'd put out there. But here *loaded*'s luck still held because the guy was a young British boxer who had moved to Canada called Lennox Lewis. The future heavyweight champion of the world.

Turning to drink in a moment of desperation would become a cornerstone of most future journalistic operations on the magazine.

Even when matters weren't going wrong. The resulting feature was both substantial and very funny and it was one of the first times when I realised that if we followed the instinct for trouble and adventure described so wonderfully in Hunter's books we could genuinely make a different type of magazine. Martin's confidence was boosted, he proved he could deliver a big story, and he returned the hero and set about becoming the magazine's star writer.

The eventual *loaded* editorial office was situated on the fourth floor of a fairly unremarkable brick building opposite IPC's main King's Reach Tower reception. The Tower was thirty storeys high and had a four-floor low rise curling off it; this meant the space directly in front of our office was effectively a bowl, with hundreds of people passing through it to and from the main reception to the street every day who often became victims.

One windy morning there was a demonstration outside the main reception against the *Angling Times* by fish lovers. About seventy people with placards and a megaphone were immediately below us and it seemed too good an opportunity to miss as we got to work with the printer competing to see who could write the most stupid fishing puns: 'Give Dace a Chance'; 'Tench Nervous Haddock'; 'Cod Help Us'; 'Bass, How Low Can You Go?'; 'Shark Life'; and on and on. Pretty soon we had a massive stack of them and we started dropping them out of the window. No one in the office felt strongly either way about the issue but the leaflets really started to annoy the protestors, which made us laugh. Passers-by were picking them up and laughing, and eventually the fish demonstrators asked the police to come and ask us to stop doing it and even complained to the IPC reception. Naturally neither of them gave a fuck but the police, who were keen readers, enjoyed the opportunity to come into the *loaded* office.

As well as being a wind tunnel the man-made amphitheatre also had great acoustics. When a brand new set of speakers and a CD of Ian McShane reading an erotic novel for women arrived within a day of each other it seemed too good an opportunity to miss. Those nearest the window made sure the cables were securely attached and just started blasting out this utter filth delivered by television's *Lovejoy* heartthrob McShane. The sound echoed off the low-rise and IPC reception and the air was totally full of deliciously delivered sex talk.

Even better than both of these was the day the first laser pen arrived. Companies were always sending us their new stuff and no one had had one of those laser pens yet. No one had even taken one to a football match; we had the review prototypes. The only time you ever saw one of these was in Hollywood action blockbusters emanating from a telescopic sight on a sniper rifle. Shining it down to street level prompted the funniest reactions. Some people would just stop and stare at it and try and walk round it but we would follow them; others would try and grab it, and by far the funniest was one bald guy in a grey suit who was utterly terrified and desperately jumping from side to side and eventually ran away. We did this for about a week. Oh, the beauty of having a vantage point, endless pedestrians and no one to come in and say, 'Haven't you lot got work to do?'

It was this sense of childlike fun that permeated the magazine that the readers loved.

Crisps World Cup

Vatican, June 1994

We became quickly adept at turning such juvenile fun into editorial. So many of the best content ideas just came from idly sitting about talking rubbish or arguing. With two issues under our belt I was sitting in my office one day when I heard my boss, Alan Lewis, down for one of his visits to the editorial floor he clearly missed since being made a suit, standing in the art area saying, 'You must be joking. Kettle Chips are far superior.'

Curious, I walked out and asked what they were discussing and someone replied, 'Alan thinks Kettle are better than Walkers.'

This was of course lunacy. At that point Kettle Chips came in massive bags, were really expensive and were only found in posh supermarkets and warehouse chains like Victoria Wines. I decided there and then we should settle it with the inaugural Crisps World Cup.

The format became a *loaded* staple, then a magazine staple, and then twenty-five years on in the age of social media, TV host Richard Osman started using it on Twitter as if no one had ever done it before. A lot of people started tweeting and messaging me saying this bloke off *Countdown* is trying to claim the Crisps World Cup as his idea.

I decided we should have a proper draw for each round, a real knock-out tasting competition and, to save on packets, just one crisp for each tasting. Two writers would taste each crisp that had been drawn together and vote which was best. We bought sixty-four different flavours of crisps, which was actually very hard to do in those days as there weren't any local Sainsbury's or Tescos, and we had to throw in a few things like apple rings and corn-based snacks, but they were knocked out early on. Then all the crisps were given numbers and placed on my large magazine rack and we went through bag by bag, round by round, until it was quite late at night, we were all speeding on chemical additives and we were down to the final.

The semis were Walkers Cream Cheese & Chive v. Walkers Beef & Onion, and Pringles Lights v. McCoy's Chilli. The final – Cheese & Chive v. Chilli – was a draw. Stumped as to how we were going to find the ultimate winner and with very few actual crisps left to broaden the tasting, we decided we needed guidance from a higher power so we called the Vatican – seriously. We put the phone on speaker and an Irish priest there who answered listened to what we were doing and replied, 'I think His Holiness is a Pringles man.'

No one could believe it. We were rolling around laughing amid the few remnants of crisps that were left. Everyone was sick of eating them, we had hardly any of the finalists' bags left as they'd come through so many rounds and we were just frazzled.

In the end we decided the winner by calling cab ranks in the towns the finalists were made in and asking them how much it was to the nearest airport. The cheapest won. That's science for you. We were so fucking stuffed no one gave a fuck about the outcome by then. In fact when I got in the company car to be driven home at about half ten I was absolutely speeding. Whatever they put in the flavouring could probably have been sold in wraps.

Given this was a last-minute idea the day before we went to press we chucked something out and squeezed it into a single page and a spread – the images of the crisp bags on the spread were minute. Like so many of the good pieces we did we just didn't give it enough space but it struck a chord with the readers, who were quick to respond to the competition on the letters page. I walked to the Coach and Horses in Soho the week it was published and Andrew Harrison, the editor of *Select* magazine, came straight over, shook my hand and said, 'The

Crisps World Cup is totally genius.' From then on I realised we could pretty much do anything. Crisps was followed by breakfast cereals, vodka, porn mags – the list went on and on.

Before we leave the subject I should at this point just give you a little more info about why Alan Lewis felt he was suitably qualified to make such a bold statement in the first place. And also what made him the perfect publisher for *loaded* and why he perhaps understood why it might work.

Midway through his career as a very successful music magazine editor with *Sounds* in the seventies and after inventing *Kerrang!* he'd left publishing to run a pub in his hometown in Berkshire. This would be inexplicable for most editors but not Alan. It's fair to say he liked a drink and I guess he just preferred being in the pub to the office. Drinker to landlord must have seemed a desirable switch. He was, by all accounts, a popular landlord, but it seems boozers eventually got the better of him. When I asked him why he'd packed it in and come back to magazines, he replied:

'You just got no time for yourself to spend with your family. You would come back from the shops on a Sunday morning with the weekly grocery shopping and the bastards would be in the car park ten minutes before opening time banging on the door to be let in.'

After this, like the Beasties' songs, food became a central part of the *loaded* contents list. We had regulars like Mick's Grill, Drop Your Bacon Sandwich and Biscuit of the Month but loads of features too. These were often visual stories like If Biscuits Were People (which was the first work Mick Bunnage and Jon Link did together before they started the cartoon series *Office Pest* and then *Modern Toss*), posters of fish and chips, bacon sandwiches and our own Sandwich Inventions. That was a great morning, as we actually got lunch out of creating a feature. While some staff went for a deliberately perverse mix of ingredients, Michael Holden came up with an absolute winner which became part of the office staple diet. Grated cheese and salt and vinegar crisps all smashed into one sandwich. Pickle optional.

The concept of culinary creation wasn't new to me. I had already invented a sandwich a year before when fucking about in Malvern on acid with Fabulous – the Pride of St James, with bread toasted on one side only, jam, sliced cheese and apple. So I felt confident when I came out with the Pride of St James but Michael's won the day with Mick Bunnage's Marmite, Twiglets and sliced white bread coming a close second.

Another *loaded* staff testing that was eventful and actually predicted a future retail trend was the Washing Powder Test. Bored of listening to corny commercials claiming their product washed the whitest, we set out to decide. We called Levi's for a load of white jeans, bought a pile of white vests from an army and navy store and set off down to Wimbledon common to re-enact the archetypal seventies advert with kids running about getting filthy. Unlike in the advert, though, it wasn't a sunny day and there was no lovely mum with a smile to do the washing.

This was the sort of mad shit we loved doing, though. We were channelling the sort of pointless but brilliant stuff we'd do as kids when the summer holidays or school nights seemed to last forever. While other magazines were sitting round in their uniform check shirts being incredibly conscientious, we were laughing out loud while freezing our fucking arms and legs off in a stream trying to recreate a Persil advert. (All except Shakey the photographer who had the sense to pull his white T-shirt over his leather jacket.) We climbed trees, rolled around in leaves, pulled ourselves over damp and grimy fences and in a moment that gave me great pleasure, jumped into a river. Not because I like jumping in rivers in winter, in fact I don't think I even jumped in. I was quietly laughing to myself as the others did because I suddenly remembered teachers repeatedly saying to other kids when we were getting in trouble at school, 'Oh and I suppose if James Brown told you to go and jump in a river, you'd do that too?'

Well yes, they did. I know this sounds weird but so often in adult life I notice the time on a clock in a public space and think, 'Only thirty-five minutes till the bell goes at 3.10.' *Loaded* just felt like revenge for all the times we'd had to do stuff we hadn't wanted to as kids, like act normal, be on time, do homework, shut up and stop talking etc. etc. The outlook of so many of the staff was juvenile, and that fed into the latent or prevalent attitudes of so many men.

More than anything, creating the content of *loaded* just felt like playing out. Pub conversations *were* the seed to the funniest stories. I realised that if spotty work experience oik Phil Robinson was staking his claim for attention by ranting about who was better, Chuck Norris or Jean-Claude Van Damme at Studio 6 where we drank, then other blokes who'd spent too long watching trashy action movies and playing kung fu computer games probably had those discussions too. I knew that if Adam Porter wanted to write about an American hippy cartoon strip about smoking drugs from the seventies like *The Furry Freak Brothers* then others would want to read about it. (Particularly in Liverpool, I remember thinking.) These personal passions, nostalgic memories and points of detail were what made up many of our conversations as men. The more we got down on the page the more we redefined what media could be about. Things that were timeless but much loved, and not new and PR driven.

Anyway, enough analysis. Back at Tim's house in Balham we continued the staining of the white clothes with Tabasco sauce, curry, beer and marker pen until they all looked suitably trashed. Then as we settled down to eat the curry and watch his Laurel and Hardy videos, a work experience and freelance writer were dispatched to the local launderette with eight different types of washing powder, a pile of change and clear instructions to use different washing machines for each washing powder and to bag each up separately so we could tell which powder really did wash whiter. As a wild card we had thrown in something called Ecover which was one of the first 'green' products that came onto the shelves. It had dolphins on the packaging and we were all delighted to see that this one rather than the heavily promoted doorstep-challenge products genuinely worked the best in our test. The dolphins won it!

It was this stupid shit that set the magazine apart from others. When *Jackass* later appeared on TV with guys just arsing around and hurting each other, resulting in hilarious filmed consequences, I recognised the thought patterns. Unfortunately we were slightly too early for hand-held video cameras and YouTube. Had we been producing *loaded* in this era the opportunities to post would have been endless.

Her outdoors

Dartmoor, dawn, no idea when

Sometime during the first year of *loaded* when the initial spring in our step had developed into a full-blown swagger and we knew what did and didn't make for good copy, we had a rare letter of (partial) complaint from a reader in the north-west. It went like this: 'You have great music and football pieces in the magazine, I really love it, but every issue you then go and do something cock like kayaking or orienteering.'

The letter was a one-off; the rest of the feedback about staff putting ourselves en masse into the hands of Mother Nature was 'Keep doing it, it's hilarious.' Something I learned very quickly from Martin Deeson's ill-fated trip to Cannes was that the worse the trip went the funnier the story would be. And the trips were great fun; the more fun we had the more it came through the pages and into the readers' hands.

Naturally we were largely rubbish at everything we tried. OK some of us were passable but the point was, none of us were the sort of blokes with a canoe or a mountain bike on the Land Rover roof, shouting, to quote *The Fast Show*, 'Let's off-road!' And that was the beauty of the articles. If four or five city dwellers found themselves in a field trying to listen to someone telling them something very important about safety on a mountain or something while still full of last night's chemicals it could only lead to amusing copy. You've all seen *City Slickers*, *Deliverance* and *Southern Comfort* – what could go wrong?

As far as I was concerned it stood to reason that if festivals were the best places to take hallucinogenic drugs, as I believed, then fields and hills and rivers minus thousands of people watching Orbital would be even better. As a kid I loved playing war in the woods, riding our bikes across the lip of clay quarries and building dens, and I had other mates who later used the same spaces for glue sniffing, and so we pretty much headed away from London regularly to combine all of the above.

In the space of three years I did something 'cock like kayaking' that I'd never done before maybe ten times or more. The people hosting the events were usually quite happy to have a group of us; it meant they got to do the activity without mixing us with the general public, plus they got lots of exposure in the mag. Between 1994 when I started *loaded* and 1999 when I left *GQ* I jumped out of a plane, slept in a cave, crawled through a stream on Dartmoor, saw a massive white owl on Bodmin, jumped into the Solent from an RIB, fired a few shotguns, upended a quad bike so it landed in my face, came last in a raft race in the Atlantic, climbed a mountain in heavy snow, got lost in a bog, tried to walk across a river on magic mushrooms, and turned over a buggy on a dirt track and walked out of the resulting crowd of dust looking like Sam Shepherd in *The Right Stuff*. The only thing that was pretty rubbish was looking for ghosts in Gloucestershire. Oh and trying to fish off the Isle of Wight in a tiny boat in rough weather with a terrible hangover was a stupid idea, made worse by accidentally smacking my head really hard on the lip of the boat. Everyone felt trip on that sick. I meant sick on that trip. Fish must have been eating our puke for weeks. Even our most laid-back writer The Loafer looked unrelaxed.

Needless to say it all made for good copy and got some of us out of the office. Some of the staff took it up a level and did this sort of thing in snow and surf in far more glamorous locations. But if it was likely to be cold, wet, slightly dangerous, country enough to take drugs and drink heavily and we'd get another coat out of it, I was in. Some of the things we originated ourselves and found someone to facilitate it, others came to us through outdoor clothing companies. At this point there was a lot of Henri Lloyd, North Face, Timberland and Shimano clothing and equipment being bandied around the office.

Reece was Beth's fashion assistant but more importantly our quartermaster and one of the true heroes of *loaded*. Beth and I would regularly be having conversations like this:

Her: 'Reece says he's going up the Three Peaks in Yorkshire next week.'

Me: 'Yes.'

Her: 'We haven't done the main fashion shoot yet and I've got the photographer booked for then.'

Me: 'Can you pull it forward or push it back? We'll be fucked without him as he's getting all the gear we need.'

You can read whatever you want into that last sentence but the fact was he was like James Garner in *The Great Escape* when it came to scrounging stuff. Boots, hats, fleeces, thermals, waterproof trousers, we had more stuff than Shackleton, and usually just to go to the other end of the country, not the world. In exchange for getting all the outdoor clothing, Reece got to come on the trip.

These trips were at the heart of what *loaded* was about, the opportunity just to fuck about childishly while actually trying something new and looking for the value in it.

We want your job

Republic of Ireland, November 1994

From the off, football was a significant part of the mag because football was such a big part of many of our lives. Pre-*loaded* it was rarely represented in the media as we fans experienced it. The sense of adventure of away trips, the stupid conversations about assembling teams of players relating to rivers (Mark Fish, Jimmy Hasselbaink) or who might have lived in a wood (Adrian Littlejohn), players behaving badly, nostalgia for long-gone kits and tournaments, iconic and cult players, great goals, nostalgic memories of our own childhood games, conspiracy theories, underdog cup wins and so on.

The first inkling of how much footballers loved *loaded* came after the *Shoot* 1994 Goal of the Year Awards at Old Trafford. Tim and I were sat with Alan Stubbs and Jason McAteer of Bolton, and Terry Christian and Craig Cash who was yet to strike gold with *The Royle Family*. Jason McAteer told us he was a big fan of the mag and we had such a good night with them that he subsequently invited us to the Irish Football Awards in Dublin. Irish football was on a high after Jason, Gary Kelly and Co. had injected some youthful excitement into that summer's World Cup in the States. One of the highlights had been Ray Houghton's brilliant volley to beat eventual runners-up Italy in New York. To us Jack Charlton wasn't just the living god he was seen as in Ireland, and a World Cup winner as a player, he was also a true Leeds legend from the Revie era. A man who had once stopped first-team training as manager of Middlesbrough to go fishing when his mate roared up in a Jag and shouted, 'Jack, there's salmon in the Tees!' He was everything *loaded* was about – fuck work, have a good time.

The squad were set to play their Northern Irish neighbours in a World Cup qualifier on the Wednesday and were staying just south of Armagh on the Republic side of the Border. The awards were in Dublin on the Monday. We arrived on Sunday night at the hotel just before last orders, checked in and found Roy Keane, who was then still a fairly fresh-faced young man, chatting to residents in the bar. With the 11.30 p.m. curfew approaching Keane left the bar but not before turning to humbly announce that he thought Niall Quinn was a much better player than him. Whether this was an early sign of the strange madness that would later come to define him as a player and endear him to a nation as a no-nonsense, fuming pundit, or just one too many pints, it was hard to tell, but as a senior player Niall stayed on for a couple more.

Jason was nowhere in sight and eventually we asked someone in an Irish tracksuit where he and the other players we hoped to meet were. 'Ah, Gary Kelly's led them on a wrecking party and they'll be a while yet.' Someone had obviously given Big Jack the same information as he started patrolling the reception looking like a shotgun ready to unleash both barrels. We were too scared to go and say hello so we just headed back to the bar and waited.

Just in time, Phil Babb, Jason and a few more players came actually pelting in and they both came up to our room. They said there would be no removing Kells from the pub as he was being mobbed by admirers. One of the true Irishmen in a team alongside a lot of second- and third-generation players, when Kells had returned to his hometown of Drogheda after the World Cup his mum's whole street had filled up like the 'He's not the messiah, he's a very naughty boy' scene in the *Life of Brian*. He'd had to hang out of a bedroom window and ask them all to move back. The great Leeds full back would eventually arrive back at our hotel in the small hours and climb in through a bedroom window, arriving so late and unnoticed that in the morning he was able to convince Jack he'd not even been out at all and had had an early night.

That first night Babbsy surprised both Tim and me by sitting up till 3 a.m. demolishing the massive bottle of vodka we'd got in the duty free on the ferry, revealing exactly how debauched the life of professional footballers could be. He'd just joined Liverpool from Coventry after a good World Cup and already he'd had his eyes opened by the difference in status that playing for the Reds had given him.

'You would not believe what goes on in the hotels, Browny, I've never seen anything like it myself.' Admitting he was more shocked voyeur than participant he proceeded to tell us so many excessive alcohol- and sex-related stories that they far surpassed anything I had ever heard or witnessed in my years on the road with bands. It sounded more like Led Zeppelin than Liverpool FC. He wasn't boasting; he was just candidly taking the lid off what really went on when world-famous young men with lots of money and confidence and fit bodies showed up in provincial cities and towns. He trusted us not to print it but agreed they'd all do an interview with us the next day.

'To be honest I'm not that bothered about getting involved with the groupies myself but you can't help but come across it when it's going on so brazenly in the rooms. We all keep our doors open in the corridor. Some of the girls have books and lists like trainspotters. These aren't like regular women you and I meet in nightclubs, this is what they're into. Shagging footballers, it's their hobby. I walked into one room recently with Liverpool and a blonde in her late thirties broke off from a blow job she was giving someone to say to the player I was with, 'Oh all right, ____, how are you, love? I haven't seen you since the cup final.'

When I asked Babbsy how he could possibly train the next morning, two days before a World Cup qualifier having drunk so much and with so little sleep, he replied, 'Oh I'll just bin-bag it,' and explained they would all fashion black bin bags into vests beneath their kit and sweat the alcohol out. As it was, the next morning we saw them briefly at breakfast and then were surprised to see them trot back in again, laughing, thirty minutes later. They got showered and changed out of their kit and their bin bags and Jason, Kells and Babbsy came and found us: 'Jack just didn't fancy it. We did some warming up and then he just said, "Ah come on, lads, let's get back in and have another bacon sandwich."' Genius.

We settled down to interview the three musketeers and, trying hard not to just ask Kells about Leeds, we went through our High Rollers questionnaire which was normally reserved for business types. When it came to the question 'Whose job would you like if you didn't do this?' they really surprised us when they all blurted out, '*Yours!*'

That night we followed their team coach down to the capital and the five of us met Dublin-based *NME* photographer Tim Jarvis in a room in the hotel where the awards were taking place. Tim Southwell and I got into some black-tie outfits (fuck knows where they came from) and Tim Jarvis quickly photographed the guys.

We then took a small service elevator down to reception. As the ground-floor light pinged Babbsy said, 'Brace yourselves.' Tim and I looked at each other and wondered what he meant, then the doors opened to a wall of people and their security man stepped out ahead of us, pushing into the biggest scrum of fans I'd ever seen. We genuinely had to fight our way through a huge pressing crowd of crazed Irish fans all screaming the players' names and thrusting pens and papers at us. It felt like the old Beatles and Stones footage or being down the front of the Jam at the Queens Hall in Leeds when I was fifteen. Their popularity in Ireland at the time was immense. The squad had recently been on the balcony at a Dublin Take That concert and when the crowd saw them they turned away from the stage and began shouting for them so much the band stopped singing.

Anyway, the security managed to fashion a route through the crowd and we burst through two golden doors into a large, dark, empty room with nothing but a long table covered in fresh booze and no one but the Irish football squad and Jack Charlton, not even FAI executives. No one. Ready to go out and be honoured for their World Cup performance, they all looked at the two strangers with their teammates and immediately asked who we were. When Jason introduced us to the captain Andy Townsend as the guys who did *loaded*, Jack overheard and the giant former Leeds stopper strode over and said, 'So you are the *loaded* boys. Did you bring any totty with you?' Jack gave us a smile and Andy Townsend confirmed we were very welcome to hang around.

This was when we realised how much the professional footballers of the day, with so much time on their hands and smart phone technology a decade away, loved the magazine. After that interview and the player-to-player word of mouth, the flow of players wanting to be in the mag didn't stop, with a brilliant mixture of current players and retired legends. Whenever the Liverpool boys came to London on a night out we would meet up with Jason, Phil, their mate Robbie Williams, Jamie Redknapp, Don Hutchison and others. They took us to the sort of nightclubs we'd never bothered with before, like the Spot in Covent Garden which was basically like a Panini sticker book for footballers and girls wanting to get to know them.

As one of the underlying aims of the mag was to enjoy the same sort of access to footballers we'd had with bands, this new development was a very resounding success. Perhaps the pinnacle of it came just before Euro 96 when I was at a *90 Minutes* mag event at the nightclub Scribes West, owned by England manager Terry Venables. Like most toilets at that time there were a lot of people hanging around who didn't want a piss and a lot of noise and laughter; the nineties was the decade when men's toilets became the social hub women's have always been. I was leaning into the closed toilet seat about to have a line when I heard the door open and all the noise go weirdly quiet and then suddenly everyone was saying, 'All right, Terry.' I realised the England manager was in the room, looked at the line, wondered what to do, did it, wiped my face hopefully clean and stepped out, trying not to retch.

Some of the boys immediately introduced me to Terry as the editor of *loaded* and asked him if he knew it. The England manager gave me his big twinkly smile, shook my hand and said, 'Of course I know it, I can hardly get the players' heads out of it to listen to my team talks.' At that point I knew the box of thirty issues I'd sent up to Gazza at their training camp at Burnham Beeches had been received.

More Kathy Lloyd, and why not?

Still London, end of '94

By the end of the year we were just rolling. From the cover lines to the features we had realised that whatever we found ourselves laughing about and discussing in the office would probably work as stories or headlines. A perfect example of this simple stupidity? After a nostalgic chat about the American sitcom *Diff'rent Strokes* we bought a Bruce Willis interview in from a syndication agency just so we could use the headline 'What You Talking About, Willis?'

We spent ages sitting around in bars and the office talking. Anyone could be holding court, expounding on something that had occurred to them at one in the morning in Soho's Hanway Street, which in turn would prompt a major, in-depth discussion about something most people in magazines would find trivial but we loved so we figured the readers would too. In terms of new ideas it was extremely productive. By now I was already being asked to go into other workplaces and talk about what was happening at *loaded* and anytime I suggested employees should be allowed to spend more time talking in the pub it always went down well.

The November issue was our best yet – it just screamed 'Buy me'. The staff had long since found their feet and every corner of the magazine had genuinely interesting content; it was packed but not overcrowded: Sting on sex, Bruce Willis on *Pulp Fiction*, Andy Weatherall on Sabres of Paradise, Kylie at Liverpool superclub Cream's birthday, and we'd explored the upper-crust world of polo, the Munich Oktoberfest

(Glastonbury for beer), and high-speed racing cars. Basically the writers going on holiday and writing up what a great time they had.

It was all underpinned by my original desire to have a magazine that mixed music and football – interviews with James Lavelle from Mo' Wax, Mick Jones of BAD II, Sparks and Sheryl Crow sat alongside Pop Will Eat Itself singer and future soundtrack giant Clint Mansell in conversation with former England man Graham Taylor who was now managing Clint's beloved Wolverhampton Wanderers. We were never, ever short of content; we were being bombarded with ideas from everywhere.

In the fashion section there was a six-page shoot with Ian, Billy and Craig from the Cult, all wearing vintage football shirts and getting in and out of the bath and an E-Type Jag at Wimbledon FC to emulate the golden era of early-seventies football. In a move other magazines wouldn't have done to their precious, advertiser-led fashion pages, we plastered ours with classic shots of Alan Ball, Bobby Moore, Allan Clarke, Malcolm Allison, Denis Law and Rod Stewart. It looked great alongside an in-depth interview with George Best. The designers produced an opening spread where the text panel looked like a huge pint of Guinness alongside a forensic portrait of George by photographer Steve Pyke, who caught George in the light of a thousand hangovers. Writer Sean O'Hagan starts: 'Today, like most days, those magic feet have carried George Best from his Chelsea home to the local pub.' It's a fantastic interview by a guy who grew up idolising him in Northern Ireland. In amid all our own over-documented thirst, there's no sense of idolising Best purely for his boozing and sex life. The writer examines extensively the impact that had on his career but the feature also revels in his pure ability as a player. For all of us the football came first; the high life off the pitch just made it even more interesting.

For anyone who thought the alcoholic drinking patterns of the men we admired were simply irresponsibly glossed over, you just had to read the in-depth interviews we were doing to see them addressed and the quality of the accompanying portraits by people like Steve Pyke, with the effects of the drinking plain to see in their eyes. Steve would go on to receive an MBE for his photographs of First World War veterans.

Most importantly, the magazine looked and felt confident and was talking to its readership with an ease that matched *Viz* and *Smash Hits* at their peak. The large yellow circle, or roundel, on the front cover, in the top-left sales hotspot beneath the logo, simply said, 'Free inside MASSIVE POSTER blah blah blah Kathy Lloyd and George Best etc'. We were using our confidence to take the piss out of ourselves but also run amok over the basic communication rules magazines were supposed to follow.

Other cover lines were inspired by simplistic ice lolly stick jokes like, 'Buzz buzz ouch! That's right, it's Sting,' and poor puns: 'Drinking Munich dry, Only herr for the beer'. As at the *NME*, writing the cover lines collectively had become a forum for attempting to outsmart each other with the wittiest or silliest line possible. It was the tone as much as the content that was selling *loaded*; no other magazine came across as not really giving a fuck about keeping up appearances. 'Blah blah blah' worked on the cover because who hadn't wanted to hand in their work half finished? There were other more subtle moments of smartarse stupidity around the mag. The overriding editorial style was we were doing all the things we'd explicitly been told not to do in class.

The 'thanks to' part of the staff list on my editor's letter page included the Vikings, David Soul and Wallace Beery scattered among people who had actually helped with the mag. Obviously none of these had. In Fiona Russell Powell's Sparks interview, a speech bubble caption on the photo of the Mael brothers says 'This page ain't big enough for the both of us*", playing on their 1970s hit 'This Town Ain't . . .' and the article finishes punctuation-less halfway through a sentence with a connecting asterisk saying '*told you so'.

These throwaway jokes amused us and connected with an audience who loved the sense of fun; they told them they were in a different world not only to men's magazines that had gone before but most magazines. Women's magazines certainly rarely showed any sense of humour and were so deadly serious. I think that's why so many women started to buy and want to write for *loaded*.

The November issue featured a really good High Roller interview with bestselling novelist Jackie Collins, one of the best we did, where you really got inside what had driven her; a piece with Sheryl Crow whose 'All I Wanna Do' had been on heavy rotation anytime assistant editor Tim got near the CD player; and the cover story was an essay by (now *Observer* columnist) Barbara Ellen on why she loved glamour model Kathy Lloyd so much, where she argued her beauty made her 'the Ava Gardner of Liverpool'. Barbara had walked in with a list of everyone she wanted to write about and Kathy was the first name on the list.

The photos were by *NME* photographer Derek Ridgers, the hair and make-up by Robbie Williams's girlfriend, the lovely Jackie Hamilton-Smith, styling by our fashion editor Beth, and Kathy brought her own basque. There's virtually no cleavage or anything in the pictures and she looks great. Hot, happy, cool. The images could have come out of a women's mag only neither they nor the women's pages of the broadsheets considered profiling Page Three and glamour girls, as if somehow they were beneath them. Whether they liked what Kathy did for a living or not, Barbara brilliantly showed why she was still worth writing about. I don't think anyone had actually considered this before but we were the first people to shoot these women in underwear that made them look stylish rather than just topless like the tabloids did.

Every issue now was just heaving with content and energy. We were now also spending a lot of time abroad.

Move it on up now

It is amazing how making money makes people tolerate you more. From the very first issue when the sales were double what they had been optimistically forecast to be after a year, IPC knew they were making money. By issue three we were selling 90,000 copies, three times more than the forecast, and had actually broken even. That meant we earned the first pound of profit in twelve weeks against a business forecast of three years. None of us were even on the staff – we were all on three-month freelance contracts.

The response was phenomenal. Contrary to the way the story would later be rewritten, these were not magazines with topless women on the cover and only very occasionally inside; the first four issues had had three male actors – Gary Oldman, Leslie Nielsen from *Naked Gun* and Paul Usher, known to fans of *Brookside* as Barry Grant. The third issue had supermodel turned business woman and actress Elle Macpherson in a dress. The fifth issue had a boxer on the cover. Men's style magazines rarely had boxers on the cover, with the possible exception of Mike Tyson. To challenge the perceived commercial and racially ignorant wisdom, our boxer was a skinny, lightweight kid from Sheffield called Naseem Hamed. Every issue the sales increased.

So very, very early on IPC was aware it had a hit on its hands. And with that came a degree of tolerance I'd not experienced on the *NME*. After the first issue came out we had a letter of complaint (one of only two) from an irate person who it seemed had come looking to be offended. The letter explained in the first paragraph that they had bought the new magazine with interest and then fairly constructively explained why they didn't like certain features of the magazine. For the second paragraph they reused every swear verb in the mag in capitals WANKING FUCKING SHITTING and it went on for a good five lines. It really was a snotty, holier-than-thou and quite unpleasant tone of voice so I just scrawled GET FUCKED! over it and sent it back to the guy.

A month later as everyone was marvelling about how the second issue had sold even more than the first issue, the MD of the group pulled a photocopy of half this letter with my scrawl across it. You could also see a black line where all the writer's swearing had been removed. There was also a photocopy of the IPC franking machine on the envelope. And he had another letter that had been sent out to as many of IPC's advertisers as possible, people like M&S who would have been in the women's and TV titles but not the lifestyle group. The MD wasn't angry because everything else was going so well and I explained I'd seen the original letter and told him about all the swearing and insults on it. He just asked me to make sure it didn't happen again. The often repeated, ineffectual words of football administrators and MPs sprang to my mind and I promised 'a full and frank investigation'.

A year later the MD of the group was having a leaving drink because he was going off to run a part of the business that amazingly included a pig farm. Up in his empty office area he had Rod Stewart blasting out and had had a few drinks when the letter came up. I admitted it was me and he just laughed and said, 'I fucking knew it!' What could he do? He was the toast of the bigwigs and I was the editorial golden boy. IPC largely kept us at arm's length and just counted the money but this acceptance of our behaviour went on throughout almost all my time there. After six months of success when we were posting independently audited proof of the extraordinary sales, *The Times* sent a journalist to do a piece about the mag and she interviewed me at lunch at a riverside restaurant. As we walked back past the local bar Studio 6 we stopped and chatted to two smartly dressed guys. I introduced her as a *Times* journalist, and one insisted he had a good idea for a story for *loaded*.

'Hey James, how about I teach you to abseil face first down to the bottom of a cliff, you and your guys do that all the way down, snort a huge line of cocaine at the bottom and then climb back up the rock face?'

I laughed and as we walked away she asked who that was. 'The head of the IPC legal department, and his number two who is in and out of our offices quite a lot.'

She looked shocked. But IPC was enjoying the money and the attention and no one was talking to us about our tone at all. They trusted Alan Lewis and I wasn't having to come in and out of the building due to being in the stables. They were delighted.

For us it soon became a truly surreal time. Speedboats, deserted islands, bags of cash, jam jars full of high-grade cocaine, limousines, freezer bags full of grass, people dressed as Louis XIV and Henry VIII. Howard Marks asking if we could collect $15k for him in Argentina. Sleeping with women we'd previously fancied in magazines and newspapers. Shooting shotguns; sleeping in caves; potholing on Ecstasy; orienteering on gak; falling off boats into the Solent; asking football managers about their underpants; jeeps; designer clothing borrowed from the fashion cupboard; unlimited sunglasses, trainers, backstage passes; travelling in helicopters; drinking straight from magnums; getting sports cars stuck in swamps; driving at a 45-degree angle across out-of-season ski slopes; being threatened by large religions; having to apologise to Her Majesty's Constabulary, Tax Office and Customs and Excise; skydiving through clouds; surfing the jaws of death in Barbados; having too many cars to drive; giving away suits and jumpers and shoes and Audis; frequently thinking we were General Patton, Led Zeppelin, the messiah, Blackbeard. That was just a typical couple of issues. That was us, the blokes who were supposed to be just writing about football and music. The ones the police wouldn't arrest because they liked the mag too much. It just went on and on, month after month. Just as we'd finish one issue we'd have to tank it all up and start again. What the fuck can we do next? Trevor's getting a cage with a great white shark outside. Good. Jon's got Michael Stipe to say he fancies the Queen. OK. James and Reece are holding up a jumbo jet on the runway in Aruba because they're so drunk they've decided they don't want to go home to London. And you know what? We weren't the only ones doing it. DJs and promoters and fashion designers and everyday boys and girls with a hunger for the sort of adventure that seems totally possible from one end of a rolled-up note to the other were also bang at it. Probably worse. Only they didn't get to share it with a couple of million people in print.

On manoeuvres with the Duchess of Duke Street

Amsterdam, 1996

By now the most overwhelmingly popular article for any of us to write was essentially 'What I Did on My Holidays'. The magazine was just absolutely full of stories every month featuring us going somewhere, getting exceedingly drunk, and then taking the piss out of ourselves in the resulting copy. That was the key really – not taking ourselves seriously. We knew young men liked to behave like this at any given opportunity, be it a stag do, a sports fixture, a holiday, a beer festival, a music festival. So the audience would read as many as we could write. There are certainly issues when I look back and think, why did we run three major features like this? Where's the balance, man? Invariably these manoeuvres also allowed us to indulge ourselves in ever-spiralling drug habits, each mission seemed to have even fewer boundaries as we pushed further and further from the fields of Wales to the backstreets of Buenos Aries.

Two years into *loaded*'s existence Shaun Ryder's new band Black Grape were playing in Rotterdam, which was the perfect excuse to go to Amsterdam. There were five of us: myself, Michael the writer, Chris Floyd the photographer, Reece the quartermaster and Adam the commissioning editor. Music, drugs, voyeurism and football. The city centre was like a living version of the magazine.

Arriving in Rotterdam we went straight into a dockers' bar and ordered drinks and bags of grass the barman was openly selling across the counter. The gig was great; the Black Grape album really did sound new, different and unique. Afterwards they gave us a lift back to Amsterdam in their double-decker tour bus.

Michael, Reece and I had spent most of the previous decade in Soho enjoying the lifestyle that went with it. Commissioning editor Adam on the other hand hadn't spent quite so much time retching in a doorway at dawn off Berkeley Square, and as Michael so accurately wrote: 'On a day-to-day basis Adam was probably the most together of us all so in many ways he had furthest to fall.' And fall he did. He got so fucked that he started doing impressions of Shaun on Black Grape's tour bus, making a bit of a tit of himself in the process. Shaun's cousin and sideman, Muzza, who I'd met in Brazil at Rock in Rio, had kindly given his seat up for Adam to collapse in and then terrorised the half-comatose Man City fan by pretending to shave his eyebrows off.

When we got to Amsterdam Reece and Shaun immediately shot off to find the devil and we had to carry Adam to our little hotel where we dumped him in his room face down so he couldn't choke on his own vomit and die. Despite some suggesting that wouldn't be a bad thing.

We asked the receptionist if he would deny all knowledge of us being there should Adam come down in the morning to ask where we were.

'The rude drunk guy? No problem, this will be funny.'

Dutch people are different to English people.

The next day Adam woke really hung-over, not knowing where he was or where everyone else had gone. He started leaving increasingly panicky phone messages and texts. When he eventually found us he leered his way into the room like he was the king of excess. He'd been a total arse but, typical of the misleading influence of drink and drugs, somehow thought he'd been on great form.

We set off into Amsterdam to a coffee shop and found ourselves looking at a clear perspex cake lid over a small loaf on a plate. Five of the slices were quite thin and then there were two at double thickness. I asked the lady in the shop what effect each would have on us and she said, 'These slim slices will give you a happy night out and these two big ones will stop an elephant.'

Before anyone had a say in the matter Reece and I immediately reached out and took the elephant stoppers. The others had the rest. We then went to an outdoor flea market where you could buy great leather coats. Looking round the market I noticed that most Dutch words just looked like a bad hand at Scrabble, then we went to the snack vans and got some chips. Sitting at the table the dope cake soon began to kick in and, despite it being a nice day, we all started shivering really badly.

'Fucking hell!' was the collective general observation and people were physically shaking with cold until Chris stepped away from the table to put something in a bin.

'Hey! It's OK, it's warm over here.'

We looked round and realised we were sitting right next to the extraction fan on the back of the ice cream van. No wonder it was fucking freezing – it wasn't the dope cake at all. It didn't take too much longer for the cake to get up to its elephant-slaying level though. In the press box for Ajax v. Den Haag, I spent some of the game crawling down the steps next to the Dutch football journalists' legs, barking like a dog. They must have been used to this happening as thankfully they just laughed about it. Walking round the centre of Amsterdam they'd see people doubled up in tears all the time.

Dutch football operated a 'mixed zone' for press to mingle with players and managers so they could get match reactions first-hand. This is great for football writers but wasn't ideal for Ajax manager Louis van Gaal when I asked him when the Marc Overmars to Manchester United deal was going to be finished.

The press all said 'What?!' The best way to tell a lie is to believe it and I was tripping so badly I told van Gaal I was from an English tabloid and Man United had leaked the deal. I'd totally made it up but the more van Gaal denied it the more plausible I sounded. Some of the Ajax-supporting journalists looked really worried and started recording my questions and then challenging Louis about it. They assumed that given we had press passes we must be legit and not just drug tourists from *loaded*. We left when big Louis with his glistening spam-pink forehead started looking annoyed about it.

Back in the centre of Amsterdam I was so fucked I started buying sheet music. Masses of it. These A4 two-sheet songbooks had all the notes and crotchets and quavers and pastel-coloured illustrated covers. I was entranced just staring at the drawings which looked beautiful and the notes which were all higgledy-piggledy, going up and down the scales like they were moving.

Then I spent a lot of cash on the company card on two rare original *Taxi Driver* posters, so it wasn't all bad. But on the way out of the shop, caught between the bustle of the Amsterdam pavement and the alluring brightness of the shops in night-time, I had an out-of-body view of myself and witnessed the spirit of a Victorian woman in a long dress and with her hair pinned up, like the Duchess of Duke Street, descend like a Dickensian ghost into my body. My voice changed instantly and I wasn't putting it on. I had been taken over by a person of a different sex and different era. When I caught the others up they thought I was messing about but I wasn't – the whole sound of my voice had changed and I had no control over it.

I was acting so weird they suggested we go back to base so I could lie down in my room. The Victorian woman talking wouldn't stop and at one point Adam looked in and saw me lying on my back with my leg in the air commentating on *Match of the Day* in a high-pitched female voice. He looked utterly terrified. I felt fine, just really weird having someone else inside me, but from the look on his face I decided I needed some fresh air and suggested we go out again.

Back at the shops Michael and I came across a Romanesco cauliflower and couldn't work out what the hell was going on; I had never seen one before. I was holding this bright-green vegetable that looked like an Escher drawing with hundreds of tiny pyramids looking perfectly geometrically formed. And there were about twenty of them. Michael came back into the shop and asked me what I was doing and then he was mesmerised by them too. 'Are these real?' he asked. I couldn't work out how my hallucination had taken on physical 3D form. Vegetables weren't high on my priority list but these looked amazing.

The woman hadn't been exaggerating about the elephant-stopping capabilities; the cake lasted a good fourteen hours. The last thing I remember was debating whether or not to go into a club called Cockring and instead ending up in a place with hospital beds hanging from the ceiling with people in medical gear dancing on them. And that wasn't the drugs.

This is largely what these trips were like. We'd leave the office in cabs joyously waving champagne bottles about and come back utterly fucked. Once I was straight back in the office there'd be a journalist from the *Telegraph*, *Newsweek* or *Vanity Fair* waiting to interview me, or someone from IPC putting me in for a conference, wanting me to explain in an intelligent way how I'd had the vision to create a publishing market no one else knew existed. The answer was simple: we behaved like arses and wrote funny articles about it. It was almost as if no one had understood men might like a laugh instead of grooming tips.

Broadsword calling Danny Boy

In the air, 1994–97

The further away we went from the office and the longer the flights, the purer the drugs. I know we weren't Pablo Escobar or anything but it was fair to say our ever-excessive lifestyle was better suited to the office, our homes, nightclubs, bars, the country, fields and festivals than airports, where safety and security were of utmost importance.

On the way to America to review the Samuel Adams brewery I was sitting at the back of the plane with Deeson and we had a plastic bin at our feet as an impromptu ice bucket. The Virgin girls had been happy to sell us bottle after bottle of champagne, I don't know if they were on commission but by the end a couple of them were just stood next to us joining in.

The magazine was becoming quite accepted, celebrated and infamous. Passport office and customs officers recognised us and speeded us through. Dentists were giving free treatments away. The relationship between the readers and the writers was like one big print-based party. Even the head of IPC, Mike Mathews, introduced us to an old friend of his, Mike Todd, who it turned out had similar refuelling tastes to myself.

Mike was now running a wine mag called the *Grape Zine* in Sag Harbor, aimed at boosting the reputation of the wineries on Long Island. It all sounded great.

Our weeks on Long Island were fantastic. Mike Todd had a stash of high-grade cocaine he kept in a grinder the size of a coffee jar. We toured the wineries as they called them and Chris Floyd took some nice shots of us relaxing there.

We were in an Amagansett diner eating a breakfast of English muffins, crispy bacon and melon one day, considering returning to Manhattan, when we came across a supermodel beach volleyball charity match advertised in the local paper, organised by Calvin Klein's wife Kelly. It was exactly the sort of luck we kept stumbling across. Martin and Chris were very excited about this and booked tickets with their own money instantly, while I was pondering what the hell a Pizza Village was in the next advert. (Houses made of margaritas?) Anyway I ended up watching exactly the same spectacle as them across the knee-high sized picket fence without spending $60 each, and yes, there really were supermodels playing beach volleyball. We had developed a sense of wonder about the place. The long grass-lined beaches, the old houses in Sag Harbor, the huge brooding Atlantic in front of us at Amagansett. The Hamptons were a great place to just hang about.

That day our friend Jennifer, who was our other guide to the Hamptons, pointed to a house across the highway and said, 'That was where I grew up.'

'What about that one?' I asked, pointing at the shut-down haunted house next door, a remarkable looking wreck. 'Ah that was Captain Mundus's house. I grew up next door to him.'

'Who is Captain Mundus?'

'He's the guy they based Quint on in *Jaws*. I'll take you to where he used to fish from.'

All around her our mouths were dropping. None of us knew that the best character in one of the greatest thrillers ever filmed was based on a real person. And so Jennifer took us to Montauk at the tip of Long Island where Mundus was based.

Down in the harbour, sport fishing boats lined up alongside each other and we found a lass from Yorkshire called Tracey organising the charter hires. As we watched white craft come in and out of the harbour, soundtracked by that constant tinkling of wind through the masts it was immediately apparent what Peter Benchley had taken from the area and put down on his pages.

We settled down in one of the wood-panelled seafood-serving fisherman's restaurants and ordered. All around were photographs of sharks' jaws being pulled open, sharks dangling from gallows scales, groups of fishermen lined up. And right next to us was a photograph of a man stood on the floating carcass of a whale, out at sea, showing his bare backside to great white sharks chewing on the whale meat just yards away.

'*That* is Captain Mundis,' said Jennifer. 'He pretty much invented shark fishing. Jealous rivals said that the day before a charter he would go out to the shelf where the fish gather and drop a fridge full of old butcher's meat into the deep, knowing the blood would attract the sharks. Until he started doing this no one had ever really caught sharks; they were considered the garbage trucks of the ocean so no one wanted to eat them. Once they saw how impressive they were it took off.'

We booked a boat and went shark fishing, starting at dawn straight after a night of no sleep with Mike. Deeson caught a shark and rightly let it go but the moment the lines started reeling out and then whizzed off at great speed was incredibly exciting. There was a shark-fishing tournament that day and when we returned to harbour there were so many dustbins of fins and a long pregnant shark with its belly slit open with babies falling out and attempting to swim away before dying, and idiots whooping about whatever they'd brought in. It really put me off and I realised that, unlike in *Jaws*, it was the humans who were a big threat to the sharks not the other way round.

Not to be taken with alcohol

JFK, 1990-something

The day we flew home was my birthday and we started drinking fine wine Mike had given me as a present with breakfast. We met a friend of his for lunch – an old boy from Pimlico who had been using cocaine since he'd been able to buy it over chemists' counters in the fifties. When we were sitting in a limo on the way to the airport with champagne between our knees, Deeson pulled out a packet of twelve medical downers, Melatonin, which he announced would take the edge off flying. They clearly said 'NOT TO BE TAKEN WITH ALCOHOL'. We both pushed two out of the foil packet and took them. He'd already been on the NyQuil and about twenty minutes of traffic later I said, 'Give me another one of those pills,' but when he gave me the packet they'd all gone.

'Where are they?'

'Shiyavhadem.'

He was slurring so much he sounded Dutch. I couldn't believe it, he'd taken eight of them and I was immediately alarmed, not only because I couldn't have any more and I had that druggie panic that without more of whatever I was taking it would be impossible to exist, but also because I genuinely worried he'd die. Sure enough a physical shudder rolled through him and he suddenly felt the urge to get some fresh air. We were in the middle of the freeway so instead of asking the guy to pull over he zapped open the sun roof and just stood up. I stuck my head out to see what was going on and there were worried and angry people shouting from their cars and beeping their horns at him. In response he was just waving at them like General Patton. Genius.

I didn't know what shitty part of which airport we were in but they were either doing renovations or I'd somehow ended up back in Russia with Pop Will Eat Itself seven years before. There was a tiny square glass shop about the size of a van with walls and shelves the height of your shoulders and virtually nothing to buy. You could stand in the middle of it and see out of the top of it. Not a proper gift shop at all. Martin wanted to get his daughter a present so he bought her a stuffed cuddly Taz, the whirlwind Tazmanian Devil off the TV. No matter how full on his assignments were he always appeared to be a really good caring dad and this was a superb present.

I liked that cartoon, I identified with it, so I got one too.

After the excessive shenanigans we'd been subjecting him to, from Long Island to Boston and then back to New York, Floydy had sensibly made his own way through JFK. The week before in a Boston hotel room during a deranged drunken exchange between the two of us Deeson, surrounded by chaos, had thrown an old fashioned heavy-duty phone so violently into my face there were key imprints on my forehead. It was an incredibly funny moment, but Floyd had just despaired and wisely checked into another room. When Johnny Depp's *Fear and Loathing* came out his Vegas hotel room looked so familiar that I called Deeson to see if it rang any bells and he simply replied 'Boston.' You couldn't have asked for a more fun travel companion. His personality electrified his writing, and he'd gamely give anything a go and turn it into engaging copy. Tim Southwell, Trevor Ward and Bill Borrows all had the ability to take you right there to the heart of whatever outlandish overseas action they were pursuing, but Deeson just gave you his whole crazed world view on the page.

At the airport check-in Deeson took umbrage at a bloke next to us in the first-class check-in lane. We weren't even in first class but he thought the guy was pushing in so he started having a go at him.

The guy looked terrified. Deeson looked like Cresta Bear in combat gear. He had his bright blond hair, huge grin, green shorts, his lucky Cannes camouflage T-shirt and trainers. It wasn't so much the aggression from him but how unprompted it seemed.

To diffuse the antagonism I suggested Martin go and cool off a bit in the bog while I finished checking us in. The airline people and the rattled first-class bloke seemed to agree. The staff had Deeson's papers and passport and had seen him with me so it was fine. Five minutes later a siren went off in the airport and there were flashing lights revolving on the top of the steps down to the toilet. People starting looking around very concerned.

Amid all the noise and concern Deeson just appeared from the centre of the chaos with Taz under his arm looking wide eyed and happy with himself and quite breathless. I quickly sensed what had happened; there were emergency doors onto the runway right by the toilets. He'd accidentally pushed his way through the emergency door onto the tarmac and set off onto the runway and then been chased back into the airport from the boarding area by ground staff.

At the far end of the Virgin lounge there were two people clearly hiding from us behind broadsheet newspapers. One of them had the telltale camera bags at his feet. 'FLOYDY you wanker!' shouted Deeson and he threw his Taz cuddly toy across the lounge and smashed it straight into Floyd's paper. It was a perfect shot from the *loaded* quarter back. We charged over like contestants in musical chairs and both tried to get on the seat between the two avid newspaper readers. The other newspaper reader turned out to be the bloke Martin had started on in the check-in queue. He looked like he had been harassed by Basil Fawlty.

They both instantly left and then this giant wearing John Lennon sunglasses, and with bleached blond hair poking out from underneath an Aussie bushwhacker hat, came in. Despite this elaborate disguise we recognised Steven Fry who we thought was still on the run. He'd had some sort of crisis of confidence and not turned up for the first night of a play. There was a mixture of concern, curiosity and anger in the British press, a lot of 'he's let the side down' but we'd been right behind him in our Platinum Rogues Premier League of Bad Behaviour, with full support for him just legging it. Who hadn't wanted to do that at some point from work? Deeson and I were straight over to get him a drink and give him our full support. 'I'm surprised you recognised me,' he said

We replied: 'Of course we did, it's a shit disguise it just draws attention to you. Anyway we know everyone else said you were a bottler for legging it but we support you.'

Who needs enemies?

Fry and his friend thanked us nervously and left immediately. A buggy cart driver came in and said we had to leave too and as all the staff had gone to the gate door, Deeson, who had once climbed into a fenced-off lake and took an alligator skull with rotting flesh still on it from Kliebert's alligator farm near New Orleans (madness - admirable though), momentarily considered the possibility of borrowing the huge perspex 'Club Class' brick sign on the lounge desk but instead just put Taz under his arm.

We followed the driver to the cart where Stephen Fry and his friend were on the back seat.

We jumped into the cart, which set off at a fair pace with the bleeps and lights going and people hastily getting out of the way. At a distance we could see Floydy lumbering along in his full denim outfit with his heavy camera bag hand luggage, looking totally worn out.

We both hailed him with loud greetings and the driver kindly asked, 'Is this man your friend, shall I pick him up?'

'No, he's a paparazzi. He's been pestering us for days, speed up,' I replied.

Which he did. Deeson had other ideas, and as Floydy looked round at us in tired recognition Martin hooked his arm out at 90 degrees and took Floydy off his feet by the throat and straight into a moving headlock. His feet left the ground and Deeson half hauled him onto the buggy and half left him trailing. The driver couldn't see any of this and just kept speeding up to get us to the gate which had announced it had closed. I could see the defeat and desperation in Floyd's eyes as he started to suffocate and beyond him Stephen Fry in his jolly swagman outfit just had his head in his hands. Thank God we reached the destination.

This was just one journey. But there were multiple members of staff going off on trips like this every month. My own grip on sanity was loose at the best of times and Tim's was the same. Martin and Michael realised they could do what the fuck they wanted because if it made a good story I would sign it off. It was like a waterfall of bad behaviour moving down the staff list.

The worst moment of international airspace disgrace came when I started the evening in Lima, Peru, got annoyed at the others when we'd been thrown out of a nightclub after they'd had our coke confiscated in the bogs and I drunkenly (pisco sours – three and you're dancing, six and you leave the country) went to the airport and threw cash about until they let me board a plane to Colombia.

Air travel, drink and powerful drugs don't go well together and it was going home that was always the main problem. However, one time one of the idiots showed up to leave Britain *with* a load of gak. We were on our way to South America and this just didn't seem smart at all. Coals to Newcastle and all that. Such was the extent of his increasing habit. Don't take drugs when you travel, they have dogs now.

I've never joined the fabled mile-high club but one freelance writer on the mag did. He started drinking heavily with a couple he'd met

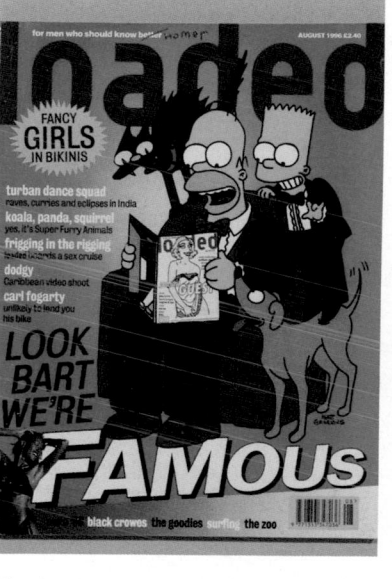

The Simpsons created this for us.

Total sell-out issue.

Two of my favourite *GQ* covers – both effortlessly cool.

Low Life, High Life: the office was a bloody disgrace . . .

. . . but we kept winning so many awards and selling so many copies no one cared. Tim and me, flanked by publisher Andy MacDuff and writer 'Dr Mick' Bunnage.

My favourite week.
Helen Mirren and me at
the Chateau Marmont,
LA, 1997.
Photo by Derek Ridgers

My favourite day. Michael Caine shooting the first *GQ* Man of the Year cover.
Photo by Tony Chambers

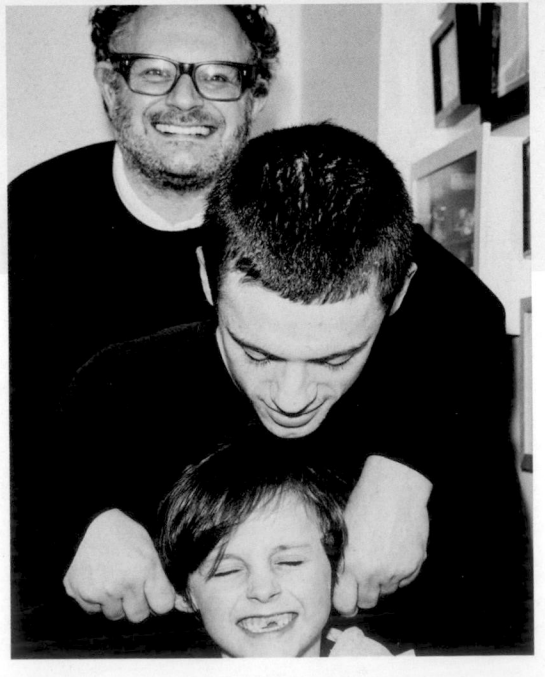

Above: Alive, sober and happy. Ronnie's room after midnight in Warsaw, 2018.

Left: Some people I helped make. Billy, Marlais and me.
Photo by Benjamin McMahon

in the airport only to discover they were seated on the same row in the same plane with only a tall gay chap between them. Thirty minutes into the journey the gay bloke turned to our man and said, 'This woman fancies you. She wants to swap seats with me, is that OK?' Obviously he said yes. Her male companion, who she insisted was just a friend, had quickly fallen asleep and the two of them, pissed as fuck, proceeded to start snogging once the lights went down.

Drink and the legendary lure of sex in airspace drove them on and eventually our man (I have to keep stopping myself writing his name here) asked the gay fella if he had any condoms. He said no but directed him towards a mate further down the plane. The *loaded* writer got up and asked his neighbour's pal but again came up empty handed. He was so pissed he then just assumed it would be perfectly all right to go up and down the plane tapping anyone on the shoulder who was watching a film and ask if they had any condoms. He even went through the curtains into club and first class. He eventually struck lucky and the pair made their way to the bogs at the back.

They were going at it hammer and tongs when there was a knock at the door and, thinking it was the cabin crew, our man insisted they both just freeze and not reply. Eventually they heard her male friend's voice and, disentangling themselves, she opened the door and the bloke just looked at them and said, 'You bitch, you bastard!'

She slammed the door in his face and went back to fucking my colleague.

When he said, 'I thought you weren't with him,' she replied, 'We're on a break.'

'Since when?'

'Since the airport.'

The women we met were as badly behaved as the writers themselves.

'I love *loaded* because it shows me how I am rather than how I'm supposed to be' – advertising bigwig, *Campaign* magazine

Soho, London, 1996

These were all operational challenges we were faced with when trapped between our own desire to get fucked up and also capture a story, and they are perhaps giving the wrong impression of what was going on back at the office.

Aside from the noise, the chaos, our narcotic self-indulgences, the title started unexpectedly mowing through awards evenings and regularly picking up Best Magazine and Best Editor categories. This was before the days when there was a men's sector at these things and we were head to head with the big guns of British publishing like the *Radio* and *TV Times*, *Cosmo*, *Elle*, *New Scientist* and so on. The judges of these prestigious awards knew what they were doing. They were often our peers, or respected editors who had gone before; they were not handing out prizes because we were getting drunk a lot and boasting about it.

At the heart of the beast was a very effective and conscientious team whose skills were recognised by the industry. The team were absolute legends; they understood the sense of freedom and creativity I wanted and just got on with it. They constantly turned out great ideas and stories, and produced the magazine with a high standard of headlines and funny blurbs. Looking back, nearly thirty years on, there appears to be an excessive use of the word 'bird', a relentless enthusiasm for defining how drunk we were a lot of the time (like in this book, I guess), and some slightly cheesy captions at times, but what the fuck, that's a 56 year-old man's perspective – at the time we were just doing what we felt like.

The sense of humour still leaps off the page now as it did then. And there was some very, very good writing. Modern broadsheet writers and authors like Miranda Sawyer, Sean O'Hagan, Jon Ronson, Nick Hornby, Barbara Ellen and others all had articles in the magazine, but it was the troop of *loaded* regulars who really set the tone and the standard.

Trevor Ward was the first to wade towards P.J. O'Rourke territory with his jaunts around South America with the Sandinistas. He was a self-confessed, high-maintenance traveller in as much as he actually invoiced us for his breakfast cereal, but from the off he created a sort of realistic travel writing that was far removed from the clichéd attempts journalists had been trying to justify free holidays with for ages. This was a time when long-haul flights to the Far East, say, were plummeting in price and our readers wanted to know where you could find cheap accommodation, like-minded travellers, drugs and parties.

Mick Bunnage's understated food column, Mick's Grill, another nod to Winner's Dinners, his Platinum Rogues Chart and his Dr Mick aggro uncle column were all regularly mentioned as highlights in the letters pages. Older, wittier and funnier than most of the staff, Mick felt very much more like my *consigliere* than subsequent assistant editors Tim Southwell and Deeson. If I was ever in doubt about an issue or approach to a story, I'd quietly ask Mick what he thought, seeking wisdom, and invariably, despite his mild-mannered demeanour, he would push for the more irresponsible of the two options. One of my favourite pieces in the mag, which I felt defined who we were and what we were about, was our response to the many 'people of influence' features newspapers like the London *Evening Standard* were always running. This was our own guide to the hundred least influential people going, which Mick and I wrote: Homer Simpson, Rigsby, Rab C. Nesbit, Arthur Daley, Stig of the Dump and so on. Anytime we needed a sharp but irreverent guide to something – like posh restaurant date etiquette, for instance – Mick would be perfectly capable of turning something out. He helped define the space the comedy could exist in, and it's no wonder the cartoons he does with former *loaded* designer Jon Link now sell masses of cards, books and posters, and appear in *Private Eye*, the *Guardian* and other places who slagged us off when they were doing it in *loaded* three decades ago. Slowcoaches.

We had a number of good sports writers like Ben Webb and Sven Harding but Bill Borrows packed the biggest punch with his brilliant cover story about going into the ring to face Prince Naseem Hamed. It was an important cover for us because it was one of our first, and I was very much aware that despite being the most charismatic British boxer around and a world champion, he hadn't been afforded *any* magazine coverage outside of the boxing press. If he'd been white I felt he probably would. Prince Naseem looked and sounded like boys I played cricket with at school. He was one of us. Only he was great at fighting, as Bill found to his peril when training to a point he felt he could spar with him. His inside guide revealed that it's not the head-shots that hurt, it's the legs that start shaking from the body blows.

Bill's father died when we were doing the mag and I came in one day to find him slumped in my office, broken. I asked him if he fancied doing a piece about being a roadie and he said yes. What I didn't tell him at that point was that it was going to be our angle for a story with Shed Seven in Japan. The fact he was prepared to do it anywhere meant, to me, he should be rewarded with the opportunity to explore the other side of the world. The feature prompted a brilliant cover line by Michael Holden: 'Sushi and the Van Keys'.

Jon Wilde was an amazing interviewer who went toe to toe with Paula Yates, REM, Ollie Reed, Richard Harris, Ron Atkinson, Damon Albarn, Alexander O'Neal and many more, and was able to get them to say brilliant things. He was also a fast and fluent storyteller, and his one-page account of all the weirdos who had populated the Welsh town he'd grown up in was so funny I simply wrote 'Read This, It's Brilliant' for the headline. His brother apparently brought the town to a standstill when he managed to piss over the top of a double-decker bus.

Mary Anne Hobbes spent a month working the door of a clip joint in Soho, and arrived every day on the back of a Hell's Angel friend's bike for protection purposes, and from there crafted a telling insight into the world of fake strip clubs, overpriced drinks and heavies marching people to cash points. It was so good the *Telegraph* tried to recruit her.

All magazines should have good columnists and frankly many don't. Jeff Barrett at Heavenly had first told me about Irvine Welsh and he needs no introduction now, but back in 1994 none of us had ever seen such scabrous writing about drug scenes some of us knew and violence we'd had the sense to steer away from. His reliance on the Leith dialect in his novels and short stories made them even harder to penetrate and all the more rewarding when you did so. The man defined a generation, and while initially looked down upon by the 'serious literary world' he wrote books for an otherwise under-served audience. To that end his work sat with *A Clockwork Orange*, *The Profession of Violence* and other cult classics. Hiring him as a monthly columnist was a no-brainer, and even if the column largely was an update on how Hibs were doing, being able to put his name on the cover every issue was a bonus. And we got his interview with Noel

Gallagher for a Christmas issue in which the cover image was just a shot of Noel's instantly recognisable eyebrows.

Over the page from Irvine was the legendary and extremely loveable Howard Marks. At that point he wasn't too long out of prison in the States, and, *Mr Nice* aside, Howard would later point out that we had given him his first proper job on release. His reputation rose as our own did but there was no denying *Mr Nice* was a brilliant book. A former policeman Deeson and I knew had first told us about trying to catch Howard many years before and then regular *loaded* photographer Steve Pyke called me and said, 'You've got to go and interview this guy I've just photographed for his book cover – he's perfect for *loaded*.' And indeed he was.

Howard and Irvine were like the lions at the gates of the features pages and it was a pleasure to have them both writing in every issue. Invariably the production editor would come to see me with a day to go before the presses rolled and say, 'Can you get hold of Howard and Irvine? They haven't filed yet.' And I'd call them, and Howard would bomb off a story about his latest stop at customs and Irv would recount tales from nightclubs he'd just been in and goings-on at Easter Road.

Our third columnist was my landlord, Vic Reeves – 'Columnist of the Year, 1753' – who essentially would do an impromptu monologue on his back steps taking umbrage with unwanted salad, lads who wore excessive amounts of branded words on their jumpers and tough guys who walked like they were carrying trays of eggs under their arms. I would record and translate these streams of surreal wisdom into a column. And he was paid in crates of Cloudy Bay Sauvignon Blanc!

All the writers across the board delivered tight, engaging and often very funny copy. And they were confident enough to come up with new stories. At one editorial meeting Adam Porter said he wanted to do a story on numbers and Jon Wilde said he wanted to write a piece about arses; the room laughed at both these suggestions but I thought they were great and duly commissioned them. There were a lot of smart people around the paper.

The beauty of the magazine was that there was so much of our own culture that had never been collectively covered in mainstream magazines before. We could include anything and everything from manga to motorised barstool races; Aleister Crowley to Dani Behr; Malcolm Allison to Frankie Dettori; school trips to Formula One pit crews; Indonesian dragons to *The Torture Garden*; *The Fast Show* to *Deliverance*-themed fashion shoots; heavy rockers like Lemmy, Ozzy and Alice to top DJs like Carl Cox, Fabio and Grooverider and Paul Oakenfold; Richard Pryor to Steve Coogan; Charlie Sheen to Brian Robson, and Jo Guest to Robert Crumb; making young Man U players look fat and Oasis look old using new technology called Photoshop.

That's just three issues I've dipped into for reminders. The mag was overflowing with top-quality content, the sort of subjects we knew our readers loved, and specifically, having been swamped with cynicism at the *NME*, we had a policy of not slagging stuff off. We'd rather leave it out and feature something else someone was passionate about. And by being inclusive like that and understanding that all of these various topics *could* sit next to each other, we guaranteed readers would just keep coming back for more and more and more.

Entrenched in social venom: the *loaded* clubbing pages

Everywhere, 1994–97

There were of course basics that women's mags and the crusty old men's mags from the States didn't go near. The boom in British and European clubbing, for instance, the Balearic scene.

Acid house and the waves of house music that followed it liberated Britain from Saturday night under the plastic palm trees of Tiffany's and Cinderella Rockerfella's everywhere. I knew people who lost their minds to acid house and Ecstasy but for the most part the club music revolution that took place at the end of the eighties changed everything for the better. It had not only captured that explosive sense of revolutionary fervour and possibility of genuine change that punk in the seventies and hippy culture in the sixties had, but had shaped and shifted nightlife across the board.

It changed the music that was played, where it was played, who created it, what drugs were taken. It changed people's lives, health and holiday plans. It was absolutely massive but was there any sign of this in *Esquire*, *GQ*, *Arena*, *Elle* or *Marie Claire*? Zilch.

This was where I knew our audience lay and I knew it was important to find someone to document clubland all over the country and not just in elitist venues in London's West End. I was asking around to find a writer who could capture what it was like to actually be in the clubs. Then Simon, the singer from Fabulous who was also writing for the style press, said, 'There's a kid from *i-D* I see everywhere, every club I go to. He's not a writer though, he sells classified ads. He's called Rowan.'

I checked Rowan out with Beth, our fashion editor who had previously been in charge of fashion on *i-D* and she said, 'Oh yes, he's a lovely guy, big clubber, but he's not a writer.' I figured given the help Tony Stewart had given me when I was a fanzine writer, and the help I'd in turn given Lamacq on *NME*, not being a writer probably wasn't a problem so long as he actually had the enthusiasm to go to the clubs. We could either teach him to write or he could tell a staff writer like Deeson or Holden what had happened and they would write it down. Much as I did with Vic Reeves.

As it turned out Rowan had done a few little reports for *i-D* and was really keen to get involved. Mixed-race, super slim and with the long thick curls at King Charles length that Weatherall and Throb from Primal Scream were sporting, he looked good, knew his stuff and was totally enthusiastic. He was like an acid house spaniel.

I explained how I wanted him to go to club nights all over the country and that we'd cover all his expenses and pay for the articles and the clubs would probably let him in free and he was up for it.

We drew up the structure of the four clubs pages he was going to look after every month. There would be a main town/city scene report like the hardcore reports in *Maximum Rocknroll* I'd read as a teenager, but with masses and masses of pictures of clubbers; a round-up of records; a second, smaller club report; a quick band/DJ interview; and a DJ questionnaire like the old *Shoot* football Q & As, but funny. We used 'Have you got any Guru Josh?' as the title for the Q & A, based on Paul Calf asking 'Have you got "Into the Valley" by the Skids,' in his TV special. That was until Guru Josh complained, even though it was years since his hit (four years, in fact – 1990 had been the time for the Guru). Ever the pragmatist, Rowan didn't want to create any bad vibes on the scene so we changed it to 'Got Any Spandau Ballet?' Every DJ in the world is familiar with the punter asking for totally the wrong song for the night so it was a well-received way in.

Writing about recorded music was one thing but writing about people dancing in clubs on drugs? Well it's an open deck really. Go for it, submit anything you want, just don't take it too seriously. Nik Cohn and Tom Wolfe were the best chroniclers of the club and counterculture scenes of the sixties that I had read – Cohn's *Awopbopaloobop Alopbamboom* and 'Tribal Rites of the New Saturday Night', the story that was the inspiration for *Saturday Night Fever* (actually about Shepherd's Bush mods) and Wolfe's *The Electric Kool-Aid Acid Test* both flew off into flights of fancy, the writers pouring streams of words out of their minds and down onto the page. This was performance journalism, explaining what the fuck was going on by capturing the euphoria of the moment. I didn't expect Rowan to reach those literary heights; I just wanted him to convey his experience and, amazingly, given he wasn't a trained writer, he did just that.

One example that came to epitomise his column came in an interview with DJ Dean Thatcher's band the Aloof where Rowan described them as being 'entrenched in social venom'. It didn't mean anything but it didn't matter. His mad, higgledy-piggledy descriptions just added to the sense that he was totally out of it. He wasn't when he wrote his copy but he was when he was in the clubs, but he was also diligently taking notes and names and really cared about making his pieces a great read. He accurately described clubbers pointing their fingers in the air while they danced as 'like spinning invisible bagels'. Whatever surreal abstract line he came up with worked and I used to sit and wait in anticipation for his copy to come in. Everyone in the subs' room did.

His writing read like someone shouting to you on the dance floor – loud, enthusiastic madness. There had never been a better period for global clubbing than the end of the eighties into the nineties and we wanted the whole magazine to feel like a night out at a club.

When the mag picked up momentum and word would get round that *loaded* was coming to town people would get very excited and start handing out drugs, getting the drinks in, snogging and even occasionally getting their tits out unprompted for Rowan's regular photographers, which was initially unexpected. We deliberately set out to visit towns and smaller cities rather than just the obvious places like Nottingham, Manchester, Glasgow, Leeds and London. Rowan and I both knew that the whole nation was having it from Newquay to Newcastle.

House music had changed that idea of exclusivity; the VIP lounges were often shit, to be honest, you wanted to be in the middle of it all. Ecstasy was an instant scene-starter. I wanted a club section where fifty people in one town would all buy the mag because their picture was in it in all their full-on, eyes-bulging, arm-waving, mouth-drying, lip-biting, laughing glory. I wanted Rowan's pages to capture the used wraps on the bog floors, the bloke trying to smash the cold tap on so he could glug away at it, the 'not a dry shirt in the house' temperatures, the screaming and slipping and endless moving of the house nation. The guys running these places – like Dave Beer, James at Cream in Liverpool, Mike Pickering at the Haç, Nicky Holloway at the Milk Bar, Lisa Loud and Charlie Chester at Flying – were like benevolent nightclub emperors. Alan Lewis and I both knew this was such an important aspect of youth culture we needed someone at the heart of the staff who lived it like Paolo Hewitt, Helen Mead, Jack Barron, Mandy James, Sherman At The Controls and Andrew Weatherall all had done at the *NME* earlier.

It was one of the most important sections in the mag because we knew the whole scene was the most important thing in so many people's lives. For the largely male readership it also helped that the pages would be full of girls having a great time and posing with their mates for the cameras.

I don't know who came up with his nickname 'Gurning Chernin' but the readers started to refer to him that way in letters, as did people in clubs, and it got to a point where it started affecting other Chernin family members. One day his dad, who was apparently partial to a bit of jazz was giving a lecture at Southampton University when he was interrupted by some students who were pissing themselves. When he asked them what was so funny one of them blurted out, 'Sir, you're not Gurning Chernin, are you?' To which he replied, 'No, he's my son.' They were stunned. His credibility had just shot off the scale.

Not everyone was going out though; a new generation was about to stay in and stare at screens.

I'm not sure we should be looking at this

The arrival of the Internet, 1994

Adam Porter joined *loaded* as a regular freelance writer after the first issue. I didn't know him but he'd been writing for the *Evening Standard* – which seemed like a weird leap – but like others he recognised the magazine could be for him as a reader and a writer. He rang me as soon as he'd read the first issue and said, 'This magazine is me, baby. I really want to write for you.'

Like a lot of the guys who rolled up, he had a weird mix of interests that were under-served by the existing media and they certainly could never be found together in one place. He was a football-loving, soul-music-living, Jewish hippy into Chelsea, spliffs and Japanese monsters. Not long after he joined I went round to sample his grass and watch the FA Cup final at his house and his living room was dominated by two 6-foot tall bass speakers from a sound system. He also had a homeless guy sleeping in his old van out the back; in this way he was very much *loaded*'s Alan Bennett. Benevolent weed-assisted hooligan was his status.

A few months after he joined I bumped into him in the revolving door going into King's Reach Tower. I wondered why he was going in there instead of into our office in the stables and he said, 'We need to get a website. I'm going to see the publishers about it.'

I replied, 'A what? What is it?' This is how long ago we were talking.

Nineteen ninety-four. They didn't exist, or certainly not for public consumption anyway. Maybe some nerds had them. Self-styled nerd Adam and his mate had secured the rights to create a 'website' for the forthcoming Tarantino film *Pulp Fiction*. I asked him to explain what he meant and he said there'd be pictures and information about the film that weren't in the film but on a computer and anyone could go to it and look at it. These being the computers we currently just used like typewriters to write articles on, and like art desks to lay pages out on. The most futuristic bit of kit we had was a scanner, which was like a reverse overhead projector. We put something under it and it came up on the screen. It was like some sort of Star Trek kit.

So Adam tried to explain his thing with Tarantino's film company in the UK and said we really should have the same for *loaded* because it was the future. We could put things up between each issue coming out, he explained, which sort of made sense.

Now if you're under forty reading this you obviously think I sound pretty fucking gormless here but this was the start of it. No regular person knew about or had websites when *loaded* started in April 1994. What followed that year was the very beginning of public use of the Internet, beyond the domain of computer geeks. I had only heard about the concept once from Deee-Lite when I'd interviewed them in Brazil two years before, and they'd sounded insane.

Adam went on his way in to try and convince IPC to let him do one for *loaded* and I just thought, 'Yeah, go for it you, mad bastard,' as he was so passionate about it. In typical dinosaur style IPC wouldn't let us have a website until *New Scientist* had one and then they wanted *NME* to have one, and like everything else it was, 'Get to the back of the queue, some of us aren't even comfortable with you guys existing yet.' So instead Adam just started writing about the Internet in the mag. Keen readers with long memories might not remember his name because, although he once stepped in and did a late-night phone interview with Pamela Anderson under his own name when none of the staff wanted to do it, most of Adam's columns in the mag were written under the guise of a stuffed primate called Cheeky Monkey, a gorilla and a duck. As I said, there was a lot of dope and toys at his house. Tim Southwell was also a big fan of Basil Brush and there were times when he'd be doing his Basil Brush impression and Adam and Pete and the subs would be talking about Cheeky Monkey like he was real and it started to feel like a children's TV show. Albeit one where people were drinking on set.

Not to be deterred by IPC's lack of dynamism, Adam got on with developing the site anyway. Once it was up and running, Adam edited the *loaded* website but before that he had to actually show the staff the Internet. He explained there were a few companies in California with names like Yahoo that sounded like comics or sweets and they would be the 'portals' to 'surfing' 'online'. It was interesting listening to him because even if it was hard to get your head round it, the way he talked about it there didn't seem to be any doubt that this stuff was going to happen.

Even at IPC conferences they started talking about the 'information superhighway' and how the 'World Wide Web' would one day replace print magazines. To which most of the people in the room would snigger. The *loaded* staff were a little more open minded, not least because some of them were already hooked on their computers, playing very basic football-manager games but also because as ten-year-olds we had watched Princess Leia appear as a hologram from a pedal bin to talk to a boy in his dressing gown called Skywalker. Somehow that seemed every bit as likely as the massive fucking shark we all feared would terrorise us on holiday or the idea that some small-time debt-collecting muscle could become boxing champion of the world.

Some techies eventually came from the bowels of IPC and messed around with Adam's computer and then we all gathered round as he put a phone into a rubber holder thing and a long, squeaking, warbling, high-pitched sound emerged and then his grey screen blinked into life and he asked people for ideas of what they wanted to look at. Within ten minutes we were looking at dead bodies in vintage car crash photographs and it wasn't Andy Warhol or J.G. Ballard. Even Adam wasn't sure if what we were doing was legal and when he said, 'Actually I'm not sure we should be looking at this,' people started moving away from the cluster behind his chair, thinking the police were going to show up.

When our website was eventually launched it was quickly valued at $20m by a credible tech industry third party, such was the madness of the early Internet days. No one realised these valuations would turn into hard cash as the bubble expanded and IPC should have sold *up-loaded*, as it was known, there and then and just started another one. But they were so busy pocketing the unexpected windfall I'd given them they never looked at the bigger picture or factored ambition into anything.

Up-loaded itself was so innocent, flat and tame. Adam had a thermometer graphic with headshots of Kathy Lloyd, Jo Guest, Rachel Bird and other women we fancied or had had in the mag and a button to push to vote for them. It was a league table of girls we liked. That was it. Headshots.

The other thing we had was the Jimmy McNulty page created by my old mate Iain Cummings who I'd been in the Butter Cookies band with in Leeds. Iain had been working in the computer industry and knew a bit about the Internet. He and Adam were the only people I knew who understood what the fuck was going on. Jimmy was a parody of the mad Scots drunks Iain had seen growing up in East Kilbride. He gave Jimmy a merchandising stall where he sold his Swearing Bracelets which was an early version of online shopping. Only no such thing existed then so the concept was you could buy them even though you couldn't. 'Hey see I fuckin' started the Amazon pal,' as Jimmy might have said.

As technology and entertainment developed and the world of computer game consoles exploded into life Adam doubled his editorial output in the mag and Cheeky Monkey and the duck started reviewing games too. No other lifestyle mag was covering these but they were clearly addictive.

It wasn't only in the office that games were taking over some of the staff's lives. One day one of our favourite photographers Martyn 'Shakey' Goodacre walked in and said, 'I've got an idea.' He wasn't prone to making editorial suggestions but he was my mate so I said fire away and he said, 'I've been playing this new game for days now, and it's totally addictive and there's a really fit babe who is an explorer in it called Lara Croft. I think you should have her on the cover.' I nodded my head, figured games were still for kids and nerds, and asked if he fancied coming to Paris with me instead with an ex-girlfriend and her mate, which he bit my hand off to do. I reckon I've made about ten identifiable editorial mistakes in my career, and not acting on his idea was one of them. (He would, I know, like me to mention here that on this trip to Paris I drank so much fine brandy that I eventually declared, '*Je suis un journaliste d'alcool*,' before falling backwards off my chair in a Montmartre restaurant.)

My very last memory of the *loaded* Internet lot was the last editorial meeting we had for *up-loaded* before I left, in which Mike Karin suggested we bought an old car and blew it up and filmed it and put it on the website. It was the first time anyone had considered putting film on the site. When I asked why, he just replied, 'It will look great and will be a laugh to do.' This was way before *Jackass* or Clarkson's *Top Gear* shenanigans but it was the same line of thinking that fuelled so many of our best editorial ideas. 'Why? Cos it'll be a laugh.' Given that within months I was having to talk to stuck-up old French wankers about jewellery ads at *GQ* I don't know if they ever did blow up a car but I hope they did.

'I used to like starting fights at parties, the hardest drug I've taken is ____ and I have legs like ... Tell me someone ... OK, David Batty'
– Helen Mirren

Los Angeles, 1997

The array of well-known people who wanted to come to our parties, be in the magazine or who we simply met along the way was huge. Naturally most of these encounters led to interviews or articles. Jonathan Ross kindly hosted one of our Video Marathon features in his living room; Jools Holland proved he actually could play 'Hound Dog' backwards – from end to beginning, not with his back to the piano as he'd first thought I had challenged him to do; Jenny Eclair was wild and funny company; Bez was always hyper-active; we even found ourselves in a bar at the NFT talking to the guy who played Darth Vader.

But whenever I'm asked about who has been the most fun famous person to hang out with I don't hesitate to say Helen Mirren. She gets the vote ahead of the Beastie Boys, Vic and Bob, New Order and Mark E. Smith, and I've spent a fair bit of time with all of them. They were/are friends. I only spent a weekend with Helen and it was the best.

I was going to Los Angeles to do a piece about the black humour TV comedy *Married with Children* for *loaded* and just before I left I saw this brilliant picture of Helen in *Marie Claire*, lying on a bed with her legs up against a wall and her hands over her tits. It was really sexy and stylish, reminded me of a fashion designer I'd broken up with a year before, and I just thought I'd like to interview her. I liked *Prime Suspect* and knew she'd been in *The Long Good Friday* but that was about it. I asked Adam, our commissioning editor, if he could get me an interview with her and, despite it being just a week's notice, she was up for it. Maybe she liked the idea of this very of-the-moment, infamous, younger men's mag everyone was talking about being into her. Maybe she just had time on her hands while her husband, director Taylor Hackford, made *Speed* and she was between projects herself. Whatever the reason, I'm glad she had time for us.

Somewhere along the way while making the arrangements Adam got a contact number in Los Angeles and assumed it was mine. He rang at UK lunchtime, dawn in LA, and upon hearing a woman's voice answer the phone asked if I was there. The reply was, 'You wish!' He'd somehow got Helen's own number and woken her up.

I was very excited when she arrived for the interview. She looked stunning, and I remember feeling like a kid in her presence, giving her an apple from the reception of the Chateau Marmont. We got on very well from the off. We hung out at my suite at the hotel for photographs and then she took me out to a load of bars. She drank, I drove. The very cool young Californians we met were very much in awe of her. The highlight of the weekend was driving her home on the Saturday night, where she couldn't open the gate of her large rented Hollywood mansion. So she very quickly and drunkenly started climbing over it in her heels. It was about fifteen feet high but she went up it like Chris Bonnington. I remember looking in disbelief as she precariously toppled over the top in heels, thinking, 'If she falls and hurts herself I'm going to have to climb over as well, and then the armed response security will show up and it won't look right at all.'

Thankfully she didn't fall but buzzed the gates open and insisted I drive her up to the house itself. There she ruffled my hair, said something very nice to me and went inside. If I'd spent any longer with her than a weekend I'd have ended up with a massive crush.

I never actually wrote the story because the work experience person transcribing it had a sudden terminal illness in her family and I never saw the tape again. Somewhere there's a tape with HM discussing fighting at parties, what drugs she has taken and when she likes to have sex.

Last summer in Italy she bumped into Suggs from Madness, who I know, and when he told her he was laughing at a radio podcast I was on, she replied, 'Oh I had a brilliant night out in LA with James.' Twenty years on that was nice to hear.

That was then, this is now

UK, 1980s/90s

Within months of the title launching it became a focal point for creative change and a flag-waving exercise for having fun. Simply having fish and chips and bacon sandwiches as pull-out, pin-up posters was making the statement: lighten the fuck up. There were just so much fun, and once we were up and running it came at us thick and fast and vice versa.

There was no doubt whatsoever that a new-found confidence was ricocheting around the country in everyday life and across multiple entertainment and creative industries. And we were a part of that. The nineties became a decade of change, exhilaration and overstimulation. It was a ten-year scramble of hedonism and confidence driven by a lost generation tired of Thatcherism and jump-started by Ecstasy-fuelled acid house who genuinely believed it was going to last forever.

Between the late eighties and the mid-nineties the creative and social shackles came off and the world as we knew it changed. In the UK cheap flights, satellite TV, email, the Internet, masses of drugs and a home-grown generation of superstars in art, comedy, football, politics and entertainment created a country unrecognisable from the one at war with itself in the mid-eighties, when mounted British police baton-charged British coal workers, and British troops died weekly in Northern Ireland.

Decades and their cultural impact don't start and end on the first day of the new year that ends in a zero, they rev up and wind down.

By 1994/5 it felt like we had the survived or escaped the 1980s with their AIDS and 'Heroin Kills' posters on every street corner, put up by a government dead set on repressing large sectors and subcultures of the population.

When Kevin Keegan ended his playing career, climbed into his helicopter and choppered away from St James Park in his Newcastle kit in 1984 that felt like the end of the 1970s, the close of play. That summer neo-Nazis attacked the Redskins onstage at a GLC festival on the South Bank; the Battle of Orgreave delivered shocking images of mounted police brutality; and even in TV fiction fireman George Jackson from *Brookside* was fitted up, a storyline so resonant that there were 'Free George Jackson' posters going up across the north. The following year was Heysel and the miners' strike ended with twenty-five NCB pit closures, while anti-police riots raged in Brixton and Broadwater Farm. This was exactly a decade before *loaded*'s first year of existence.

In the intervening years there was of course acid house, the Roses, Mondays and Madchester; the ubiquitous grooves of Jazzy B's Soul II Soul and the smoking sounds of Portishead and Massive Attack – they released brilliantly innovative albums that became a constant background soundtrack, interrupted only by the punk dance of the Shamen, Prodigy and Underworld's more notable singles and then replaced eventually by the arrival of Blur and Oasis; inflatable bananas on the terraces in 1988; the Berlin Wall coming down; and by 1990, ding-dong, Thatcher was gone. Italia 90 happened. Leeds were promoted. Sky Football and *The Simpsons* made cable TV worth investing in. Then came sharks in formaldehyde and solid-concrete house art and a sense of fun emerging all over the place. All of this was nourishment for the generation who would start and read *loaded*.

In the eighties and early nineties those in charge seemed to have no sense of how the other half lived at all, and those that were seen as enjoying themselves the right way and were championed by Thatcher and her ilk – the champagne-drinking yuppies – didn't innovate anything – they all just made money and boasted about it. But by the mid-nineties the emerging story in the alcohol industry wasn't about the top end of the market – the champagne drinkers – but the mass market; the infantilisation of alcohol with Hooch and then Red Bull mixed with vodka, basically lemonade and Spangles with a kick, took it out of the upmarket wine bars and into the fields and corner pubs.

The change was unstoppable. New Labour replaced old Tories; Oasis, Pulp and Blur replaced Stock, Aitken and Waterman; Vic Reeves replaced Jimmy Tarbuck; festivals replaced the Radio 1 Roadshow; cocaine replaced heroin; *Absolutely Fabulous*, *Father Ted*, *Partridge* and *The Fast Show* replaced *To the Manor Born*, *'Allo 'Allo!* and *Are You Being Served?*; Gazza replaced Ray Wilkins; the Spice Girls replaced Phil Collins; and on and on.

Last orders were called on the decade – and we were smack bang in the middle of the scramble for as much drink as possible. It didn't go unnoticed beyond our own shores. In 1996 *Rolling Stone* sent former Orange Juice member turned writer, Steven Daly, into our office for a comment for his article 'Britain Is Drunk'. It was, and all the better for it. Nowhere more so than in the offices of a magazine specifically designed to be like being on tour with Happy Mondays or the *Dance with the Devil*-era Rolling Stones.

Imagine you've had the only job you ever wanted for your first job (*NME*) and then after that someone says invent an even better one, and everything you ever liked went into it. *Loaded* really did feel like working in Willy Wonka's chocolate factory. Just before we launched I'd watched a BBC2 lecture by a McKinsey management guru in which he said all big companies must have ninety-nine straight guys and a weirdo to do the new product development. I simply and deliberately reversed the formula and had effectively assembled ninety-nine weirdos and a straight guy. So that culture of 75 per cent fucking about in search of the story or the laughs and 25 per cent turning the story and the laughs into something we could share with the readers on the page worked very well. The bottom line was we never thought we were better than the readers and we never wanted to produce anything that was less than our best. And we were happy to take the piss out of ourselves from the word go. Apart from not making any money out of it and having no mental health support it was the perfect set-up. Everybody was having too good a time to really worry about basics like that.

Like a good football team, the *loaded* team almost transformed into one being. Being 'the *loaded* guys' offered us a sort of individual anonymity as well as an air of notoriety. It gave us an aura of possibility and confidence: who are these mouthy, drunken bastards? They don't look too rich, who the fuck are they? As well as producing the mag we inhabited this weird world where people were amazingly excited about the magazine. It was like getting a double chocolate digestive that had stuck together. (I had by now my own column called Biscuit of the Month.)

We all loved *loaded* but Tim had total belief in and passion for the magazine. This enthusiasm was his strength. I don't know if it was because he didn't like other people getting more attention than him, but he thought working on *loaded* put us on a par with celebs. One time at a Take That party he thought Robbie was showing off too much (erm, it was his party?) dancing on a bar top so Tim just walked over and pushed him off. Right off, boom, disappeared behind the bar. 'Big bloody show-off berk,' Tim probably thought. It didn't go down well. Our other ex-*Smash Hits* writer The Loafer was there and said Robbie got up and was furious, saying he could have hurt himself and not been able to do gigs.

I liked Robbie, he was just a cheeky young lad having the time of his life. Oasis and Blur were absolutely storming it, music wise, but Robbie was very much the mainstream pop man of the moment. At some amazing party at Ally Pally he and I were talking and he said, 'James, you've been at all the best parties I've been to since I became famous but the difference is when you get up in the morning, there's not a load of paparazzi outside your house waiting to see who you went home with.' Thank fuck for that.

It took Americans to capture what we had going on and package it up in a magazine, *Vanity Fair*, give it a title, Cool Britannia, and send it back as a ready-made, and indeed remarkably accurate, label for the times.

Whereas Britpop had been a head-to-head battle for chart supremacy between Oasis and Blur – just as Slade and Glitter had gone toe to toe in the glam days – with an undercard of Verve, Pulp and a few others, Cool Britannia encompassed the true variety of talent that ranged from fashion to art to music to comedy, film, food, fiction, DJs, politics – and yes, to magazines. Well *magazine*. Ours. There was a clear creative resurgence, a confidence that made those of us thriving in the mid-nineties cocky and bright and drenched in self-belief and excessive celebration.

Whether it was at the Atlantic or Vic Naylor's or Marco Pierre White's, Quo Vadis or Damien Hirst's Pharmacy bar with giant E's for barstool tops, the nightly froth was whipped up then blown away by a generation who knew they were having the time of their lives. What I liked was that it wasn't exclusive to these bars though. Every city I went to had really vibrant exciting scenes and people dead keen to show us it.

Nor was the period, the scene, the moment confined to the arts and media. Smack bang in the middle of the decade came Euro 96 with its collective euphoria, its hit song, its English superstars fulfilling their function of 'going close'. Before the tournament Gazza, Shez and Co. had apparently brought shame upon the nation for their drunken dentist's chair antics, and yet just weeks later they were heroes no one could get enough of.

There were helicopters landing in school playing fields around the Wembley area bringing high net worth individuals and celebrities to hastily assembled villages of hospitality tents as the world of corporate branding exploded. Me? I took the tube. It's fast if you know which one to get. People remember Gazza lobbing the ball over Scotland's Colin Hendry and then volleying it into the back of the net, and his outstretched leg just centimetres away from helping us beat the Germans – a cross I was in line with at the ground – but for me one of the finest moments was just staring at the scoreboard as we beat Holland 4–1. Twenty years before, they'd been the best team in the world. It almost felt magical.

Many of those at the heart of the scene had backgrounds similar to my own. Lee 'Alexander' McQueen confessed on Frank Skinner's chat show to having started out on the enterprise allowance scheme, which Primal Scream had still been on when they made *Screamadelica* and 'Loaded'. That was one moment of identification that stuck out. The new acts – Oasis at Knebworth – and the old – Sex Pistols at Finsbury Park – were lighting huge fires of inspiration at both ends of music's timeline. I DJ'd at the Pistols gig and was one of the few who watched the infamous punk rock scoundrels from the side of the stage – after the first song Lydon announced, 'Finsbury Park has never looked so good' and then bounced to the back of the stage and just grinned in delight at his mum and her chap who were stood there looking proud and intrigued.

There was no plan or strategy to what or how much good stuff was happening; maybe the ex-comprehensive school kids were having a field day *because* we'd left school with nothing on offer. So the drive required to achieve it had made the success so much sweeter. Frank Skinner spinning around at the *loaded* cover shoot with his eyes closed playing the just-recorded tape of 'Three Lions' was a vision of a man fulfilling his dream of becoming a pop star, it massively overshadowed his decent career as a comedian and *Fantasy Football* host.

So many of us who sped into the mainstream with our creativity intact found this big, wide-open space where we could actually do what we wanted to do. We all had our own influences and motivations. Six months after my mum died I was still down and out – emotionally beaten, not homeless – when I saw Abel Ferrara's stunning *Bad Lieutenant* in a cinema in the Haymarket, the heart of the London establishment. Walking out I saw Adrian Edmondson and his wife Jennifer Saunders together in a car at traffic lights. The film's apparent freedom and this glimpse of two brilliant comic actors filled my head as I walked home to Tower Bridge, where I then lived pre-Jim's flat. That moment illuminated the reality of possibility. How the hell had he been able to make a film like that? And have it shown in a mainstream cinema less than a mile from Parliament and Buckingham Palace?

And I think everyone who had that Cool Britannia spotlight on them had experiences like that, because the mid-nineties were bright with self-belief. And *Vanity Fair* saw that. It was a time where for once the best things were in the mainstream and not the underground and the sidelines.

I loved the throwaway, stupid things we did in *loaded*, and the impressive, well-written articles too, but I was equally thrilled when I was told *loaded* had become the fastest and biggest-selling magazine at Britain's number one newsagent's – WH Smith in Waterloo Station. Anyone can be cool and obscure but to get away with doing something you love in the full view of the public eye was sweeter.

So when the *Vanity Fair* writer, David Kamp, arrived and engaged me in a conversation that made me realise this was a feature that would likely come close to telling it how it was, it was extremely welcome. Because the broadsheet writers often reported on us but largely believed we were some species of weird wild animals.

The photo shoot for the Cool Britannia edition was not a great experience – with not enough outfits for us all to appear as *Clockwork Orange*-style droogs, and too many cocaine hangovers doing the rounds of the assembled *loaded* staff, I took a pair of pink leather shorts and a black shirt and struck a pose. It seemed better to look nothing at all like Kubrick and Malcolm McDowell's Alex DeLarge than some sort of Carnaby Street interpretation as the stylist had seemingly thought would work.

The interview though, as I said, was interesting. Kamp accurately wrote: '*Loaded* magazine has perhaps done more to foster this hyper-real Englishness than anything else. It's a men's magazine ... that makes no attempt to be cool. ... James Brown is a banty, diminutive, Dickensian-looking Yorkshireman of 31 with dark corkscrew curls that protrude five or six inches from either side of his head. ... He has been named editor of the year thrice in *Loaded*'s three-year existence.'

What he essentially meant was I'd been brought up on chips and looked like a *Beano* character. It was right and nice to be featured in that round-up but essentially it was another photo shoot and another interview – it just happened to be in a great magazine.

There were so many parties and so many new famous people enjoying themselves that you just ran into the same famous people over and over again: Coogan, Vic and Bob, Robbie, the *Fast Show* guys, the Gallaghers, Zoe Ball, Sara Cox, Anna Friel, Martin Clunes, Rivron, Keith Allen, the club runners, club DJs, Howard and Irvine, all the bands I knew at *NME* and on and on. There were so many agreements to appear in the mag being done in bars and bogs and at festivals. The first time I met Liam Gallagher one to one was on a sofa in a private bar in Soho. I had a beard, fleece and hiking boots and was covered in shit. We'd just come back from sleeping in a cave on a deserted island in Scotland for a week and were utterly fucked. Obviously most people go home and get changed but we'd just gone straight out to refuel. He asked who I was and when I said, 'James, editor of *loaded*, you came to my birthday party last year,' he looked at me and didn't actually believe me.

Just as the phrase 'lads' mags' didn't appear until at least a year after I had left *loaded*, so the most '*loaded*' afternoon I experienced happened years later. Interviewing Liam for one of those monthly magazines that relentlessly fucks the corpse of the same sixties/seventies rock bands every month, I had a text from a mate who said he was in a bar interviewing Gazza and did we want to come over.

Gazza was many sambucas to the wind, had numerous bags of Haribos everywhere and was insistent that Liam sing him something. This wasn't going anywhere, with Liam replying, 'Do I ask you to do some keepy-uppies or headers?' and it started to get slightly fractious until, knowing which children's TV shows he watched with his son, who was the same age as my son, I started the opening lines of the theme song to *SpongeBob SquarePants*, to which Liam stood up and chanted, 'SPONGEBOBSQUAREPANTS' and took over the rest of the lead vocal.

Suitably pleased, Gazza went on to tell the most remarkable array of stories which involved him dating and then drunkenly pissing off Liz Hurley, getting caught shoplifting in Spain, and insisting he could get Liam a great watch from a mate of his in Newcastle. Gazza was an amazing storyteller and thought nothing of spilling anecdotes that didn't exactly portray him in the best light. So much so that he began to remind me of Unlucky Alf, the *Fast Show* pensioner who would invariably end up falling into a roadworks ditch to the cries of 'Oh bugger.'

I had promised the members' club we were in that I would vouch for Liam's behaviour as he was still banned from previously smashing up the snooker room. As it was time for both of us to go and collect our sons from primary school we got up and headed down the stairs, only for Liam to say, 'Hang on' and run back in and all I could hear was 'LIAM, NO!' from multiple voices, primarily female, and then an almighty whoosh and loads of shouting and screaming and the Oasis frontman jogged back down the stairs to catch me and said, 'Come on, we better scarper.'

Upstairs Gazza was dripping wet from a discharged fire extinguisher and I could only imagine him saying, 'Oh, bugger.'

The fire extinguisher cost me £185 on my club bill and I was asked to inform Liam that he was once again banned.

Being worn out and covered in shit was the consequence of taking the *loaded* editorial team into nature. Behaving like we did in clubs, only in a field, and then coming back utterly shattered. That exhaustion from what should have been a relaxing weekend on an island was perhaps the slightest of hairline fractures. But there was just too much good stuff going on to realise that the intensity might start to wear people down. You can see how intense and relentless it was just from reading this, but this is a fraction of what was happening every week.

Night after night we were being treated like Ray Liotta as Henry Hill in the restaurant entrance scene in *Goodfellas*. Nothing like this had ever happened before. A British magazine had not been famous like this. The breadth of the editorial coverage meant we were invited to parties and launches across the board; we went out every night. I'd only stay in Sundays to rest. I'm not sure who came up with that idea, but to quote our column of the same name: good work fella.

There were so many different things going on that it was like being in a firefight of fun. It really did feel like going on tour, and then we did go on tour. I figured we'd given the readers so much free booze they should buy us a drink and we went off on a Buy Us a Pint Tour just to meet the readers, and we met some really great men and women across the UK. Much better than doing focus group research which thankfully, because of the unexpected sales, we never had to do again.

The magazine was rightly celebrated as a brilliant publication. The industry thought so as they gave us so many awards, the readers thought so as they turned up in their hundreds of thousands. The advertisers thought so too as within eighteen months the issues were just under three hundred pages thick and featured things like a shiny six-panel gatefold Marlboro ad. It was loud and noisy and action-packed with content and had little resemblance to the way it's been painted since.

The only letter of complaint we ever had from a woman read simply: 'Dear Loaded, I know you are a funny magazine but please can I have my husband back? He disappears for ages on his own and all I can hear is him laughing.' Lots of women liked the magazine because they recognised their husbands, boyfriends, brothers, mates and workmates in it, they knew the tone of voice. Knew we were cocky but often hopeless without them. They were perfectly familiar with the sometimes lazy, frequently self-deprecating attempt to have an easy life. The cheekiness, the bad jokes and the droning on about football.

The only time a woman came up to me in person with an issue about the magazine was a student activist on the Buy Us a Pint Tour who, once I'd listened to her views and talked to her politely about them, subsequently proceeded to try and pull the charismatic Deeson. Beyond that it was just writers in the *Guardian* who were perfectly entitled to their opinion because every time they voiced it our sales went up.

The *loaded* staff weren't men who were unfamiliar with women; we all had girlfriends, there were women around on the magazine – styling, writing and so on. The advertising departments were half women and we spent plenty of time in the bars around King's Reach Tower with other female editors and magazine staff who liked our company and the mag. Most of the awards I picked up will have been given to us by committees made up of numerous female editors and publishers because there were just so many female senior editors in publishing.

I asked comedian Jenny Eclair to edit an issue because she was extremely acerbic and popular on the live stand-up circuit; it would have been like *Elle* or *Marie Claire* asking Bill Hicks or Jerry Sadowitz to edit an issue. Didn't happen.

We all knew women who were into music, obviously, but as I will say elsewhere music and clubbing just didn't appear in women's mags as features and in-depth sections. And I knew women who were into watching and playing football too.

By the time I left after three years the publishing department told me that the independent body the National Readership Survey believed over 10 per cent of our news-stand sales were to women. That's about 30,000. There was nowhere near that many men buying a woman's mag. It got to a point where every week a woman would accost me in a bar and say, 'You're never going to believe this but . . .'

And I would finish the story for her '. . . you love *loaded*!'

'Yes!'

'Great, can I buy you a drink for buying the mag?'

At the heart of it we were a very, very good editorial team and we had a very good array of contributors. The readers who loved it inspired us too. The confidence and editorial freedom just bursts out of the issues. Have a random idea, execute it, make it look good and readers will enjoy it. There was easily enough in each issue of *loaded* 1–36 to make three magazines per month, with the content given more space. It was rammed with things that just wouldn't have featured in the style-obsessed mags that came before. In among the footballers, musicians, comedians and so on were features on real male interests other than just fit women we fancied. We knew enough about men to know that even if you didn't want them on the cover, loads of people liked motorbikes, cricket, snooker, rugby, kickboxing, golf, horror, cult fiction, old TV shows, computer games, pubs. All this was obvious but it was more everyday than necessarily aspirational, as all previous mags had been, and within those scenes there were great stories to tell.

Christian, the production editor, suggested an interview with Will Carling, who I wasn't sure about – maybe a bit too mainstream, captain of England etc. etc. But he was keen so I said yes and then the *loaded* luck and fate colluded and we ended up with an amazing cover that sold loads. One of my favourites, as it was quite unexpected. Christian was actually with him mid-interview when Carling received the call that news of his affair with Princess Diana had broken. By pure luck, Steve Pyke had shot him with a bright-red glowing background. It made for an interesting and absolutely of the moment story. 'Wicked Willie' ran the cover line, with an extremely devilish image.

The concept that old icons had great stories they wanted to tell absolutely worked. We played cricket with Peter O'Toole, went on an Eastern European film set with Ollie Reed, talked multi-country pub crawls with Richard Harris. And it wasn't just cinematic hellraisers. We sent darts commentator and all-round legend Sid Waddell to interview Ian Botham, who had once been Britain's most charismatic sporting icon but had disappeared. A dark, moody portrait allowed me to write 'The Forgotten Man' as headline. Darren Gough had another great opening spread: 'Batsmen, This Man Can Seriously Endanger Your Health'. They were using these features as textbook examples on IPC training courses I was being obliged to attend because of some HR bollocks.

'Anyone got anything to say on this spread?'

'Yes. I wrote it.'

Adam Black's side job as a table tennis coach paid dividends when the dad of one his young clients turned out to be Gazza's agent, and

Gazza agreed to do a cover interview when he joined Rangers in exchange for fifty videos for his stepson Reagan. We duly blagged them from HMV, and Gazza was utterly delighted.

Years later Ronnie Wood told me our much-loved Jimmy White cover was the *only* print Jimmy had on his snooker room wall. Same sport, but in the young and up-and-coming sector Ronnie O'Sullivan looks *so young* on his six-page feature as he ignites the world of the green baize. Tim played golf with Mike D of the Beasties. We all played football with stars of music and TV at the Phoenix Festival which we not only helped organise but won two years running.

When Eric Cantona went over the advertising hoardings to drop kick that idiot Palace fan it was titled as a 'Bacon Sandwich Dropping Moment'. Cue another section, Drop Me Bacon Sandwich, and a sarnie-shaped book that followed. With Good Work Fella, our column thanking people for things we liked which originated with Tim's car mechanic Shady Ady, and Bunch of Arse (a Basil Fawlty line) which was our column of things we didn't like, we popularised phrases that actually entered common use for young men, and advertising creatives borrowed them too for their campaigns. In fact it was an ad guy in trade magazine *Campaign* who first said, 'I love *loaded* because it tells me how I really am rather than how I'm supposed to be.'

The plundering from the magazine was so frequent in terms of style and design and actual images that we could only take it as homage. We would do a monthly gatefold cover with someone like Claudia Schiffer on one side and Ruud Gullit's great Holland team, George Best, Kenny Dalglish or the Clash on the other, but after a while we just started to subvert it with a bacon sandwich, fish and chips, a crisp, an oil painting of a steam train, a battleship poster. The weird images they used to have on men's and boys' birthday cards. Within weeks of the fish and chips poster Channel 4 appropriated the same type of image to put on a billboard to advertise their Friday nights, right opposite the *Guardian* office. Sol beer copied our use of 'Scorchio' on a poster campaign and I had to point out to them we'd taken it from *The Fast Show* who yes very much *did* own the intellectual property rights to it when the two parties started getting legal over it.

We filled the mag with things that would never have been considered elsewhere: Deeson spending a night in a kebab shop – working not eating; a profile of the man who invented the AK-47. International festivals were a godsend – Michael Holden went to Thailand just for a national water fight and Bill Borrows went to Spain for a tomato fight. All made for great copy.

Alan's old *NME* pairings worked well too – my friend Jim aka Vic Reeves interviewed both Mike Leigh and Phil Oakey of the Human League for us. Tarantino sat down with Dennis Hopper, which is one of many pieces that, looking back, would have made great covers. The breadth of content was so wide I could interview Arsenal star Paul Merson on one page and on the next Jon Ronson would interview someone who'd been a follower of Charles Manson. Martin Deeson would go high-rolling in Atlantic City with Tony Bennett, while Rowan would be interviewing Mr C from the Shamen.

Kylie Minogue, Stuart Lee, David Seaman and Renegade Soundwave all happily featured in our swimwear issue and Vic and Bob appeared on the cover looking fantastic with crowns of ribs on their heads: 'You Can't Beat Your Meat … well you can here.'

Not wanting the readers to miss out we invited them – pre-smart-phone – to send in their pictures of them with celebs and we received so many it became a monthly column. The best of the month won a camera and the others published won beer.

We were constantly challenging ourselves editorially as well as narcotically. When former *NME* colleague Paolo Hewitt delivered us a Noel Gallagher interview I put a large photo of a bread cake/bap next to him on the cover and wrote 'And a roll with it'. It was just silly, fun and playful. I didn't like writing an editor's letter so started designing it then stubbing fags out on it, photographing and printing that. We burned through one, poured sweets over another.

I scribbled next issue pages out on napkins in felt tip and that would be printed. Freelance sub Danny Plunkett secured a full-time job for the headline 'Schiffer Brains', first used for a numbingly uninspired conversation with Claudia. Disrespectful, but an amazing pun. And whoever wrote 'Fatman and Knobbin' for the Barry White on sex cover line will have been toast of the moment. Everyone was capable of writing a headline because they were often just jokes or good puns. Even the original picture editor Robbie Martin waded in with 'HIB Positive' for the feature on Hibernian-loving Irvine Welsh, and later 'Affray in a Manger' for a Christmas cover story where we sent Rowland Rivron to Dalston shopping centre to pretend to be drunk while being Santa.

Such a cavalier, slapdash attitude occasionally had its consequences. On a tour of forty pubs in Dublin, having half a Guinness in each, Deeson managed to confuse a Family Pub of the Year with a similarly named hostelry that a taxi driver had described as a den of thieves that should be bombed. Which Martin duly reported. That simple drunken mistake cost us £20,000. Five ad pages. It was unintentional but it made us laugh.

Creating the mag each month was the heart of everything we did, so much more important than the drug excess I've written about in this book. That was essentially just young men in our own white-lined Disneyland but the magazine production was brilliant. Everyone bought into it and did their best and you can see that flying off the pages.

When we did a *Deliverance*-inspired canoeing feature in Wales, young work experience Phil Robinson actually got on to directory enquiries, took down the numbers of all five John Boormans in Ireland and called them until the director of said film answered and was happy to do an interview.

Jane Garcia called me from LA and said, 'O.J. Simpson's wife was murdered last night. Can I write about it?' We were in the last week of production so I binned something and made space for Jane, who was a brilliant contributor with great ideas. That was Tuesday. On Friday as we were laying it out, O.J. went on the slowest car chase ever and we suddenly had our images. We were running like a newspaper, and apart from the *Guardian* we were the first UK publication to go really big with that story. We couldn't find a headline that linked a guy we only knew in the UK from the *Naked Gun* comedy movie with a violent double slaying. Sitting on the bog staring at the headline-less layout with about fifteen minutes to deadline, I finally got it and came running out whooping, 'Murder on the Orenthal Express' – Orenthal being the O in his name.

The only feature we could never come up with anything for was the one on *The Fast Show*, whose catchphrases had already been done to death. In the end we took a totally irrelevant headline from *Rugby World* with an asterisk explaining how we'd failed to come up with anything suitable.

One day a Mujahedeen commander called the office asking for twenty copies of an issue a young photojournalist had managed to interview him for. A very strange moment.

We had fun in the fashion pages, laying out grids of gloves and black socks – all looking identical. We did big shoots based on films, stars, TV shows we liked – who does a fashion shoot based on the Comic Strip's *The Bullshitters*, which was in turn a homoerotic take on *The Professionals*? Former Fun Boy Three and Specials frontman Terry Hall agreed to model 'What to Wear To Court'. Elsewhere we did a spread of a bloke in a donkey jacket and black beanie, looking like one of the original Dexys, just to model holdalls. Beth's pages were so imaginative and she engaged the audience brilliantly and was happy to execute our daft ideas that allowed us to meet old heroes.

Ralph Ineson – later Finchy from *The Office* – and Sacha Baron Cohen (wearing donkey jackets) both modelled for us when they were young, up-and-coming actors.

The covers built sales and popularity: Frank Skinner, Jack Dee, Jo Guest looking happy and confident, Judge Dredd, Suggs, Chris Tarrant. My favourite was *The Simpsons*. Tim wrote a great piece with Matt Groening and he offered to draw a cover for us. I felt the best thing to get him to do was draw Bart and Homer reading *loaded*, to which I added the speech bubble 'Look Bart we're famous'. Inside we had the pull-out poster of every character that had ever appeared at that point.

There were Simpsons producers who loved *loaded*, invited us round to their writing house on the Fox lot in LA, and had the mag on subscription. It was the same with Letterman's guys, who would eagerly send me T-shirts in return for copies. When *The David Letterman Show* came to film in London and climaxed with Peter O'Toole celebrating *Lawrence of Arabia* by entering the set on a camel which then drank a can of beer, we decided to just put that on the cover as a Great Moment in Life – depicting Letterman himself with a hastily drawn marker-pen crown. Steve Reid had the confidence to produce that because I'd already scribbled glasses on a grumpy cover shot of Kevin Keegan when Newcastle United were flying high but he hadn't wanted to do much in the shoot but sulk. A pity, because the piece was very upbeat and optimistic as all our stories were. There was no cynicism in *loaded* – it was essentially a fanzine for men.

I was able to mine my childhood for ideas, my favourite being when we bought some of those Sports biscuits that featured little stick men doing various athletic and sporting endeavours and then actually reviewed their technique.

I was lucky enough to visit Tokyo with Paul Smith, where he was mobbed like the Beatles at a fashion college. Young people queued up for ages to meet him in his shop where one of the PS employees had the amazing name Cherry Orchard of the Beautiful Free Century, or Cherry for short. 'My parents were existentialists,' she told me as I wondered whether it was feasible to fall for someone purely on the strength of their name. I also discovered sake, which was eventful.

The *loaded* team climbed the Three Peaks (well one and a half of them) in deep snow against the advice of locals, warily eyed each other up with shotguns while clay-pigeon shooting in Wales, upturned quad bikes and nearly destroyed ourselves and came last in the brilliant Portrush Raft Race.

The ad team were constantly hitting us with totally the wrong ideas. They repeatedly sent the one man we all really liked, Chris West, to talk to us, but even Westy couldn't convince me to cover-mount a T-shirt with no neck hole in it on every copy to promote Polo Middle Bit mints. Where was the value in giving readers T-shirts that don't work? Nowadays they'd make ten and let social media do the rest. IPC was trousering so much money they'd consider anything.

Another time, pressured by a fragrance industry keen to spend money, they finally talked me into allowing some perfume and grooming copy into the women's issue we did – brilliantly edited by Jenny Eclair (she chose Sean Bean for the cover because she thought he was hot). Writer Barbara Ellen, model Kathy Lloyd, fashion designer Pam Hogg and fashion editor Beth tried to control themselves/not retch as the male staff appeared topless, covered in an array of men's fragrances. Unfortunately the product of the company that had actually pushed for coverage was described by Barbara in the article as smelling like rapist's sweat.

Citizen Cocaine

River Wye, 1995

We were on a roll, accumulating millions of pounds for IPC and awards, infamy, free crisps and high jinks for us, but the reality was that there was a real human cost to pay too. Our article about our River Wye canoeing trip featured a brazenly open reference to staff cocaine use. It was the first time there'd been such a blatant admission, and IPC – who had long since stopped looking at what we were actually printing before going to press, apart from making libel checks – were really worried.

The publisher, Andy, and my boss Alan came down to Studio 6 where we drank, pulled me aside from the rest of the gang and said they thought the drug squad would be on their way to the office right now. No one should have drugs in the office. I guessed probably four people but when I went outside and asked the staff everyone got up – it was like an 'I'm Spartacus' or 'I'm Brian, and so is my wife' moment. The look on the publisher's face was priceless.

We went back and put everything into a bag and then stashed it in my car. I wish I'd kept that bag, actually. My own desk drawer had so much loose stuff in it I just pulled the whole drawer and went and put it in the bogs. The whole caper seemed pointless to me. The police did pop in occasionally but just to get copies when they realised they were on the road *loaded* was produced on.

The drugs were prevalent because culturally at the time they were prevalent across the lives of so many people. The E boom changed everything. When the first ever delivery of skunk arrived in our office via a friend of the pop group EMF it had such a powerful stench that the following week, without prior arrangement or discussion, everyone brought in Tupperware boxes and biscuit tins like a school home economics class.

Editorially, from the off, the lives of Bukowski, Pablo Escobar, Keith Richards, Hunter S. Thompson and the many others who'd ridden the river of alcoholic excess and/or white line highway fascinated us. *Scarface* remains to this day the most popular film in prisons, as it was back then in our office. Nowadays *Breaking Bad*, *Narcos* and all the trafficking documentaries have normalised excessive drug trafficking, dealing and use in the media; we were just being honest about what was going on in our lives. When our contributing editor Bill Burrows went out to interview Hunter in Woody Creek, Aspen, the once great man called the office, leaving crazed, insane, screeching messages of approval and abuse.

We were enthralled by the culture, the rock and roll trail into self-destruction that had been made to look glamorous by Iggy, Belushi and so on. Having worked in music and journalism, two industries where heavy drinking and more were not only accepted but even encouraged, I knew no different. It was a choice, true, but it looked and felt so much better than just going to work and being good boys every day. A couple of the staff didn't partake, but largely our drug and drink use felt as normal and regular as other offices having sandwich deliveries or a canteen. Every morning I would start the day ramping myself up with excitement by jumping around Jim's flat listening to a bit of *Kiss This*, the Pistols' live album, on full blast but by the end of the day I was usually so fucked that I was extremely appreciative of Andy and Joe who ran the IPC car service and would come and collect me in the early hours from anywhere in London. They were life savers and I imagine we were running up a fair-sized bill with them. One night at a really popular bar in Leeds the staff lined up a whole row of shots, set fire to them and then gave us them for free.

Upstairs they had a present for me – a full-size cardboard cut-out of Elvis's white rhinestone suit with my head on it. They poured a line out the length of my upper torso which I was happy to help them remove. We were very easily pleased.

Yet between the intensity of the production process, fuelled by my belief that the films I'd loved as a teenager – *Animal House*, *Quadrophenia* and *The Blues Brothers*, and later *Withnail* and *Performance* – were reasonable templates for working practice, and the actual physical and mental impact of so much alcoholic and narcotic intake, people did start to drop away. Christian left first, then Tim, both stepping away from the fire, then Michael experienced a breakdown after a month of writing too many features, one of which involved flying to four different continents in a day with a heavy rock band. Then he went on holiday to Ireland where he ran into some of the "Gulf War speed" flying around at the time, spent nine days awake and was hospitalised for months, during which time I had to keep telling IPC they couldn't let him go and had to keep paying him. Second production editor Jason didn't last too long, then the Shark Deeson (he could digest anything) and I would eventually head for pastures significantly better paid and I too would seek a lifestyle change. I was very fortunate in the way I was helped. After that Beth and her fashion assistant Tom Stubbs were involved in a serious motorbike accident at fashion week in Milan which resulted in her having an acquired brain injury and partial paralysis in her right side which means she has needed 24/7 care ever since.

There was no doubt we flew far too close to the sun, so close the soles of our Airwalk trainers were melting, and IPC was happy for all this to go on because it was absolutely coining it in. A few of us started to feel resentful that although we were having a great time, the company were making a fortune and we were on pretty standard wages that in no way reflected the success of the title. Yet when I said I wanted to get a lawyer to negotiate my wages I was told, 'Anyone who brings a lawyer to a personnel meeting will be fired.' It was bullshit.

I was being offered so many jobs in TV, Australia, Fleet Street, and with six-figure fees, that IPC's tightness really started to fuck me up, and when you shower a resentment in paranoia-inducing drugs it isn't a good combination. We were having the time of our lives but it was also starting to seriously affect our lives. Deeson's article and the trip to the River Wye were both brilliant but it was almost a tipping point. It started to feel like those bands and artists who were ripped off by managers. I know IPC paid for the mag and distributed it and did all the back end but the staff were seeing nothing beyond a basic wage. Not even circulation bonuses. And I had come up with the idea, created it, and the team and I were the creatives.

What I really needed was a rest, a senior designer or editorial adviser to say, 'Stop putting thirteen features in, nine will do. Let it breathe a bit and calm down.' Some sort of structural support like a proper senior executive assistant to make sure my life was in order, which it wasn't. And by then at least four of us very much needed rehab and everyone else needed a holiday.

We were fucking worn out but what a way to be worn out. We created an utterly brilliant magazine; there had never been one like it. Twenty-five years on people stop me and say, 'I loved *loaded*.' Yep, we did too. And I wish it was set up in a way where the original team could have stayed there and grown old with it as they did with *Rolling Stone*. But shit, I was in a hurry.

Trading places: from *loaded* to *GQ* to rehab

Rio, 1997

The crispest, whitest envelope I have ever seen is resting on my office phone. Inside is a letter on Condé Nast International headed notepaper from a Jonathan Newhouse to discuss an international opportunity at Condé Nast Publications (CNP). 'Dear James, I have tried to contact you by telephone over the last two weeks but no one ever picks up . . .' I laugh. This is certainly true.

Condé Nast publish upmarket glossy magazine titles like *Vanity Fair* and *Vogue*; they do not carry articles like 'How to Organise a Piss-up in a Brewery'. I wonder what he wants. A week later I am sitting in a restaurant called Scott's, in Mount Street, Mayfair when an energetic man with a close black crop, smart suit and a big smile hustles his way through the tables and thrusts his hand out. He seems very pleased to meet me and I instantly like him. He proceeds to tell me about his role in charge of his family publishing company worldwide outside of America and about growing up on Staten Island. When I ask him what the overseas project he wants to discuss is, he says, 'British *GQ*.' I'm a little disappointed as I've no interest in the title which has no relevance to my life and is everything *loaded* launched against – it has Government ministers on the cover, FFS. I had hoped for an interesting international launch.

'You already have an editor,' I point out.

All I know about the editor, Angus McKinnon, is that many years before, Francis Ford Coppola held up his *NME* feature on *Apocalypse Now* at a press conference and declared, 'This man understands my film.' It was a story passed down the generations at the *NME*.

Jonathan explains they feel they need a change. They want someone who can make *GQ* central to the exploding men's sector I had started. He loved the humour and energy in *loaded*, mentioned Jon Wilde's brilliant interview with legendary actor Richard Harris and Deeson's piece on the Shetlands Up-Helly-Aa Viking bonfire festival. Referencing the latter, he asked, 'How *do* you fuck a skate?'

That was the moment I decided that although I didn't really want to leave *loaded* for *GQ* I'd probably enjoy working for Jonathan.

I explained I was going to Brazil for the Grand Prix and if he wanted to make me an offer I would call him when I came back. I was regularly being approached with job offers by newspaper proprietors and executives, TV stations and publishing companies abroad, and my instinct was that I didn't think I would go for this.

James will be raped and murdered

São Paolo, 1997

One of our freelancers, Adam Black, worked at Lynne Franks PR and he seemed a perfect choice to hire as a foil for all the PRs who were now calling the office. His appointment as commissioning editor had worked out well; hiring a PR to deal with PRs meant they spoke each other's languages and he always knew how far he could push our editorial requirements on a story. We were being absolutely bombarded by people offering stories, from TV shows, films, sports stars, comedians, snack foods, alcohol brands, outdoor wear, fags, clothes, computer games, cars, books, comics, travel destinations . . . it was genuinely relentless. And all of them took second place to the stories we came up with ourselves.

When the offer involved overseas travel, Adam had to assess how many of us could go. The smart PRs understood that if they left us alone to have a good time we would write a great story and the readers might get a good impression of whatever the fuck the PR was supposed to be getting into the mag. Eight editorial pages in *loaded* with their brand cropping up across the photos had an AVE3 (advertising v. editorial × 3) value of about £75,000. If they spent ten grand taking four of us somewhere it was a better return than spending anywhere near that in ads.

Adam hit the mother lode when he walked into my office in spring '97 and said, 'Hey, my friend Tania at Saatchi's is going to take us to the Brazilian Grand Prix with the Jordan Formula One team. Eddie Jordan is supposedly a cool guy and they are the party team.'

Deeson, Adam and I decided we would go to São Paolo; we just needed to take someone else to write about the cars and someone to take the photographs. Do the work, basically. We invited Zed Nelson to take the photographs as he'd got us the last shot of Ayrton Senna on the grid in the race in which he sadly died, and the production editor, Jason, because he was a petrol-head who had previously worked on *Car* magazine. *Loaded* would be left in the capable hands of staff writer Michael, who had recovered from his hospitalisation and was no longer acting like Dennis Hopper in *Apocalypse Now*. In the production room were Derek Harbinson and Danny Plunkett, both excellent editorial guys and future editor and features editor.

Adam added: 'She's agreed to five people and she's going to give us expenses! The money's all coming from the cigarette sponsor.'

Deeson and I looked at each other and knew exactly what that might be spent on.

A week before we were due to go, *loaded*'s new publisher Lucy was sitting on the big blue sofa when Adam walked in with a very expensive-looking Bill Amberg leather suitcase with the Jordan logo discreetly branded on it, and hanging from the strap was a small but very heavy Theo Fennell silver Formula One car on a key ring. It looked like the most expensive *Monopoly* piece ever. Inside the bag were travel documents and $4,000 in cash.

As I examined the contents the publisher was sitting there with her eyes wide open, wondering what the fuck was going on.

The only thing I knew about São Paolo was that it had a massive prison population and Helen Mirren had told me that when she had flown there the lights of the city had seemed to go on for the final hour of her flight. I really liked South America; it was a magical place for obvious reasons and I carried on in Brazil where I'd left off in Peru with the pisco sours. On the first night in São Paolo I was happily downing powerful alcohol that was coated in sugar and salt and Eddie Jordan's team were joining me in singing a Gary Glitter hits medley. This would be one of the last times you could innocently sing Glitter songs in public without drawing some sort of disapproving comment; later that year he'd be arrested and imprisoned after a computer repairman found indecent images of children on his computer. From that point on the term 'hard drive' entered the British vocabulary.

Outside, on a high, I bounded over the road and bounced over the top of our people carrier. Not the bonnet, the roof. I thought I'd land on it but cleared it and just kept going all the way across. The *Daily Telegraph* cricket correspondent Simon Hughes was on the trip and rushed round to find me lying on the pavement, laughing.

'How the fuck did you do that?'

'I can fly, Si,' I explained, patting myself down.

The alcohol was a major influence on my Peter Pan complex. I had a high tolerance for South American cocktails because they tasted like the ice pops I'd lived off throughout summers in Headingley.

Deeson, Zed and I ended up in a huge nightclub full of small dance floors and mini swimming pools. We'd arrived in a branded Grand Prix vehicle with an official guide and the club manager was under the impression we were actual European Formula One drivers, mainly because I'd told them we were. Someone gave me a pure grass spliff and, seeing a white light shining up through a deep blue pool, I just plunged in wearing my lightweight Paul Smith suit. I thought it would reduce my temperature and calm me down. I climbed back out and a bloke started following us round with a mop. He was very friendly; it seemed like they were used to it.

At this point I'm four personalities removed from sober James. The spliff and the drink power-whacked me. Some people suddenly get stopped by drugs, but in my case it works the opposite way, speeding me along into insanity, like I've been fired from a finger and thumb rubber-band catapult. It is like any common sense is floating away from my body like a hot air balloon lifting into the sky. Looking down at the idiot below flailing, retching, laughing and shouting, in one big tangle of noise and thick curly hair and Italian mod-style wraparound Ray-Bans.

One of the things I liked about Martin Deeson's writing in *loaded* was that he seemed to be able to get into the same state but still write about it. I would just set off on operation fuckwad to get into the most extreme situation possible. Which was largely why I liked festivals and South America.

I climb into a minicab and ask the basketball-player driving it to take me to the best place in São Paolo to buy drugs. I also make sure I give him the note I've had the hotel concierge write out for me in Portuguese on an official compliment slip: 'I am very drunk. Please take me to the hotel, you will be paid there.' I've long since come to terms with how my nights abroad end up so I have one of these made out for me by the concierge wherever I go.

We pulled up at a sloping street corner thick with people milling around, women and men selling themselves, haggling and shouting as open drug sales are going on. The super-tall driver is scoring some coke for me when I see a really small woman with a bleached-white cropped feather cut and ask him to see if she fancies coming back to the hotel for a drink. I really like the idea of being in the bar with these two when the others get up for breakfast.

She looks in at me in my dripping suit, senses things are OK, and agrees. I'm just sitting there babbling away to two people who don't speak very good English and we then get to my magnificent hotel. It has a huge atrium, and despite being 4 a.m. it is well lit and people are at the reception. In the middle of the floor is a toddlers' village with a picket fence and toy houses, and bouncing around in there are huge, soft-looking, floppy-eared rabbits. I'm wondering what the fuck this is and the people behind the reception are looking at us, thinking the same. Here's the sopping-wet, stinking-drunk deranged English guest, a 6 foot 8 taxi driver and a tiny bleach-blonde lady and the manager looks at me with polite, almost familial, concern, and I can see in his kindly eyes the phrase, 'Are you sure?' I turn and pull out a huge pile of the Saatchi cash and give the driver and the lady $200 US between them. They are delighted, totally quids in for bringing a friendly wet drunk home.

I say goodbye and pick up a lovely big floppy-eared giant American chinchilla rabbit and go into the lift. Then I head straight to my room where I strip out of the wet clothes and just walk back out naked holding the rabbit, which feels so nice in my arms, and go next door and bang on Deeson's door.

'What!?'

'Come on, get Zed, we can do rabbit racing.'

'You're naked, wet and look like Jerry Sadowitz! Go away!'

It's funny how hangovers declare martial law on your body and mind. Just shut you down with a vicious threat of repercussions. In England I don't really get them any more; I know how to manage them with a litre of lemonade before bed, lots of sleep, and pink lemonade Snapple at the office. In South America, however, it is another level of punishment because it involves jet lag, major dehydration because of the heat and too many sweet alcoholic iced drinks. The next day at the Brazilian Grand Prix I am slumped in the boiling hot sun against a pillar in the F1 VIP hospitality area wishing for a firing squad while our party are helping themselves to the finest buffet I have ever seen. There is lobster everywhere. The fruit has film-star looks. High end champagne bottles rest in buckets of ice. None of this is going to run out. It is here for the benefit of the sponsors who pour money into the sport like a broken tap. The lovely buffet is an irrelevant tease because my brain and body aren't letting me anywhere near it.

Down in the pit lane we meet the young Scottish Mercedes McLaren driver, David Coulthard, a keen *loaded* reader whose eyes light up on introduction, and who invites us to the post-race drivers' party.

Because of Ayrton Senna, the Brazilians love Formula One and their *verde e amarela* national flags are everywhere. I'm impressed by how well organised and structured the backstage is. A bit like a stadium-sized rock 'n' roll tour, the infrastructure is the same at every track, regardless of the country. For a moment I wonder whether I could actually go on a tour of the F1 circuit like I did with the Cult and U2; then I remember each race is two weeks apart and everyone goes home for a week in between. There would be no chance to soak yourself in rock 'n' roll tour momentum.

Start time approaches and there's a genuine build-up of excitement, expectation and volume but once the race starts and they all scramble away it is just so bright, noisy and repetitive that I head behind the stand and delicately find a shadow to sit in. The air is thick with the stench of burning rubber and I take out my pen and pad and write, 'Formula One is the sound of billionaires screaming.' That is the sum total of my Brazilian notes but it is what the piece will be about.

While everyone else is watching cars flashing past and laying waste to the buffet and bar I wander back to look at a brand-new BMW yet to be launched – the Z3. I'm not particularly into cars but it looks great. Earlier they had had one racing round the empty track to promote the forthcoming Bond film *Tomorrow Never Dies*. When I ask Jason, our car expert, how much it will cost, he says: 'You'll never get one. It's already sold out before it's even available. The waiting list is two years.'

His attitude annoys me; it is totally at odds with the spirit of *loaded* and the conversation rankles. It's something I've noticed from the second generation of writers and staff. They've joined a hugely successful magazine so they're a different type of person to the ones who joined a start-up no one gave a chance to. They've no sense of how we started with nothing but a 'yes we can' attitude, from my very first sheet of paper describing the mag in 1992, through the development time, to finally existing and being a massive success and attracting global attention and copycat titles. Now here we are, five of us with someone else's cash in our pocket, in Brazil watching a grand prix, downing as much champagne and food as we want, creating a magazine that a million people a month read, that's been voted the industry magazine of the year twice, and he's saying, 'You'll never get one.' I know anything is possible. Even though I don't have the sort of money required to buy one, I tell him I will get the car. Just to prove a point.

That night at the party Coulthard is dancing with Deeson who is after a few quotes. It's a bizarre scene watching these two men with massive grins, dancing and talking quite intimately. One's worth about twenty million and lives in Monaco. The other's worth about twenty quid and lives in a squalid Camden basement round the corner from where *Withnail* was written.

The next morning, as we arrive at the airport for a flight to Rio for a few days, our driver, a nice student doing a temporary chauffeuring job who I have tipped heavily, turns to everyone in the people carrier and, as if I'm not there, says in a concerned voice: 'I like James, he has been very kind to me. However, if he behaves in Rio like he has behaved in São Paolo he will be raped and murdered.'

Everyone else is laughing but I am stunned. As farewells go it's a hell of a send-off. As we head into the domestic airport, the others can't wait to get to Rio and I'm just wondering at what point this will happen.

In Rio the chaps all head out to see the Big Jesus but I decide to stay in the pool and think about the *GQ* job offer. Because IPC wouldn't give me a wage that reflected the unexpected success of the mag I'd vowed to take the next big job I was offered. Even though I didn't have any interest in *GQ* I knew I could actually do this job whereas I wasn't sure my nocturnal lifestyle would suit editing a national newspaper or a colour supplement. I sat in the pool with my arms out along the edge, mulling it over. There was a lot to consider.

I loved *loaded*. It was such a brilliant job in terms of what we got to do but I was absolutely worn out and fucked off that neither I nor the team were sharing in the profits. I was struck that no one above me had congratulated any of our many new award winners at the latest company awards. I was pissed off they wouldn't let me have a royalty on a series of party compilations I'd been discussing with Colombia A & R man Rob Stringer; they thought they should have all the money even though Rob wanted me to select the tracks. And now this . . . if I got drunk I'd be raped and then murdered. Jesus fuck me. I knew I had absolutely no control whatsoever over my behaviour when I was out and running. It was the same in Sydney, Lima, Newcastle, London – wherever I went I'd end up super fucked. It would start out fun but end up just unpleasant and dangerous. My lifestyle just accommodated this extreme consumption, the success somehow legitimised it. It went with the territory I had defined.

I started to think that maybe *loaded* was going to kill me. Young staff writer Michael had spent half of 1996 in an institution. Even before that, Christian had melted down and left for the sake of his own sanity. The drugs some of us were using were getting harder and darker than we were admitting to in the magazine. I decided that if Jonathan Newhouse's offer was good I'd consider going. If only for a rest.

His offer knocked me off my feet. I'd been taking some advice from my friend Hayden Evans, agent for Leeds United's Gary Speed and David Batty, and he'd suggested I ask them to build in loyalty payments and regular sales bonuses. And they had. The basic was a 120 per cent increase on what I'd been on for the previous two years at *loaded*. Every six months I achieved a 10 per cent news-stand sales increase I'd get another £10,000, plus £20,000 for every year I completed; a Cherokee Jeep; health insurance; an unlimited expense account; biannual trips to New York, Paris and Milan; and on top of that an immediate one-off golden handcuffs signing-on fee equivalent to my annual *loaded* salary in dollars, offshore.

I was really shocked. He just wallpapered me with money at a time when I'd been wrangling for months with IPC just to get half what the newspapers and TV companies were offering me.

I still wasn't 100 per cent sure – should I go just for the cash? Then there was one final motivator and it didn't come from Jonathan Newhouse. IPC censored the content of the next issue of the magazine without even telling me. For a laugh, with a month to go to the 1997 general election, we'd put a page in announcing Deeson and I were going to stand for Parliament against rogue Conservative MP Alan Clarke in Kensington and Prime Minister John Major in Huntingdon. Our manifesto for the Fight for Your Right to Party Party read:

- Young people: we will make it like it's never been before!
- Old people: we will make it like it used to be.
- Off-licences will be open twenty-four hours, booze delivered to your door.
- Marijuana will be legalised.

That was it. Most of these pledges entered mainstream political life over the next twenty-five years anyway. With four weeks to go we hadn't actually formed a party, we were just fucking around and making ourselves laugh.

However, the people above us panicked and took the page out at the printer's. When the issue came back and I asked them what happened I was told, 'Oh, it isn't politically balanced because you aren't standing against sitting Labour MPs.' What? I couldn't believe it – we were making them millions of unplanned pounds and suddenly they decided they'd start taking things out which were harmless. That was the tipper. I thought about all that enthusiasm for me to join CNP and decided if IPC wanted to edit the magazine rather than me they could.

I called Jonathan Newhouse and asked if I could bring two people with me. He was delighted.

'Yes! Who?'

'Martin Deeson and Mick Bunnage.'

'Deeson and Dr Mick? Yes absolutely!' How much would they need?

I added £20,000 on top of what they were both earning and said that should do it. Then I had to let them know that I'd effectively sold them to another company.

Deeson's eyes lit up. 'Yes! Decent money at last. I've always wanted to work at Vogue House!'

'Good. He wants us to go over to his house in Holland Park tomorrow night to sort it out.'

Jonathan took us down into his basement kitchen which was backlit, sharp and very minimalist. He was accompanied by Condé Nast's MD Nicholas Coleridge who, like Mick, was very quiet. Jonathan talked a lot about what he liked about *loaded* and what he felt *GQ* lacked. He said, 'At Condé Nast we want our editors to be bold, outrageous, passionate and talented.'

'This is why you want me.'

'Yes.'

The meeting felt like some of the record industry pitch meetings I'd had with Fabulous, but in this case with proven talent to trade. As the meeting wound down, Nicholas asked Martin, 'Could I possibly have one of your beers?' I looked across the table to where Deeson was sitting and he had every bottle of alcohol empty or opened in front of him, like the Manhattan skyline. We all shook on it and said we'd resign that week.

Piling back into my car we all just shouted, 'What the fuck have we just done?' It somehow felt like a very *loaded* thing to actually leave *loaded* for a laugh and more cash.

Hovis has left the building

A roof in London, 1997

The next day I walked down to the river with Alan and told him I was leaving. He asked if I was going to *FHM*. I laughed – no chance, who leaves the Stones to work with Cliff?

He said he didn't want me to leave. I guess in hindsight he knew how early it still was in the magazine's lifetime, just thirty-six issues in, and he said he'd try and get me some more money, but I told him it wasn't about their tightness any more. I'd already accepted the job.

At the end of the afternoon he sadly relayed the message from those above him that, 'There'll be no more money for James.' I think they thought I was still trying to negotiate with them. I told him I was going to tell the staff and Andy, the publishing director of the group, came over to my office and said, 'You can't just announce it, it has to be done properly.' This little controlling panic underlined why I was glad to be leaving the company, if not the magazine. As far as I saw it I'd just made them millions; now I was off I could do what the fuck I wanted.

The next day I drove south over Blackfriars Bridge and looked across at King's Reach Tower, the Oxo building and Waterloo Bridge in the morning sun. Oasis were playing, just as they had been for so much of our *loaded* lifetime, and there were tears in my eyes as I thought about saying goodbye to the staff. It just didn't feel right that this thing I had clearly sketched out on an A4 sheet of paper after my *NME* discussions five years before was making absolutely millions and the team and I were seeing none of it. The simple fact was that other people wanted me to work for them more than IPC did. The staff had been absolutely brilliant and we'd had such a good laugh. It really had been like being on tour with the Beasties or the Mondays.

My boss Alan and his boss Andy came down to our office from the Tower and I asked everyone to go out of the fire escape and onto the roof which had hosted smoking sessions, sex and spin bowling lessons. (Never concurrently.) This space was the nearest equivalent we had to a meeting area. A couple of the sharper staff had sussed something was up when they'd seen Mick, Martin and me behind the closed door of my office. I never closed it.

I looked round at the staff. There were twice as many now: twenty-two of us compared to the nine who had produced the first issue in a room two floors below. I told them I was leaving and there was just a sense of shock, and when I added that Mick and Martin were coming too everyone looked even worse. Alan spoke a bit and then Andy gave some corporate speak.

The Loafer and Porter had tears welling up. It really did feel like a family breaking up, albeit one with a young, volatile father. I'd come up with the idea for *loaded* six months after my mum had died of an overdose, when I was pretty much in a sense of shock, fucking around with Fabulous and covering up my feelings about it with drugs, and then it had just exploded like no one could have imagined. Now I just needed a rest, some tangible reward and a better environment to work in really. IPC wasn't offering any of that so it was hard to put that into words with the bosses there.

Afterwards in my office I told Tim it was his time to be *loaded* editor but he said he wanted to do his own thing. With Christian and Tim gone and Deeson, Mick and I on our way, the people who had defined *loaded*'s tone of voice would all have left within three years. There would, however, be more booze and snacks to go round. No one would ever again be cruelly chewed out or ordered to acquire drugs, drink, planes, helicopters, coats, fishing rods or indeed anything, on the promise of having it refunded on expenses again.

IPC released a press statement thanking me for 'helping them launch *loaded*'. It was embarrassing and typical of why I wanted to leave. They had put their machine behind my idea of a magazine for men who liked football, music and having a laugh, and Tim's enthusiasm for surfing, sport and Laurel and Hardy, but they'd had nothing when I arrived in the new projects room, just the remains of an ill-thought-out news magazine for teenagers. I'd given them almost everything *loaded* would become on a sheet of paper after my *NME* interviews, Alan had added girls and fashion, Steve had designed the logo, and the boys and Beth had brilliantly breathed life and soul into it.

And that was that. There were loads of yellow message slips from the *Sunday Times*, *Independent*, Press Association and so on asking to interview me. For all their slagging us off, the *Guardian* still had the best media section so I did an interview with someone I knew there; the story translated roughly as 'James Brown grows up'.

IPC told me that as *GQ* was in the same market as them I would be confined to garden leave for my twelve weeks' notice. The irony was that despite *loaded* taking an eight-figure sum over three years, IPC had never paid me enough to even afford a garden in London. I now lived in a one-bed attic flat off Brick Lane.

The money Jonathan Newhouse was wiring me as a signing-on fee was going to buy me a house in a nice Islington square. I stripped various clippings and pictures from my wall and stuck them in a book: photos of us at the acid awards evening drinking dry ice; Vague club cigarette cards of Betty Page, the Undertones, Vera Duckworth and Bob Dobbs; a single-stick Kung Fu chewing gum wrapper; a postcard of Dylan Thomas; a tiny punk badge saying 'I've been sick with Dr Mick'; a fax from Onken saying they were going to send us a load of yoghurt opposite a fax from Paul Weller's sleeve designer asking me the name of the Charles Sobhraj serial killer book. I also stuck in art editor Jon Link's 'May the Fourth Be with You' wedding invite (the first time I'd ever seen that pun); a nice pic of my recent fashion-designer girlfriend Kait with fashion editor Beth; the photo of John Paul Getty and his wife from *Vanity Fair* that had lured me to Marrakesh; a list of staff IOUs from money I'd lent them; a clipping of Noel Gallagher and Gerrard (from Fabulous) when they were Inspiral Carpets roadies; a press box pass from Southampton–Leeds; *loaded* promotional George Best and Rod Stewart postcards; a cartoon invite to the premier of *Pulp Fiction*; a faxed photo of me in a massive ankle-length silver Adidas manager's coat with a message saying 'I think the Suggs issue is great' from *Arena* editor Dylan Jones who had been on the Paul Smith Japan trip; a *Media Week* clipping from 18 August 1995 saying, '*Loaded* Overtakes *GQ* as Leading Men's Mag'; fan letter/fax of encouragement from the editor of *Vanity Fair*; a letter from Mal Young, producer of *Brookside,* on headed notepaper thanking me for the cover with Paul Usher (Barry Grant), saying it would go on their corridor of fame; an interview with me from *Newsweek*; a really nice photo of my new girlfriend Kaz at Top Withens in the Pennines; and finally the 'How to Spot a Socialised Psycho' article Deeson had stuck to my door. That was it. On the cover I scribbled, 'From my desk at close of *loaded* play, May '97', stuck the first front cover over the top and closed the book on four amazing years of my life.

The only person I really knew who had anything to do with *GQ* was Paul Smith. When I told him about the job he paused, then replied, 'James, it's so wrong, it's right.' Fifty per cent truthful. If there'd been any way someone from the City could have helped me take *loaded* out of IPC in some sort of buy-out I'd have gone for it, but it was what it was. What with not being a big fan of getting raped and murdered, it was time to move on. I assumed going to *GQ* would reduce the chance of that happening.

Martin and I had a low-key farewell drinks and they presented him with the framed artwork of a cartoon version of his trip to Cannes, and me with a great image of the Leeds 1974 League Champions saluting the Kop. When the boys wrote a farewell note to us in the next issue the powers that be made them remove it, and when the next editor Derek asked them to put me on the mailing list, Robert the youngest exec on the publishing side, who I'd known since he was on sales at *NME*, told them that wasn't going to happen. Cheers. Instead the staff published a photograph of me naked in the background of the next editor's letter. No one else would really know what it was but I did and it made me laugh a lot.

Two weeks after I left *loaded* I received a terrible call and a reminder of how fragile all our lives and lifestyles were. One of our friends and contributors, Gavin Hills, had been killed while fishing off rocks with his brother Fraser and Tom Hodgkinson, the editor of the *Idler*. An unexpected swell had caught him, smashed his head on the rocks and then quickly taken him face down and motionless 40 yards back out to sea. There was nothing Tom and Fraser could do. He'd gone.

With his rosy cheeks, endless enthusiasm, and strong belief in whatever he was into, Gav was popular and much admired. He was close with Adam Porter, editor of *up-loaded* and photographer Zed Nelson. As soon as word went round about his death, about fifteen of us descended on his flat in Broadway Market by London Fields. People were shocked and bewildered. In his food cupboard he had a jar of dried pasta in the shape of pairs of tits. On his wall he had a huge poster of Sir Matt Busby that I had once slept beneath with a Subbuteo pitch for a blanket.

I had first met Gav a few years before, backstage at dawn at

Glastonbury when he was dressed as Richard the Lionheart with Nutella smeared all over his face. I thought 'What a great look, who is this?'

Now writer Miranda Sawyer, who had introduced us that morning, was stood in front of me, knowing about my mum and asking what I thought happened to people when they died. Suddenly we all felt very young. Like we weren't equipped for real life. Or death.

During his talk at the funeral, Tom from the *Idler* had mentioned how many hours he and Gavin had been up all night eating crisps, and afterwards I asked him what the fuck that was about. 'I didn't want to say taking coke in front of his parents.' It felt like the end of our post-rave, extended media childhoods.

By this point *loaded* had four keen heroin users, coke was as prevalent as Coca-Cola, the office stank of poppers, skunk and sometimes freebase. When we weren't fucking around in the office or in pubs and clubs we were out in the countryside or abroad for stories, acting even worse. Gavin was a contributor and a comrade, the only other writer out there in media world who felt like he was one of us, but he'd died in the fucking sea. It was too surreal a death for any of us to even consider that going closer to the edge of the rocks might be some sort of metaphorical warning. I thought changing my environment might calm me down but if anything it was to put my excessive drug and drink behaviour in even starker relief.

Spunk Towers

Hanover Square, London, 1997

Rod Stewart was one of many people who couldn't understand why I'd left *loaded* for a publishing backwater like *GQ*. He brought it up when I interviewed him a few months later for *The Times* magazine.

'James, why did you leave *loaded*? It was so good.'

Me: 'At Vogue House there are 460 employees, 50 of them men, many gay or ancient. The rest are great-looking posh girls.'

Rod: 'Ahhh, James my son, you are in Spunk Towers.'

It was a beautiful sunny first day of May 1997. Election day: Tony Blair v. John Major. Leeds were having a grim season under George Graham, but England under Hoddle had just beaten Georgia in a World Cup qualifier at Wembley with goals from Shearer and Sheringham. There was a tremendous sense of excitement around the country, the collective buzz of Euro 96 was still there, the Verve, Blur and Oasis ruled the airwaves and it felt like time for political change. Blair had announced himself to the *loaded* generation by playing head tennis with Newcastle manager Kevin Keegan eighteen months before.

I met Peter Stuart, the *GQ* publisher, at his favourite Italian restaurant, Cafe Venezia, off Savile Row, where the staff treated him like a king. Peter was a small chap in a royal-blue pinstripe suit, with a massive personality and an array of self-deprecating one-liners. He said he had a flat near Harley Street which took him twenty minutes to walk to work from but forty to get back because by 6 p.m. he couldn't walk straight. He had a permanent smile and a handshake ready to extend to whoever he was introduced to. His favourite line was, 'She had marvellous breasts, two on the front and one on the back for dancing.' He felt like a Kenneth Connor *Carry On* character.

His job, he explained, was to entertain and sell the concept of *GQ* to advertisers and his deputy Maria would follow up on the deal he'd sketched out over lunch. Organised by his PA, 'the lovely Sophie' – he'd introduce all women as 'the lovely . . .' – he was on a permanent charm offensive – always charming, sometimes offensive. He had immense pride in his job, magazine and company. It was clearly the best position he'd ever had and he lived it to the full. 'We're going to be a team – you make great editorial and I'll get us great ad deals, and we're going to have a bloody good time doing it.'

He would give me a 'flat plan' with the pages already taken for ads, and say, 'The rest is yours, fill it with whatever you want.' The concept was, 'Ads first but we won't fuck with your editorial.'

After lunch at Cafe Venezia we headed to Filthy McNasty's and Peter sat down at a table next to two girls I recognised. I didn't know them too well but I knew an undertaker they did drugs with. Their pinned eyes lit up when Peter started buying all the drinks. He had no idea of their drug of choice and it was the first of many unusual *loaded*/ Condé Nast cultural crossover experiences to come.

Election day 1997 was halfway done and Filthy's was filling up. The Charlatans' brilliant 'North Country Boy', with Tim's Dylanesque drawl, was blasting out of the stereo, Tony Blair was riding into office and Peter was hammering anything wet in a glass that came over the bar. He eventually headed off back to Mayfair and I went to an election party at the Duke of York in Holborn, owned and run by Farika, who Michael from *loaded* went out with. All the crew was there. It was a great night of dancing in the basement when everyone knew Labour had won. It seemed strange heading into what was clearly the CNP blue corner just as the country was going red.

Enthusiasm for my appointment came from an unlikely source. The next time I saw the Beasties they told me they'd been waving *loaded* around at Si Newhouse (the owner of CNP) for ages, saying it was the best mag in Britain and that he should hire me. Apparently they knew him through their parents.

At a CNP drinks party in the boardroom for some old crocodile from Cartier the following week I'd never seen so much grovelling, but apparently the guy had a massive budget to spend across the entire company. He didn't seem too impressed with my bubblegum T-shirt from D Mob. 'You look like you're going to play sport.' I was – my mates the Exiles, who I played with every week, were about to kick off in Regent's Park; I'd be fucked if I was wearing a suit before I even started working there. It was clearly going to take me some time to acclimatise.

If it wasn't for the lines of slim, stylish, attractive and extremely healthy-looking young women pouring through its doors you probably wouldn't notice Vogue House – or Rogue House, as I liked to think of it – tucked away in a park square just south of Oxford Circus. Inside, the commissionaires, the two Peters, in their white shirts, steel hair and big grins constantly look like they can't believe their luck. All they have to do is welcome all these really nice guests and employees and sign for endless flower deliveries. The whole luxury goods sector communicates through high-end bouquets.

Behind them is a display of CNP's glossy magazines – *GQ*, *Vogue*, *Tatler*, *Vanity Fair*, *World of Interiors* and *GQ Active*. Above them is a mezzanine floor with a balcony that takes you from the *GQ* floor through into the boardroom decorated in immaculate and instantly recognisable iconic black and white photographs taken for *Vogue* over the years by Bailey, Donovan, Duffy, Lichfield et al.

It is from this balcony that on week one I watch Deeson awkwardly introduce the CNP MD to a Scottish writer we knew who had once nodded out face down onto a three-bar electric fire that had left him looking griddled.

Walking back away from the boardroom and across the balcony you would find the corridors leading to the *GQ* advertising and editorial offices. Weirdly they were lined with framed paper shopping bags from fashion retailers. That's right, shopping bags behind framed glass. Designed to show the advertisers and staff how the company saw high-end retail as art.

Martin and I had a lot of work to do. There were certain basic elements I'd learned from *NME* and *loaded* that I needed to introduce quickly at *GQ*. I'd been significantly involved with two very successful titles where the sales had rocketed.

A magazine is only ever as good as the people creating it and most importantly they have to function as a productive team, with everyone making sure they put in as much good stuff as possible. And for that to work you have to have the right combination of people in terms of personality, experience, worker type and talent. The magazine staff has to share the lifestyle and passions of the target audience and within that team there also has to be a degree of diversity that allows you to inspire and grow the target audience.

Some magazines you can rebuild from the bottom by empowering junior staff and attracting fresh young talent. Others you have to change by restructuring the top end. As soon as I met the *GQ* team I understood why the magazine was so distant from contemporary male culture; both needed fixing, the top and the bottom. They were actually a long way from the lifestyles of their supposed audience, the rich young city boys who'd all been buying *loaded*.

The month I was announced *GQ* had Gary Oldman on the cover and Primal Scream as the second lead cover line, both *loaded* staples from three years before, but they had somehow managed to make it feel dull. Like an old gentleman's club. There were features on spanking women, port and how to play bridge. Just fucking weird – there weren't any labels like 6876, G-Star or old school Adidas in sight. Mention Back to Basics and they'd think of Tory policy not the night club.

When it came to editing features, three or four senior staff would all have a taste of the piece and pass it on to the next one. No serious editor in their right mind would allow such a communal approach. It wasn't the Watergate investigation they were editing, it was how to cook an aubergine while wearing an expensive watch.

The powers that be were keen for me to clear out 'as much dead wood as possible'. Thankfully deputy editor, Simon Hills, was an asset and a really nice guy. Qualities I want in a deputy are loyalty, editorial ability, mental stability and the confidence to challenge me privately. Simon had all of these. Despite having friends on the staff he understood the importance of giving me an honest briefing. I asked him about his own plans and he said he'd help me settle in for a few months then he would seek a new challenge. This seemed fair and I appreciated it.

At my first staff meeting I said I didn't care who the readers were, where they lived or what they did, so long as more of them bought the magazine. Within a few days this quote and the news that I'd addressed them with my sunglasses on appeared in a newspaper gossip column. I knew I needed to change the personnel as quickly as possible either by moving them on or getting them on board. We paid off some and thankfully others left.

GQ had a three-month production schedule which meant it was impossible to feature topical content. At *loaded* I'd run it like the *NME* or a newspaper, updating it throughout the monthly publishing cycle right up to the day before going to press. During our first meeting the managing editor started explaining, 'What Michael says is . . .' I had to stop her right there and point out that not only was Michael – their previous boss but one – no longer in the job, he wasn't even alive.

There'd been a new editor since then. Right there I saw the problem. It must have been difficult to progress without feeling disloyal to their late boss. Men's magazine publishing had changed and *GQ* was no longer market leader in a field of three high-end titles.

I'd been shocked that the recent issue with the model Caprice on the cover had sold only 70,000 issues at the news stand when their audited circulation was 118,000. My last issue of *loaded* had sold over a quarter of a million – with Harry Hill sitting on a badger on the cover. Like any declining product, if the magazine was losing sales it was either because there was something wrong with the publication itself or the commercial landscape around it had changed. In *GQ*'s case it was both. *Loaded* and *FHM* and, further down the scale, *Maxim* had totally changed the buying habits of young men; millions were reading magazines now, but even with all this new footfall *GQ* wasn't benefiting from any overspill sales. It was badly adrift.

Simon Hills kept describing freelance writers as, 'He's not a great writer but he has good ideas.' Or, 'He's not a good writer but has contacts.' I met about six people like this who 'weren't great writers but . . .' and then after I'd gone to the pub with one of them with an army background who explained he could kill a man – I guess he meant me – with a pencil, I asked Simon not to introduce me to any more people like this and said that from now on we would concentrate on recruiting actual good writers with strong ideas and contacts.

I called Tony Parsons who had written great, provocative columns years before in *Arena* and he was delighted to be back in a men's mag. I hired Bill Prince and Iestyn George who I'd been on *NME* with, and brilliant fashion and culture man about town Chris Sullivan who had been contributing to *loaded*. And then as editorial assistant I hired a fitness fanatic called Morgan Rees who'd been a good intern on *loaded*. Bill brought soul music expert and experienced magazine hand Lloyd Bradley in, and within a few months we had new faces in the office.

They had a strong mix of editorial skills and cultural knowledge that livened the place up.

I'd met the *GQ* art director Tony Chambers before at a Lenny Kravitz shoot/interview for the *Sunday Times*. Tony was a really bright, enthusiastic Scouser who'd arrived just months before me and was ambitious, design wise. I told him I wanted it to look bold and confident and he and his team just got on with it. Tony excitedly said, 'Have you met Geezer? He's great.' And he introduced me to Dave Gyseman who did the production and liaised with the printers. Suddenly the three of us had a little gang of probably the only people in the building who knew what free school dinners were. There wasn't a single day over the next eighteen months when one of them didn't make me laugh.

What soon became apparent was that Condé Nast was a brilliant place to work. MD Nicholas Coleridge's publishing meetings were clipped, clear, to the point, and he got through the whole of the Condé Nast portfolio of titles in the same time as just one IPC *loaded* publishing meeting. Every day I encountered things that were just better than at the Ministry of Magazines. They cared about their titles more. They were better designed. The whole company had more class.

It was very posh but far from uptight. There was a nice reception; a tiny tuck shop selling coffee, smoothies and toast to all the girls; there was a fantastic boardroom with an attached kitchen full of cake and strawberries dipped in chocolate at all hours; a storeroom full of very expensive booze next to my office. In the basement was a parking space with my name on and the Cherokee in it.

The first time I met my new PA Alex Hearn she told me there was a mirror on the back of my door and it came off if I needed it for anything other than to look at myself. I raised an eyebrow and we both just laughed. She explained that when she'd been briefed about my arrival she had replied, 'So, fasten my seatbelt again?' Alex was a lovely, super organised and curious person. Sometimes I'd see her walking round Hanover Square on her lunch hour in a dream looking at the clouds. Probably wondering what the fuck she'd done to end up having to sort my life out. Ticket to Paris, Milan, New York, Leeds? She'd sort it. Lunch at the Ivy, Caprice or the Groucho for five of us? She'd sort it. Champagne? She'd sort it. Cup of coffee for Paul Weller popping in? She'd sort it. She was so discreet, charming and effective.

One morning, not long after I'd joined, I discovered that six of the staff were big fans of the Cult, so as light distraction I lined them up along the art department wall for some synchronised air guitar to 'Love Removal Machine'. Half the subeditors, writers and art team were stood with their arms out ready to rock when Alex glided quickly over, turned off the stereo and whispered, 'James, Si's in the building and on his way down right now with Jonathan.' Condé Nast was Si Newhouse's company; he was an almost mythical figure, based in New York, often mentioned but rarely encountered.

I looked at her to see if she was joking and she averted her eyes over my shoulder with such speed that I just spun round and held out my hand to a surprised Si and proceeded to lead him and Jonathan down the team of confused staff members, introducing them like the captain introduces his teammates to the royal family member before the FA Cup final. The staff wondered if the whole thing had been a set-up; Jonathan wasn't sure how I'd known Si was on his way down. Alex had saved the moment. I have no idea what they would have thought if they'd walked in on the staff screaming, 'Baby baby baby baby I fell from the sky,' miming chunky guitar riffs.

If *loaded* had been like John Landis's *Animal House*, joining *GQ* was like Landis's *Trading Places*. Zed Nelson came over to photograph me for some *Guardian* supplement. I'd hardly seen him since Brazil and I met him outside the CNP car park where a huge truck was offloading a BMW Z3. It had a silver exterior, black fabric convertible roof with ox-blood leather seats and polished cherrywood dash. Inside it smelled fantastic. I had never had enough money to buy anything like it before. The weight of the door and the sound and feel as it clunked perfectly together with the body of the car was impressive enough for Zed and me to both do it repeatedly.

We were both laughing at the significance of the purchase.

'Dude, this is the car Jason said there was a two-year waiting list for. How on earth did you get it?'

'Tony Yeboah?'

'Who?'

'Yeboah.'

The Ghanaian superstar striker with the massive arse and cannons in his boots at Leeds was leaving but he'd already ordered the exact car I wanted and didn't want to take it to Germany. When I'd mentioned wanting one to my LUFC agent friend Hayden, he'd said, 'Ah, I might be able to help you there.'

Simon already had a full issue of *GQ* ready to go but I had to choose the cover and we went with a really stunning session they had of the American supermodel Tyra Banks. Tony said we had to run it past Nicholas Coleridge. 'Don't worry, he never wants to change anything. He just wants to see it, have his say and then we send it off.'

The cover looked fantastic but when we got into the MD's room he was humming and hawing. I'd never had to run a cover by anyone since the first three issues of *loaded*. Eventually he asked us if we had anything else more commercial? She was beautiful, the photographs were really good and she was one of the most famous models in the world. It was *GQ*'s hundredth edition and this was by far the stand-out image in it.

It was my first couple of weeks, it was Simon's issue, and I was keen to start getting the sales up. Nicholas's response was weird. We walked out and Tony said, 'That's really strange, he's not done that with me before.' The only other cover he would do this with was Lauryn Hill.

With only Paul Newman, Ian Holm and Paul Whitehouse interviewed in the mag, we quickly reshot the cover to feature *The Fast Show* star, who I'd known in Bow a decade earlier, with a napkin printed with the rest of the contents listed on it, a huge jelly, a splodge of cream on his nose and a colourful kid's party trilby on his head. The hundredth birthday issue was a whopping great edition at 308 pages thick, with so many ads, and even a letter from someone on behalf of the Queen congratulating the magazine on the milestone. Despite all this it sold just 75,000 copies at the news stand. Tyra would have sold far more; the photos would have made the sort of cover you'd drop what you were doing to buy.

A guy called Dave Hannigan had written in saying he'd made a TV doc about Manchester United captain Roy Keane in Ireland and did we want the interview from it? Editorially this was great news. When I announced this in the editorial meeting the editor of the front section asked, 'Who is Roy Keane?' She wasn't joking. I asked Weller if he would appear on my first cover and Julian Broad shot a great portrait of him in a strong blue shirt with a mod RAF target cufflink for detail.

I just went hell for leather to fit in as much more lively and interesting content as possible. Anything that would put a footprint on the letter from the Queen's mate. On the front we mounted a modern house and dark beats CD with tracks from the Orb, David Holmes, Death in Vegas, Bentley Rhythm Ace and loads of other artists from Deconstruction, Wall of Sound, Heavenly and XL Recordings.

My editorial turnaround was really deliberate and obvious. I was choosing some material to make the magazine more interesting, some to make it more commercial and some to shake out any staff who shouldn't be there. Deeson wrote a piece in appreciation of rebel icon Che Guevara, comedian Lee Hurst interviewed Arthur Scargill, Zed brought in a harrowing but stunning set of photos from the Elvis Presley Trauma Centre in Memphis dealing with gunshot wounds. Joe Corrie and Serena Rees from Agent Provocateur came in and asked if I'd be interested in running a photo from their new range. Joe had a cheeky grin and his dad, Malcolm McLaren's looks, and Serena's plastic miniskirt was crackling on the office leather sofa. I looked at photographer Tim Bret Day's campaign and just said, 'Can we have all of them?' They were delighted. 'Fifteen Pages of Sexy Chicks in Pants' ran the cover line. It also helped us speed up the production process and reduce the issue costs.

The day I was writing up my Weller piece at home on a very tight deadline I managed to lock myself out. Nick Kent came round to interview me about Oasis for a French TV documentary and the first thing he said as he dragged his skinny body out of an estate car in his leather jacket and little white vest was, 'I'm glad you've done well.' The next thing he said was, 'Your door's just shut!' It was mid-morning on a lovely day so despite only wearing a pair of jeans and a shirt and no pants, socks or shoes we did the interview in the square. Everything felt great. Nick dropped me at Filthy's, still barefoot, and Alex biked over final pages for me to sign off, while I waited for Kaz to finish teaching at her new school, and come home with a key.

In fashion the up-and-coming and fantastically named model Charley Speed and some pals dressed as schoolboys. It wasn't going to blow anyone's minds but I didn't have any issues with it. The fashion director was a bit like someone's batty old neighbour but it was well executed and she kept the ad clients happy by being hand in hand with them. Every month they were given a steer on who had spent what and how many 'credits' should appear for each.

With all this content we sold 110,000, which was 35,000 more than the previous issue and an immediate 10 per cent uplift on the same cover-mounted promotion issue the year before. We had ignition.

The second issue followed instantly. We'd scrapped the three-month lead-in time but with no obvious cover contenders lined up I called my old landlord Jim, aka Vic Reeves, and asked if he'd consider revealing his then unknown art to the world. Twenty-five years on he's now a respected artist. When I asked our designer Ash Gibson what the regular interview section, *GQ&A*, was, he replied, 'A rich Milanese and someone famous with nothing to do with fashion talk to each other. So, Giorgio Armani meets Eric Clapton.' It was a very funny summary. But fuck that. We arranged Howard Marks and Shaun Ryder, which was a great read. There was a gripping crime story about a bank robber in America by New York correspondent Edward Helmore. And an in-depth piece about Ken Bates's redevelopment of Chelsea and his hiring of Ruud Gullit – his wife wrote in saying it was the most balanced piece she'd ever read on her husband. Which I guess was a polite way of thanking us for not calling him an out-and-out cunt. We had a profile with a thirty-year-old Stelios, founder of new company easyJet.

Claire Grant joined as managing editor from the *Telegraph*. Her job was to look after the budgets, liaise with the ad team, the flat plan. It was a serious job and she was excellent at it. So much so that after about four weeks she came to me and said, 'James, I can't sleep, all I keep thinking about is everything we are doing.'

When I replied 'Good,' she seemed shocked. 'Claire, if you're up all night thinking and worrying about how fast we are moving, that's good. I want people who become consumed by it.'

I drew three rectangles in a U shape on my whiteboard and told her, 'This is a slow-moving oil tanker and we are turning it round through this U-turn. This bit when we are side on to the current is when it is most dangerous, that's where we are now, and we have to move fast to get us going back in the right direction.' She liked that there was some method to the madness.

Madness? When I puked into a bucket after a lunch of the wrong powder I then placed it in the writers' area for want of anywhere else to put it. That appeared in *Private Eye* and had the desired effect of loosening up the log-jammed staff list. It was uncouth and unsubtle but I was trying anything just to burn off the dead wood so we could crack on.

GQ was just rammed with all the usual fashion and luxury goods and property ads but also pages that reflected out of touch, ageing concepts of masculinity. It was as if acid house, Alex Garland's *The Beach*, *Trainspotting*, Channel 4's *The Girlie Show* and Euro 96 had never happened. Many of the ads looked like they'd come from the seventies.

At the start of September I went to Australia to be the guest speaker at the Australian Advertising Awards. While I was there Condé Nast Australia arranged a very civil, welcoming and quite unexpected drinks reception for me where the boss toasted me with a glass of Moët & Chandon and said, 'When there's a problem at Condé Nast we throw champagne at it.' These words would soon come back to haunt me.

Maggie Jones's is a friendly, rustic, restaurant in Kensington. On a Monday morning I am there with Peter Stuart and Martin Deeson, along with Barbara Ellen, previously with *loaded* and *NME*, now a *Mail on Sunday* columnist. We are getting hammered drinking white wine from huge, unbranded bottles with long glass measuring sticks so you can be charged by the volume consumed. We go on to a vodka bar and then head back to Vogue House which is totally the wrong thing to do. As the car drives us down Oxford Street Barbara climbs up through the sun roof and is sitting up there shouting at shoppers and tourists, until Peter pulls her by the legs back into the car.

We arrive at *GQ* like a cartoon of Asterix and Obelix beating up Romans – a cloud of fists, helmets and swearing. It is mid-afternoon on a Monday, people writing articles and selling ads look at us in shock. Barbara and I lock ourselves in the wine cupboard and drink another bottle.

Martin takes Barbara into the fashion department where she insults everyone and slaps John Morgan, the gentlemen's style editor. Hitting men when drunk had been the subject of her opening column in the launch issue of *loaded*. They charge back into my office and start physically fighting over the ownership of a £10 note. Peter Stuart and I are just watching and laughing as a heavy glass ashtray flies across my desk and cracks a corner panel of the window. Then something even worse happens. I am about to display just how badly my judgement is impaired by alcohol.

I pick up an empty bottle of champagne that we'd already laid waste to and hurl it through the main office windowpane while saying, 'This is how you break a window.'

It is fucking nuts, there's glass everywhere. I look out of the smashed window and see the bottle has travelled over a cashpoint queue and buried itself neck first into the windscreen of a parked minivan. My immediate thought is it is so lucky no one was hurt.

Amazingly, Alex sees the van is from a company a good friend of her husband's owns. She contacts him immediately and explains there's been an accident with a bottle falling out of a window and that it will all be paid for. Within minutes an old boy from the upper echelons appears in the open-plan office entrance looking furious. This was not the time to point out Jonathan Newhouse had said he liked his editors to be controversial.

Alex suggests I leave the premises so I relocate to Filthy McNasty's with Barbara where we are joined later by Tony and picture editor Louisa, who assume this is probably my leaving drink.

The next morning I sober up to a call telling me not to come in till Thursday when the MD gives me a written warning that if anything else bad happens I'll be in breach of contract and fired. Peter, Martin and I are then sent to Susannah Amoore's office. Susannah is the Condé Nast HR gatekeeper, with a card index of people she will or won't hire, and is known to ask which school potential employees have attended. I think the only other person to cross the threshold from my school is the brilliant Alan Bennett who often waits in reception for his chap who works on *World of Interiors*. Susannah is so intimidating that after her initial meeting with Mick Bunnage he scarpered back to *loaded*.

In her office I take the middle seat of three, with Martin and Peter either side of me, for what turns out to be more of a scolding than a bollocking, but Peter really gets it. 'Peter, you are a grown man, a Condé Nast board member and you are leading these boys astray. You should be ashamed of yourself. I'm holding you responsible for this incident.' Barbara is 'never to set foot in Vogue House again,' and then after warning us about the terrible dangers of alcohol she asks, 'Do any of you need help?' At exactly the same time the other two say, 'No!', I reply, 'Yes!'

They leave the room and her tone immediately and surprisingly softens as she explains that someone close to her died due to alcohol and that if I am serious she will get me some help. This development is actually a fucking huge relief. No one has ever asked me if I need help before, and I do. By the end of so many nights over the previous year I'd been trying and struggling to find some sort of value to the state I'd end up in but to no avail. Too often I'd end up feeling utterly lousy, incapable of going home, ending the night in holes in the ground in Soho with people I didn't really want to be with, thinking, 'How the fuck do I stop all this?' A night that started out good would always end up shit. Paul Smith, Damien Hirst and Frank Skinner have all said things to me about my drinking and using, but this is the first time anyone has offered to help.

Alex is kind enough to support my emotional mood swings and now some of the older women at the company, Brigitte in catering and Sandy Bowler, editor of *Brides*, who walks around in her wraparound shades looking like Bono, take the time to talk to me caringly. Maybe they recognise the lost boy. When I asked my friend Sarah Lavelle, who worked upstairs in production, about this recently she replied, 'They could see you were in a terrible state, but you were doing so well professionally lots of people just didn't see it.'

Susannah dispatched me to the company doctor in Sloane Street who in turn sent me to a Harley Street psychiatrist with a big fringe and Dr Strangelove accent. He said they had grounds to claim my rehab on the company insurance scheme and sent me to see an addiction therapist called Clive Meindl. The first time I went to see Clive was on a dark Monday night in October 1997. 'The Drugs Don't Work' by the Verve was all over the airwaves and ace alcoholic columnist Jeffrey Bernard had just been buried. (Deeson and I had once visited him uninvited in Middlesex Hospital with biscuits when he was having his legs amputated. He was confused but appreciative.)

These two factors – the song and his death – were probably some sort of sign but I failed to notice. I was gripped by an almost childlike fear of not getting to the appointment and when I arrived it seemed the lights were on but no one was home (at the health centre not me, although a case could have been made). The doors were locked. No one answered the bell so I scaled the side of the building to try and attract the attention of anyone inside. I was desperate enough to consider walking through a door towards a different way of life. The problem was it didn't seem to be open.

While up the drain pipe I realised if the time was right the place must be wrong. In the opposite direction I found a very discreet private hospital that looked like a small luxury hotel opposite the Imperial War Museum. On the third floor was Clive looking like Radio 2 DJ Steve Wright: 'Oh, you must be James. I didn't think you were coming.'

The remaining thirty minutes of my first session would turn out to be the first step of a journey that changed and possibly saved my life.

Through excess or misadventure I figured I would seriously slip up sooner or later. I had no idea what I was really doing beyond following a route Belushi, Iggy, Hunter Thompson and Co. had somehow made seem attractive. Clive told me a little about how he saw people with all sorts of addictions from anorexia and bulimia to gambling and drink and drugs. 'They are all different ways of changing how you feel.'

I'd never considered that before. I took drugs and drank because I liked it, because my mates did, because I thought it added to my personality in some way, because some substances relaxed me, others over-stimulated me. And yes, now that I think about it, probably because I wanted to cover up the feelings I had about my mum.

Clive gave me a cross-addiction questionnaire on food, sex, drink, drugs and, weirdly, sport. I scored high marks on the sex, drugs, drink and food addictions; then he pointed out that doing well was actually ticking as few boxes as possible.

The sport questions made me laugh, 'Do you hang around sports centres looking for a game?' He explained that someone with a problem with exercise would think it equally weird that people snort cocaine off dirty toilet seat lids.

Once he saw my questionnaire results he suggested Condé Nast send me to a residential rehab immediately. This came as a bit of a shocker. His suggestion brought up all sorts of questions for me. Would it be like the mental hospital I had visited my mum in? What sort of bed would I have? Would I be able to go out to a pub?

He showed me some brochures for places called Promise and Farm Place which looked like nice country house hotels and suggested I go for thirty days this coming weekend. What? There was no way I was doing that. I wasn't against the concept of it but I wasn't sure that I would be able to come back out and re-establish enough influence to take charge of GQ in the way I had already done. The momentum would be broken. But far more worrying was the return of a feeling I hadn't had for over a decade.

'What if I don't like the food?' Clive must have thought I was being self-important but I wasn't. This wasn't the Editor's Editor of the Year asking this, the wild man of publishing, this was the vulnerable kid inside. The idea of an institution, albeit a very comfortable-looking one, reminded me of the terrible tension I felt going into school dinners for so long and those feelings just came hurtling back. I was also beginning to feel really worried about not being in control of my environment.

I hid the personal insecurities behind the professional and just said I didn't think I'd have enough credibility to return and carry on with the job. So we agreed I would see him twice a week for an hour on Monday and Friday but if I missed a session without giving notice I had to go into residential care.

When he then asked why I wanted help I said, 'All these hell-raising greats in *loaded* that no one has appreciated for years have actually almost all destroyed themselves and their careers. I don't want to be like that any more.'

I gave him the list of the guys I loved: Peter O'Toole, Richard Harris, Keith Richards, Ronnie Wood, Hunter Thompson, Hurricane Higgins, Ollie Reed, Keith Moon and how I realised while publishing their many tales of self-destruction and debauchery how much damage they did to themselves and their careers.

'Well I've worked with one of them and you're right, they understand that too.'

That was it, I was in. If he had been counselling someone off that list I was fine about spending two hours a week with him.

I was really lucky to have had Susannah, Clive and the company insurance scheme. Susannah was delighted I was taking it seriously. Not that it slowed me down; we were going to the Ivy so often that Deeson was collecting napkins to use as tea towels. I could handle hangovers – the cloudiness slowed me down, which wasn't a bad thing, and the darker, cynical outlook had influenced the generic black humour that worked well at *loaded*. But at Condé Nast I felt like I'd walked out of a jungle in camouflage into a harsh glare in a white landscape. My drink problem stuck out massively.

Attempting to control my drug use, I tried to impose a 9 p.m. drug curfew, which lasted three days. Then I tried 8 p.m., which was another waste of time. So I decided I wasn't going to buy drugs any more but then people just gave them to me for free. They wanted to do drugs with me or give me their drugs. It was just what I thought sounded great in the Bob Woodward Belushi book *Wired*. Be careful what you wish for.

'It would be rude not to,' was a common phrase said by a generation of enthusiastic cocaine users as they received a mirror, CD case, wrap, book, tray or album sleeve with a five-bar fence of lumpy white powder on it. If they had any sense they'd happily roll up their own tenner or fiver or twenty or playing card or travel card or if they were really flash pull out their own little silver straw and snort. If you were alert enough you'd notice that notes that were handed round with the coke frequently had blood and mucus on one end and I really didn't want to be getting into other people's blood and mucus. For a while I had some plastic Australian dollar notes, made to last in a beach and surf culture, and perfect for rubbing remnants off once you'd opened them up again.

As I was struggling to get some sort of handle on my own drink and drug use, a mate was going the other way. He had married someone with an even bigger habit than himself and they were soon locked inside their own cocaine cocoon. In his notebook was a list of twenty dealers with different London post codes, a single name and a number.

This was the first time I actually felt sad about what was going on. I didn't see him any more because he was caught in his post-code cocaine list. I was still drinking at Filthy's – on bad nights on my own – alternating volleys of vodka and ice followed by tequila and then on repeat until I was numb. The former to stop me feeling anything and then latter to kick-start some sort of reaction.

Seeing Clive twice a week was an unusual yet welcome experience. I'd never wanted to see a therapist because I just knew there was so much inside I didn't want to revisit.

After the third session I sat in my car outside the clinic and felt like a really heavy rucksack had been lifted from my back. I felt raw and nervous but I was definitely feeling lighter. The week later felt like I was removing concrete overcoats. Meanwhile magazine life was racing along.

'You've never had it so good' – Michael Heseltine

Vogue House boardroom, London, 1998

A year before, I was lying awake in a tent in a graveyard in Gloucestershire giggling with The Loafer, Reece and Shakey, looking for ghosts, but what my life has become now is equally as ridiculous. Condé Nast is a lovely place to work but it feels like Marie Antoinette's world.

The people are very nice to me but I don't share their enthusiasm for the chitter-chatter of the aspirational luxury goods world. If there's one thing I'm trying increasingly to master is 'how to look interested when you really don't give a fuck'. The boardroom is the social and commercial hub of the company and an evening rarely passes without a reception there. CNP are proud of their editors and magazines and we are thrust forward at every opportunity to update everyone on how well everything is going.

The pages of *Tatler*, *Vogue*, *GQ* and others are luxury goods magnets and the boardroom is regularly full of Condé Nast staff, plenty of great-looking girls, fine wine and Brigitte's amazing canapés. And here's Peter Stuart in full effect, going to sell all our pages to everyone. More than once, Deeson and I look at each other and say, 'It's amazing how he's like this and he's not even on cocaine.' Here he is asking me a question. Have I met Bambi Cartlidge-Fawkes from some marvellous company in Mayfair?

'No, Peter, I haven't but let me shake their hands and exchange cheek kisses and you tell your funniest self-deprecating jokes, the full routine if their budget warrants it, and I will smile and laugh a lot, because you are genuinely funny, and I will say something flirtatious (to them, not you) and then the truth about the sales increasing and how, yes, it will be lovely for us all to have lunch if it will help you bag more cash.'

And the non-work conversations are fast and fleeting and far from subtle. 'This is amazing. Where are we going next? Have you got any gear?' Or, 'No, I won't come and snog you in Nicholas's toilet. I'm married and anyway your husband is looking at you.' This is the world we now live in. And it is a very different world. Half the job is editing the magazine and half the job is doing this. Turning into an exploding greeting card to suck money from those members of the international upper classes who through actual interest or some unfortunate luck with their inheritance have to actually work.

And whereas at IPC whenever they tried to get anything like this together it would be greeted with as much enthusiasm as fresh sick in a kiss, I will do it because Jonathan is paying me fucking loads of money. And also because the champagne is fantastic and the food is astonishing and my senior staff Tony, Claire, Martin, Bill and even the legend Chris Sullivan, if he's just arrived at work by 5 p.m., are also gripping hands and laughing and smiling and going through the process because it really is bloody good fun. And Condé Nast really know how to plan and time these things so they never drag on and the bigwigs probably have five more events to attend on Savile Row, South Molton Street or Mount Street. Nicholas the MD has explained to me how to get in and out of multiple external client events a night. 'Show up at the very beginning when the host can see you and is delighted you are one of the first there and then as the place fills up and you've quickly said hello to everyone at the company hosting the event, slip away and on to another one.' Living the dream.

Lunchtime is no different and each magazine publisher regularly books the boardroom to schmooze companies and dignitaries. They regularly host someone from beyond the world of publishing and it frequently seems to be a Conservative MP. Oh joy of joys, I have been invited to join Jonathan and Nicholas and editors and publishers to meet the leader of the opposition, head of the Conservative Party, William Hague and his wife Ffion. Hague is going through his baseball hat in Portobello Road identity crisis and there are plenty of rumours floating around about his private life. One of them is that Johnny Morgan, our own special editorial ambassador to the luxury goods world, is advising him on what to wear. When I ask John if this is true he does admit, 'Yes, William is known in our circles.' As well as Ffion, William has also brought his judo partner, Olympic gold medallist Seb Coe, along. I was always an Ovett man myself but even so it seems a little awkward to see the popular middle-distance winner sort of kowtowing to Hague.

Talk turns to the imminent election for London mayor and William Hague asks me who I think would make a good mayor. My answer is not a politician nor a celebrity but John Bird, who started and runs the *Big Issue* – maybe a compassionate businessman of sorts. I have never met John Bird but I have been impressed by his project which has been turning homeless beggars into licensed magazine vendors for six years but despite changing the streets of London William is surprisingly unfamiliar with Bird. Talking to former Tory ministers doesn't come easy and Jonathan can detect the edge in my response to Hague's ignorance and we all jollily roll along to dessert.

Next time it's the old lion's mane of publishing and politics himself, Michael Heseltine, former deputy prime minister and minister in the Thatcher government that dispatched fleets of cockney police into the county I grew up in to beat striking miners and their families around the heads with batons. He had once brushed Seb Coe aside to talk to

Deeson who was on duty for *loaded* at the party conferences. Now a back bencher in opposition, he also owns the large publishing company Haymarket so I'm hoping the conversation might be more interesting.

Whereas Hague was sitting at the other end of the table from me Heseltine is sitting almost directly opposite me, which is unfortunate when he starts slagging *loaded* off and saying, 'Magazines like that wouldn't exist if we still had conscription.'

'Well we have the man here who invented *loaded* – James, he now edits *GQ*,' says Jonathan. I very politely give him both barrels, pointing out that his comment makes no sense as many of the boys in the armed forces actually enjoy *loaded* and have taken advantage of the special discounted forces subscription offers. He then claims my generation have never had it so good, to which I point out that if Thatcher and their pals hadn't laid waste to the British economy, making it an employment no-go land for school leavers throughout the eighties, my friends and I wouldn't have had to end up inventing things like *loaded*, Oasis, or before us acid house raves, to entertain ourselves. And that it was only three years ago that Major was referring to young men in Britain as 'yobs and slobs'.

The Condé Nast boardroom is silent but for us batting these exchanges back and forth. Having spent my teenage years doing this I know that telling the truth to those who have rose-tinted interpretations of their own actions will shortly prompt some sort of abuse but I am surprised when he becomes personal and starts to have a dig saying, 'Well you yourself look like you've never suffered.' To which I point out I'm from a comprehensive school with a free school dinner ticket and that any success was in spite of and not because of the Conservative governments.

And that ends there. For once I am calm and firm and he's a little rattled. No blood or feathers are meant to be shed in the Condé Nast boardroom. And on to a lovely dessert we go.

It is not just Tory leaders of the day who pass through our offices, but also men of the future. Here comes jolly fat rugger blond Boris Johnson, last heard of driving off to Belgium in a borrowed car for his *Telegraph* motoring column, with my Greenwich flatmate Jimmy the *Telegraph* photographer wearing my rare Airwalk trainers from the Beastie Boys' Los Angeles store X-Large. Jimmy spent many a night telling me how hilarious this big posh blond bloke he went driving with was, and at last I meet him. I'm a little underwhelmed as he arrives to profile me for his weekly interview series. The only thrust of his conversation is, 'This magazine is for blokes who want to buy puff juice.' By puff juice I eventually understand him to mean fragrances. And while I have little interest in it myself beyond a single bottle of Issey Miyake that sort of smells like you could drink it, I'm surprised that this is the only thing he wants to talk about.

To his credit he at least writes what we talk about as opposed to broadsheets who send snide writers to effect some sort of hatchet job. People really seem to have a problem with me editing *GQ*, as if it's bad enough that I'd first created a magazine that was more fun than any other print media going, but that I should now be enjoying the upside of Condé Nast is beyond the pale. Little snippets appear regularly in the gossip columns of various papers and *Private Eye* – Condé Nast is a very leaky ship. There is a constant fascination with goings-on in Vogue House. When you can't even buy a pair of sandals to go somewhere insanely hot without the *Evening Standard* spotting you and commenting in print, 'Surely it should be trainers,' you begin to wonder how thick some of these people are. But fuck 'em.

There are others more put out by the attention I am getting. One morning Nicholas summons me to his office and asks me if I've 'seen this ridiculous thing in the *Daily Mail*'. I have no idea what he's talking about but he explains that a power list has been printed and the thing that is especially silly is that I am higher up it than him. I genuinely don't care; these lists don't mean anything. I'm none the wiser, but it turns out the list had been a Channel 4 and *Observer* joint venture and the *Mail* had just picked it up. My life hasn't changed because I have been named 236th most powerful person in Britain by a series of experts including Roy Hattersley, and to put it into some perspective I doubt Mrs Thatcher and the Pope are fucking put out that I am higher up the chart than they are.

Alex calls the *Observer* to see if we can have a copy for the files and this subsequently appears in another gossip column saying I ordered ten copies and pinned them all along the corridor of framed shopping bags to wind Nicholas (and presumably the Pope and Thatcher) up. Like most of the stories that appear none of this is even based on the tiniest grain of truth. The only time we ever pinned anything up in that corridor were the words 'Monkey Tennis'. Genius was in our midst in a Travel Tavern in Norwich and it had needed celebrating. The powers that be called me in to inquire what monkey tennis was. Where do you begin?

The final days of Citizen Cocaine

London, January 1998

At the start of December Clive suggested I give myself a cocaine limit for the month. When I suggested fifty lines he just laughed so we settled on twenty-four. It was the first time he had suggested I do something physical to curb my intake. I guess he knew that laying down guidelines or rules too early into our sessions would have just pushed me the other way. We didn't discuss alcohol limitation because that just seemed pointless, I guess. We were heading into the Christmas season – a lot of *GQ* lunches, and three or four parties at least a night. Working at the heart of a city running on booze. People would visit the capital for celebrations as treats, revel in the lights and bars and the clubs and the atmosphere on special occasions. That was our daily life. You don't want your shot of grappa the nice lady in the Italian café off Hanover Square set out for us free after lunch? OK, I'll drink all six of them.

I didn't sit with a bottle in my drawer, it would come in on a tray sparkling and inviting, smiling and beguiling. Someone who could have walked out of the pages of *Vogue* would wander in and take me down into the boardroom. There was never, ever a scramble to get served, no money exchanged, no shouted conversations with bar staff. There was always someone at the front of a queue happy to pass a drink out without even being asked. Or a bartender who would see me come in and just hand a bottle over or pour a glass and leave it by the hatch with the bottle and the bucket of ice and a smile, knowing

I'd sort them out later or shake their head and say it's on them. That was the best perk of being well known for *loaded*. Free drink forever. The alcohol was like air. When people who stop smoking used to say they had nothing to do with their fingers, that's how I'd feel without a bottle in my hand.

The cocaine control actually went pretty well initially. I really did want to stop feeling how I did at 3 a.m. with shitty gak and gurned-up, repetitive conversations with strangers. I had managed to get to the *GQ* party at Chris Sullivan's old club the Wag in the third week of the month having just done nineteen lines. I actually managed to keep it together for the party but afterwards in a suite I'd hired for DJ Dave Beer and our mates from Leeds, the whole thing just went out the window.

I was in the kitchen with Howard Marks and a chap who'd been serving up out of a restaurant bar who gave me a big clear bag as a present. It had parmesan-sized lumps in it (the real wedges, not the milled, shaking-pot stuff). I asked Howard if he fancied some and he said, 'Oh go on, then. I've never done this before.' Which surprised me; when I recounted this to mutual friends years later they told me he'd said the same thing to them too.

There were twenty people in the room with grinding jaws and increased irritation levels huddled over wraps and bags. We looked like those monkeys in frozen ponds in Japan.

Clive said he thought a massive blow-out might have occurred sooner so he was glad I'd taken some benefit from the trial period.

Heading down to Mumbles in south Wales on Christmas Eve to join the in-laws for Christmas, I dropped Chris Sullivan, the *GQ* style editor, in Merthyr Tydfil. He loaded up the Cherokee – which I still had alongside the BMW, and two other cars I'd been loaned that I'd lent to other people – with more Christmas presents than I had ever seen. 'You know this is the first time I've had a regular job going into Christmas in years. It's made a massive difference.' It was really touching, seeing this great man with real humility behind the wild stories. I was really glad we'd both left *loaded*; this was the physical difference right there before us.

I arrived in Swansea in the early hours, high from driving in bad weather and a pre-drive livener and then I silently sat up until dawn discovering father-in-law Roger's cricketing autobiographies and cocaine don't go well together at all. You need a Jimmy Greaves or George Best for that type of thing.

As soon as we got back to London after Christmas I went out and bought sixty-four bottles of Chablis. 'In case some people come round,' I explained to my bewildered wife.

No one was coming round, I just dreaded running out. She replied, 'We're going on holiday next week.'

Big Trouble in Little Dix

Virgin Islands, January 1998

There were moments in my life by now that had me seriously wondering what the fuck was going on. Weekly rehab meetings, free drugs and drink, Savile Row suits, four cars, an expense account, posh lunches; politicians, musicians, great writers and models popping into the office; free and regular first-class international travel.

At Christmas my office filled up with unanticipated gifts from the leading fashion houses and luxury goods companies; over thirty boxes and huge posh shopping bags full of cashmere jumpers, leather boots, bags, gloves, wallets, scarves, fragrances, watches, cigars, silver business card holders, bottles of fine wines and spirits. The luxury goods business was in overdrive. I gave a lot of it away to staff but years later I'd occasionally find overlooked goods wrapped in tissue paper at the back of a cupboard.

The peak of this unexpected gift avalanche were Prada skis. I couldn't ski, and gave them to the editorial assistant, Morgan. The fashion editor of *Tatler* was extremely alarmed and offered to swap a Prada cashmere jumper for them. But I enjoyed giving them to him, he was delighted. Years later when he was editor of *Men's Health* he gave me a column and a beautiful water rowing machine.

Kaz and I went off for a couple of weeks to the British and American Virgin Islands. I needed a break, but instead we were sued by the Beatles – well, one of their sons. One morning Alex contacted me to explain a very serious litigation had come in regarding Oasis and that

I had to talk to the company lawyer. I'd had a lot of dealings with the legal department at *loaded* but the conversation I had over the phone with the hitherto unknown Condé Nast libel lawyer was surreal.

In our latest *GQ* cover story the Gallaghers had libelled George Harrison's son Dhani, and the former Beatle's family weren't taking it lightly. Our writer had been with the brothers on the day they'd got really pissed on Steve Lemacq's Radio 1 show and Liam had challenged the grand masters of rock 'n' roll to fight him on Primrose Hill. It was madness – Oasis were selling like the Beatles and behaving like the Sex Pistols.

In the *GQ* interview they'd claimed they'd met Dhani Harrison, George's son, on a flight back from the States, outdrunk him, and he'd been taken from the plane in a wheelchair. It turned out they'd made the whole thing up. So the CNP lawyer was asking me why no one had fact-checked it. I was really surprised. I explained, 'You don't just call up a world-famous person and say, "Hey, were you telling lies?" Would *Vogue* do that to Versace?' This sort of crazed shit appeared all the time in the *NME* or *loaded*.

Anyway that cost CNP £25,000, one of just two times a magazine has been sued under my editorship. I really liked that issue too. The story was strong and the photographer had caught both brothers laughing and falling out of shot on either side of the page with just enough leather jacket, fringe and eyebrow to know it was them. The golden rule in covers is eye contact but I chose the shot for the very reason it didn't have any. It wasn't even in colour but it just looked so confident to do that and caught them as they were and I felt we should be.

On the way back from the Virgin Islands Kaz and I stopped off in New York where I got into a fight with a street dealer in St Mark's Place who tried to rip me off. After that a guy I'd been hooked up with said: 'You really didn't need to go through that, you could have just asked me. Do you want me to get you some better coke than this street stuff?'

'Yes, I'll have $1,000 worth.' He said he'd bring it over the next day. I wasn't the biggest buyer of cocaine in the world by any means. I wasn't a soap star or a gangster with a lot of fast cash to burn. I figured the grand's worth would last me a week.

Back at the Schrager hotel I lay in the tiny designer room on the bed filling the whole floor and spent the rest of the night watching the blades of the fan going round above me. I was pinned down, sweating, my legs twisting from side to side and my body dragging behind the turmoil in my head. My mind was flying down deep valleys of doubt and back up hills of need. It was the same shit over and over again. No matter where I was, what I'd done, who I was with. If cocaine was involved I'd end up like this, inside my own head, dissatisfied, clawing at something solid that wasn't there. It was like running on a turntable, sliding with gravity, those dreams you can't escape from. Only I was awake and my circumstances were the result of my own actions. I thought it gave me status, a carelessness that was attractive, but it wasn't – I was just another cocaine cunt.

The momentary euphoria was nothing but a false promise, hounded afterwards by a desperate, scraping need for more. Even on the other side of the Atlantic where the quality of the coke was markedly better I found myself with the same fault lines running through my mind. Whatever concerns were in my head, whatever I cared about or was worried about was just being intensified.

White room, white fan, white walls overbearingly close. White gak crusting up my nostrils, drying out my saliva, my teeth grinding out a frantic Morse code, tongue sticking to the roof of my mouth trying to spin up more spit. Only the negative thoughts sharpened in this state. The big ideas, the hopes, the ambitions, the ideas that had seemed so important four hours before just shifted away and lost their power and allure. Things you thought would unlock the future were just cast aside – wasted, unwanted and valueless.

Kaz, who could probably see this going through my mind, said, 'I think we should go home.' I knew she was right. That if I bought the gear I probably wouldn't be coming back for a while.

This is a clock. At the six here, this is bottoming out. You die, are hospitalised, sectioned, homeless, raped, have nothing left.

Churchill Clinic, London, 1998

That unpleasant white dawn in the Paramount hotel was Sunday. We flew home that night and the next day, Monday, 2 February 1998, I went to see Clive opposite the big guns of the Imperial War Museum. I had no idea where those barrels were pointing but it might as well have been at me. I thought everything else was about me.

I told him the details of another stupid drug night in a far-off location and the scuffle in St Mark's Place. Maybe it was because it had come after some weeks of relative sobriety, maybe he was tired of my binges getting worse, maybe he didn't want me to be stabbed or shot on his watch, but for the first time he said something to me that was prescriptive rather than a question or guidance.

'You sound scared of yourself, James.'

And that was it; everything that had been hiding my true feelings dropped away and I recognised exactly how I felt. (I would later come to understand this was called my moment of clarity.) I was fucking terrified of myself because I had no control over myself. In that rotten strip of street life, dealers and giants in São Paolo. In the slanted traffic and lights and threats of King's Cross, Sydney. In the cellars of Soho. Wherever I was, usually somewhere nice, I would head for the worst possible places I could find because something inside felt I should be there. I needed to be fearful, because that's how I'd arrived in the world. Fear was my constant companion. Of getting caught, found out, fear of eating as a kid, fear of not eating as an adult, fear of the Ripper, fear of being jumped. I'd walked home at night for years assuming someone would be about to jump out at me and planning how to get a car between me and them. As Clive said those words I finally realised I was the person that was waiting to jump out at me. I was the one doing the most damage to myself and the biggest threat to my own mental and physical safety. I was scared of myself.

What he said made me think of about how I felt around 4 p.m. every day in Condé Nast – an unidentified nervousness. The bulk of that day's work would be being done, another section ready to go to production and in my head I'd be fearful about where I'd be in eleven hours' time. Knowing the tide was coming in for me. And initially I loved that feeling, of untying the boat and knowing it would drift, but lately it had been shadowed by this greater sense of fear and I didn't like where I might go.

I explained to Clive that feeling of the tide coming for me every day and how he was right about me being scared. He then said something he had never said or tried to force upon me once in the four months I'd been seeing him.

'James, you are an alcoholic and a drug addict.'

'Are you sure?' I asked, and we both laughed.

'Yes, I knew it the day you first arrived here late and sat down and told me why you were here. I knew it when they first told me why you were coming. I've just been waiting for you to realise it yourself.'

'What's going to happen?'

He drew a large circle in the air with his hand and explained.

'This is a clock. Down here at the base of the clock is the six. When you hit that it is known as bottoming out.'

'What's that?'

'Bottoming out is when you can't go any lower. You die, are hospitalised, sectioned, homeless, have nothing left, are raped, murdered.'

I was really alarmed; this sounded terrible. This was the second time someone had predicted I'd be raped and die in a matter of months because of my using. He had never used any real recovery words with me before. It suddenly seemed quite blunt and ominous.

'Where am I?'

He pointed back at his imaginary clock.

'You are just coming up to the five. Just before twenty-five past. You still have a good job, a wife, a home, people who care about you. You've got further down to go but you're heading here towards the six faster and faster.'

The utter terror of what he told me about myself cleared everything else from my mind. I felt like I'd been put on pause. My fear of what life would be like without drugs or drink suddenly seemed a lot less worrying than what lay ahead with them. There didn't seem to be much more space to keep riding my luck. I was aware I was leading a charmed life. I'd been in worse places and conditions than I've gone into here, but what was now apparent was that the problem was me, not where I was or who I was with. I was at the centre of all this.

Clive drawing that clock gave me some objectivity. Since the summer and the champagne bottle through the window we had spent hours together processing my drug use and my feelings. All the sensitive emotional junk that was piled up inside. The experiences I'd been trying to cover up. For two hours a week he'd offered an emotionally intelligent alternative to the repeated nights which would find me sat slumped in doorways at dawn in Mayfair, lost and demented. I realised he knew so much more about what was going on in my life than he'd yet acknowledged and that the key had been for me to reach that point myself.

After Clive described that clock, I decided I'd actually listen to what he had to suggest and I'd try and stop drinking and using drugs. He had always been clear to me about his own experience of addiction so I asked him how he and others managed not to use or to drink. He explained that a lot of people used the concept of belief in a higher power, and how that higher power could be anything you were prepared to believe in. It could be nature, a group of other addicts, a spiritual entity. We talked about the concept of the individual being just a small part of a much greater universe and the fact that the world didn't actually revolve around me. You can imagine this came as something of a shock. Self-obsession mixed with drug-enhanced paranoia had led me to believe otherwise.

He also said that if you accepted things happened for a reason, and looked at that reason and what you might get from it, rather than trying to manipulate and control everything, things might seem easier. But he also told me not to worry about anything too much and to just try to steer clear of drink today, and then ideally the four days until he saw me again on Friday.

I stepped out of the Churchill Clinic into a dark cold Monday night in London, wondering how the fuck was I going to be able to do that and knowing that the alternative seemed unthinkable.

The next morning I was shivering at the thought of the ominous nature of what lay ahead. I knew I had no willpower; my whole life and identity pretty much revolved around drinking and taking drugs, my job was just something that existed within that and facilitated it.

My friends were part of the ride. I didn't socialise with anyone who didn't use, with one exception, and he could capably sink twelve pints and go for more. My biggest and most immediate fear was it was going to be boring being sober, assuming I managed it.

I just knew I had to change. The desire to change was greater than the desire to carry on. For the first time, I had clearly seen how someone else, an expert in addiction, saw me. And I didn't like it and didn't want what he said was coming. I felt like something had changed inside me.

It's hard to convey my sense of desperation, given that my professional and social circumstances were so luxurious, but that's how I felt. Everything that went on outside was irrelevant; it was inside where the problem lay. I started thinking back over the conversation with Clive about the concept of handing over your will to a higher power. It seemed surreal. I wasn't having any truck with the concept of God but he very clearly explained the old white man with the long beard as portrayed in Christianity wasn't what he was talking about.

'A higher power can simply be a group of people sharing their issues and discussing them. A group is a higher power than an individual. Nature is a higher power.'

I stopped him there and said, 'I'll take nature.' Again, I was arsed if I was discussing my problems with a load of strangers in a group.

Somehow the concept that I was just a tiny part of nature and that whatever happened in my life was probably going to happen anyway and was just a minute part of a bigger natural scheme over which I had little real influence, resonated. I knew my ego, my fear, my aggression, my ambition, my addictive behaviour were part and parcel of my personality and that, combined with some ability as an editor and writer, they may have helped me get on in life professionally but I was in a fucking state as a person.

The idea of abdicating responsibility and letting go of what was going to happen was novel to say the least. I was a control fiend. I'd listen to the ideas in the staff meeting and then just go with whatever I wanted anyway. This really pissed them off.

So I considered this fucking weird magic he was suggesting and decided maybe a tree opposite could help me. Still shaky from jet lag and the big weekend in New York, I was looking out of the Velux roof window at a massive old tree behind the house opposite thinking, 'That tree is going to help me stop drinking and taking cocaine!' This is how fucking desperate I was. The mountains, the rivers, the seas had all been around way before I showed up to become the centre of the universe. So that was it. I officially stood down as the most important person on earth and put my faith in a tree.

Clive had told me not to worry about what had happened in the past or what might happen in the future and to just try and focus on the day ahead. At work I quietly told Alex and deputy Bill I didn't want any more drinks in my office or any hotel rooms I'd be staying in. I wasn't going to make a big thing about it because I figured the more I set myself up the further I'd have to fall. I explained to Susannah I hoped I'd hit a turning point; all I had to do now was get on with the day ahead. Which, it's fair to say, would be different.

It looked so long.

The idea that all this time existed between about 6 p.m. and 2 a.m. where I had nothing to do was a real shock. It was half the day. I'd have all sorts of stress flying around without an obvious way to demolish it. I called my mate Geoff in Leeds and asked him how he dealt with the pressures of teaching thirty teenagers every day. 'I stop off at the driving range on the way home and get a basket of balls, imagine a pupil's face on the ball, someone that's been a fucking pain in the arse. Then I just smash it down the range and I feel better.' This seemed like a great idea and although I wasn't struggling with individuals so much as myself I decided to give it a go.

Fuck knows what this must have been like for my wife. 'I've given up drugs and I'm taking up golf.' But I vaguely remembered reading once that Iggy and Alice Cooper had got into golf when they stopped drinking. I imagine they were playing in lovely courses overlooking Los Angeles, not a badly lit gravel driving range behind King's Cross station but Iestyn gave me some Wilson clubs he'd been sent to review in the sports section, and so that's where I drove to straight after work every night.

Within days without drink I was so tense I headed down to Champneys in a hotel in Piccadilly and got a massage in the spa there. It was fifty quid but much less than I'd been spending every lunchtime on drink. After a few weeks of this I went to Nicholas and asked if I could charge these to expenses. To his credit he said yes.

At the next few meetings Clive and I started to discuss sobriety, not drinking and using, and it was a bit like day following night. The underlying issues were becoming more prominent but instead of acting on them we were going through ways of responding without drinking. At one session, when Kaz and I were both there, Clive pointed to a chair across the room and said, 'Imagine there's a drink on there. Now, between you and that drink I want you to place five things you would like to do instead of drinking.'

I mentioned a couple of basic things and then, knowing I wasn't alone in the room, acknowledged that being sober meant we could probably have a baby as there was no way I'd wanted to be a father drunk. I also really wanted to play football regularly again.

Clive went on to expand about cross-addiction which was when the obsessive nature of the recovering addict just jumped from one substance or practice to another.

We studied what triggered urges to change the way I feel. He explained how people often talk to you in a certain way because they have a personal issue with something else themselves and that affects the way they approach you. He explained the importance of understanding, 'That's their stuff'; the importance of taking the time to think before I responded rather than immediately reacting.

He gave me a leaflet about stopping being judgmental and what came with that, just having some acceptance. When I started to actually practise the latter it was a real relief. I'd grown up in a very judgmental house; my dad had an opinion on everything and voiced it a lot. Just going to Condé Nast and discovering a lot of posh, rich, upper-class people were actually very nice had blown apart prejudice I'd grown up with. So not feeling I had the right to judge everyone, that I should be more accepting, initially made a big difference.

Next up we talked about lying. For five years I had competed in the British Liars' Tournament on home soil and abroad. I liked making things up. When I first met Kaz she spent the first two weeks looking at our fashion assistant Reece, marvelling at how well he walked despite having a wooden leg from a landmine in the Falklands. Given how amazing my previous years had been at *NME* and *loaded* I didn't need to make stuff up.

Clive pointed out that if I was going to be late somewhere, just call ahead and be honest and explain why, don't come up with some bullshit. This too was an extremely liberating suggestion.

Although day by day there were constant challenges – trains, planes, pubs, parties, restaurants, all places I'd drank – week by week I began to feel different. Changing the way I felt by changing the way I thought meant I spent less time trying to change the way I felt by drinking. For the first six weeks my gums kept swelling up into huge lumps as the toxins came out. I found I couldn't fall asleep naturally till very, very late. Clive said this was because I was so used to drinking and drugging myself to sleep.

I would sometimes find myself heading towards toilets in bars and restaurants out of habit, not necessity. Often my impulsive nature would kick in as I walked up Savile Row after lunch at Caprice and I'd respond by buying a shirt or tie at Richard James then a new chocolate bar called a Twirl which was basically a double-barrelled Ripple with better chocolate and wrapping. Within a month I had masses of brightly coloured shirts and ties and my waistline started filling out.

After a while I took his advice and started hanging out with other recovering addicts and I was amazed by the similarities of other people's thinking to my own, even though they were from different backgrounds, sex, race and so on. I was also surprised by how so many people, regardless of their different walks of life, had experienced the same things as me. They'd grown up feeling different, paranoid, fearful, having constant, intense, negative conversations with themselves. How they were driven by an overwhelming desire for more of whatever they needed to cover up their feelings of shame inside.

Most significantly, I heard people talking about having a hole inside they just felt they couldn't fill. This was something I massively identified with. Then one day a new friend, Jay, who also didn't drink, told me about a place he'd been to called Middle Piccadilly in Somerset. It was a healing centre Princess Diana used. Intrigued, I looked it up and decided to go down and check it out. There I did a treatment called metaform which involved vibrations and crystals and bowls and a brass bed and wires and humming, and the lady who did it, Illiana, said, 'Now I just want to let you know, James, I went to America for six months to spend time with the Native Americans who developed this practice, just to check out it isn't a load of bollocks.'

And she was right; for me it wasn't. That hole of negative energy inside me that I'd been trying to fill for years had just disappeared. I couldn't spend too long doing this sort of thing, I had a magazine to turn around.

Man of the Year

London, 1998

GQ's sales were building nicely and subs were going up but it was all coming purely from the magazine. The title seemed to have no specialist marketing department, and Peter's current strategy to promote the mag was a trade show in Olympia and a sticker on the safety car at the Formula One.

In America, GQ was a far more established brand. They had a star-packed televised concert and dinner for their GQ Awards, and Peter wondered if that was something I'd be interested in. 'Yes!' Anything to get people talking about the mag. We decided we would just start it modestly as an editorial feature the readers could vote on and a party, but we should do it quickly. Someone commissioned a very nice award involving the GQ logo and one of the Condé Nast events team booked the Café de Paris in Leicester Square for the party.

In the next issue we gave the readers a multiple-choice shortlist of contenders and we had a really strong response in the postbag. I counted and tabulated all the votes myself because I was intrigued to see who they had gone for: Michael Owen (sports), Irvine Welsh (writer), Chris Evans (radio), Arsène Wenger (International Man of the Year), Ewan McGregor (actor), the Verve (band), Robbie Williams (solo artist), Louise Redknapp (services to mankind), Vic and Bob (comedy), Sir Paul Smith (fashion designer), David Beckham (most stylish), Norman Cook (DJ), Johnny Vaughan (TV) and Sir Michael Caine (legend). I gave Tony Adams of Arsenal the Editor's Award for his surprisingly honest biography, *Addicted*.

We then set about tracking down the winners, interviewing,

photographing and filming them receiving their awards. In a hotel in Hertfordshire Arsène Wenger thanked us for his Best International Sports Figure award and then gave the champagne to his agent. Robbie Williams was rehearsing and in good form and seemed genuinely pleased to receive his. I appeared as a guest on *The Big Breakfast* handing Johnny Vaughan his, and co-host Denise van Outen was on the latest cover which gave me an opportunity to wave that around. All these people were popular and mainstream but still had a bit of cool about them – which was where the magazine needed to be to build the readership. I gave Louise Redknapp her award at Lee Chapman and Leslie Ash's excellent Teatro restaurant and club on Shaftesbury Avenue. It was just after lunch and she was quite keen to get into the magnum of champagne she'd won. We'd had her on the cover which had sold well, and once she started talking about opening the bottle I could see why all the younger boys in the office liked her so much. She was just really lovely, with a flash of intrigue in her eyes.

Thankfully I was saved from temptation and an afternoon crush by club owner and former Leeds player Lee Chapman who was guiding Michael Parkinson round the dining area. Beckoning me over, he said, 'Michael, do you know James Brown?'

'Of course I do, one of our finest modern Yorkshire exports. Hello James.'

I was quite shocked. Meeting people who were super famous when I was a kid was always more impressive than people who were popular now. It felt a little surreal; normally you'd see him on the front cover of the *Radio Times*. I said hello with a big grin and we shook hands.

Ewan McGregor was establishing himself as a star in quality British films like *Trainspotting, Brassed Off* and *Little Voice*, and having won the Best Actor Award we arranged to shoot him together with Legend recipient Michael Caine. We did the shoot and then filmed them giving each other their awards. For the Caine interview our deputy editor, Bill Prince, came up with the brilliant idea of selecting photographs from throughout Caine's life as prompts for anecdotes. Michael really enjoyed it and was quite emotional when he saw one with John Wayne and multiple other stars. He'd never seen it before and asked if he could get a copy. He explained that John Wayne was the first star to befriend him when he'd gone over to Hollywood as a young actor.

Then Bill showed him a still of him in his iconic black mac from *Get Carter* and Caine started up: 'Now a couple of years ago a good friend of mine from my childhood rang me and said, "Maurice, you've got to get this new magazine, it has photos of you every month from your best old films." And that was *loaded* magazine.'

And Tony and Bill and others round the table started laughing and pointed to me and said, 'That was him!'

'Really? Well, James, thank you then. You really are the guv'nor.'

I was just sitting there laughing. A few days after the interview Caine called me and asked if I'd mind not running a quote he'd given about Richard Harris as he'd remembered he'd done something similar before and Harris had got upset about it. One by one I was crossing paths with my childhood heroes. As a little kid at middle school in Leeds in the early seventies the headmistress had asked me which film we should have at Christmas in the hall, James Bond or *The Italian Job*, and I went for the latter without even thinking.

Most of the people I'd written about at *NME* were the same age as me, but since the success of *loaded* had propelled me onto chat shows and magazine and newspaper profiles I'd crossed the line from writer to written about and in the process I was meeting all sorts of interesting and successful people.

The first *GQ* Man of the Year Awards party was really informal. England cricket captain Nasser Hussain, singer Ian Brown and Irvine Welsh were among the guests and everyone just danced and hung out like a normal party. No formalities. The most important thing was it took the title off the page and into events and gave the title and the wider press the opportunity to write about what we were doing. I believe it is still going.

GQ to LLL

We were changing British *GQ* in a way that would make it the new template for the editions around the world. New, modern, confident, popular, and it desperately needed doing. The first time I had to go to the States for fashion week I was taken to the Four Seasons for lunch by Art Cooper, the editor of American *GQ*. While we were eating, Tina Brown, the editor of the *New Yorker*, actually left her lunch with Henry Kissinger and came over and said hello, which was nice and a bit weird. She should have brought Henry over, as I knew he was a big football fan. Tina had modernised *Vanity Fair*, a magazine that, when I was younger and still at the *NME*, I would sometimes buy for the covers and the cover lines, which were a cut above.

Sadly the same couldn't be said for the US *GQ* which was still very much the template for restrained, formal masculinity. It was so stiff most of the covers looked like the star was dressed in wood. I had hoped to be able to use some of their content to get some bigger names into *GQ* quickly but sadly there just wasn't anything in there in any way in tune with the speed and the energy of the British men's sector. We took one cover of Sharon Stone which was a simple 'at dinner with' and the dinner had gone awkwardly. James Ellroy, the great modern American crime stylist, had a monthly column but the format made it impossible to run – it was like free-form jazz. American *Esquire* was notably better at the time.

Art was a nice guy, though, and like so many at Condé Nast, extremely polite and welcoming. He must have had immense patience to deal with the fashion weeks we were required to attend.

A black, chauffeur-driven German town car smoothly pulls up to the edge of the crowd in a cobbled Parisian street, you stride out past the hopefuls skittering around the fringe of the queue and straight to the British PR who is stood with her company counterparts from Europe and America. She recognises you, leaves whoever she is talking to and nods at you, hastily crosses you off a list you can't see on a clipboard hugged close to her chest, she says something into a headset and the rope is opened and you are into whatever historical building their seasonal fashion show is being held at. It's taken less than two minutes from car to catwalk because you are a Condé Nast editor, while some of those people outside have been blagging and waiting for hours. And to be honest it's totally and utterly wasted on me because I couldn't give a fuck. Nowhere in my list of ambitions has there ever been an entry that says I want to wait around for too long in front of a shin-high bench and then watch sixteen scraggy young guys with carefully ruffled hair and skin the colour of papier mâché paste stride past me at a forward-leaning stoop dressed in this season's shades of slate grey where the jumpers are too long and the trousers too short, and because we are ahead of the season they are modelling for, they are wearing overcoats as spring turns to summer and linen vests in winter. It's painful and this is before smartphones so dead time really is dead time. Perhaps an indicator of how far this process is from the real world is best summed up the time when, having once been badgered at *loaded* to attend fashion week, we sent the nicest guy on the writing team, who wouldn't say a truly bad word about anyone, and he came back and described the world's leading fashion writer as looking like a pig. The only hope is that the music might be half decent, but apart from one time Arthur Baker blasted out the Jesus and Mary Chain for the Fake fashion company in a genuinely blinding DJ set, you'll be lucky if you get some ambient interpretation of the opening bars of a Cure hit or some tropical birdsong.

Everything at CNP is pointed towards advertisers so I am ushered to fashion shows in London, Paris, Milan and New York, introduced to designers, go to some dinners. Fans of hanging around before watching people strut up and down catwalks would be delighted but I was not. In Paris, sensing my lack of interest, the fashion editor pointed at the male model's feet and said, 'Ooh, football boots,' as the guys strode past in the new vintage Camper trainers. She was making an effort. We both were. In Milan, at the Armani event in a huge black aircraft carrier of a building, she had the huff because she was put in the row behind me. I'd have gladly swapped with someone in the back row and she could have had my seat no problem. I offered, but it wasn't the done thing, apparently, and Arnold Schwarzenegger was conquering the stage, waving presidentially in a spotlight, underneath a huge silver Armani logo. Another night we had dinner in one of the late Gianni Versace's homes where Boy George was annoyed because he wasn't on the top table. I found it bizarre that he even gave a fuck either. I was more interested in the fact the floor was scattered with heads from very, very old statues and wondering where he'd got them from. Shit at small talk with strangers from another planet while newly clean, I'd be counting the minutes to get away.

In New York at the Kiehl's shop, which was an interesting set-up with vintage skiing shots of the founder and his classic old motorbike, they said we could help ourselves to whatever we wanted and the fashion editor picked up two bottles of product but both Chris Sullivan and I were still on '*loaded* blag' setting and left with a full wire shopping basket's worth. She looked shocked but the Kiehl's ladies couldn't stop themselves giving us stuff. Just round the corner from my old favourite hangout – the Hat, on Stanton and Ludlow – we watched men in cashmere hoodies pimp-roll in a shop where a decade before real pimps and dealers had run the block.

There was one exception. Peter Stuart took me to one show in New

York for a brand that wasn't known in the UK in 1998. I spent most of the Victoria's Secret show gob-smacked. England just didn't have this type of thing. I was on the front row and someone later showed me a press photo of me leaning forward off the edge of my seat looking up at a procession of supermodels with wings and underwear and nothing else with such a big grin. At one point Karen Mulder looked down at me and laughed at how happy I was.

The highlight of the fashionweeks, though, came in Milan where I attended a Dolce & Gabbana party in a park. I got there very early, was introduced to the designers in their little VIP area, and was just wondering how the hell to avoid a load of preening fashionistas when the editor of *L'Uomo Vogue*, recognising a fellow dissenter, said he had no intention of sticking around and offered me a lift back into central Milan. I happily agreed and we fought our way out of the big queue of people desperate to get in. The car park was filling with an excitable jam of minibuses, cars, taxis and Humvees and when we got to his car I was surprised it was a Mini. The guy was well over 6 foot 2 and he looked at me and said, 'I know, I like the design,' and we just laughed and climbed in. Looking at all the traffic it became clear we weren't going anywhere and then he said, 'Do you like *The Italian Job*?'

'Yes, of course!'

And before I could say anything else he put his foot through a 90-degree turn up a small grass bank and straight over a zebra crossing where traffic was waiting both sides and just turned right into the empty lanes on the opposite side of the road and scooted back into town. It was the most audacious and amusing experience and we were laughing like kids being chased all the way home. So that was the best thing about fashion shows – leaving them.

We love you Leeds! Leeds! Leeds!

Elland Road, Leeds, 1998

Remaining sober meant there were just so many hours in my day, and with *GQ* starting to pick up momentum and build significant sales, in my infinite wisdom I decided to use the nights to start a fanzine. No one in their right mind would do this but I'm a Leeds fan, so clearly I'm not, and it was to Leeds United that I took the idea of getting all my various professional journalist mates who supported Leeds to chip in and make a great mag for them. They agreed and Hayden negotiated a really good budget out of them and about ten of us sat down in chairman Chris Akers's boardroom in a tiny office he ran the club out of – across Regent Street in Argyle Street. I was really surprised that's where he was based but he had MD Jeremy Fenn running things in Leeds and Adam Pearson was on the marketing side. I had assembled people from all sorts of magazines, from *Kerrang!* to *loaded* to *Empire*, but the best idea by far came from Mark Waites, who was just starting up an ad agency called Mother. George Graham had just walked out on Leeds to go to Tottenham and Mark suggested we create a waterproof sticker with his face on that you could put at the bottom of your toilet bowl, with the legend, 'He shat on us once, you can shit on him always!'

Amazingly we put this in the first issue and no one batted an eyelid. In fact the new chairman Peter Ridsdale was just getting into his stride and he came over to me one game and said, 'I can't be seen to approve of that sticker in public but it was very funny.' From then on we set up a larger office even nearer the *GQ* office, subletting from a stockbroker's on Regent Street and cracked on creating a really well-produced, well-written, well-designed official magazine with strong interviews and lashings of irreverent content.

Irvine Welsh paid tribute to Billy Bremner when he died in the same language in which he wrote his books and that brought a few complaints. And I co-wrote a column called True or False in which we insisted Ian Harte couldn't read; there was an old well below the centre circle; the goalposts had a cheese filling; and Tony Yeboah's arse had been used as a mould for Ghana's national skate park. The latter prompted calls of outrage to David Mellor on 606, and listening to him read out all the lies we'd made up in disgust was tear-inducing. We made sure every issue featured some content from every era, from Revie's onwards, and having pro writers and designers and production staff made it a must-buy (once we'd voluntarily calmed the language down a little). I got them a proper distribution deal with the company who distributed *GQ* and we built it up to selling 24,000 copies a month. David O'Leary's appointment, his promotion of young players to the first team squad and subsequent international shopping spree meant we were never short of a great cover star. All we had to do was go up to the training ground at Thorp Arch, near Wetherby, and interview and photograph them. Only two people ever let us down: Harry Kewell refused to come out and be photographed with the six other Australasians for an Aus/NZ special we were sending 10,000 of down under; Viduka just stood there and called him a wanker and said we'd do it without him. And Neil Jeffries, my deputy editor, went down to the Charlton training ground to be stood up by Mervyn Day because he didn't fancy it.

Back in the *GQ* office, the team and I were improving the title content and sales was bumping along nicely. We ran a fantastic cover with Eric Cantona in Maori warpaint by his friend Richard Aujard and had interesting actresses like Anna Friel and Beatrice Dahl on the covers. A year after I had been appointed was a good time to take stock. It was like a different magazine – fresh, contemporary, confident, and with sixteen new members of staff there had been a major personnel overhaul. Subscriptions and news-stand sales were significantly up and we'd eaten into all the free issues and overseas estimates that had been propping the ABC figure up with real sales. September '98 had All Saints' Mel Blatt as the cover star looking deadly while pregnant. Unlike the *Vanity Fair* Demi Moore cover she was face on and staring, with great eye contact: 'I'm a pop star, I'm pregnant, deal with it.' Strangely the father of her child, Stuart, had once been in Fabulous for a few months before he'd left to make the natural leap to Jamiroquai.

Inside I was happy with the array of content, specifically a ten-page special called 'Changing Man', illustrated by Pete 'Monsterist' Fowler and pulled together by Lloyd Bradley. The feature reflected what had happened to me over the last year, how I'd changed. It pointed out that by the time you were in your early thirties if you hadn't matured naturally, life would do that for you. You'd have a baby, get promoted, lose a parent, get married, buy a property, whatever. It was a funny and well-researched look at what life used to be like and how it was destined to change. Elsewhere Sky News crime correspondent Martin Brunt wrote a hefty and well-informed account of Britain's most wanted man, Kenneth Noye. Jo Levin's lead fashion shoot looked strong with regular good-looking guys against a red-brick estate. Deeson and I had been back to South America for another Grand Prix jaunt with Jordan again, but this time I hadn't been fucked out of my head. Deeson, Tony the art director, photographer Derek Ridgers and I all jumped out of a plane to go skydiving and Martin wrote his funniest piece since we'd left *loaded*. Elsewhere Norman Jay, Bernard Sumner, UNKLE and Vinnie Jones all appeared – it was a magazine that knew what was going on. Vinnie wasn't in as a footballer but an actor, his first part being a new British film reviewed in this issue: '*Lock, Stock and Two Smoking Barrels* taps into a spirit of pure exploitation that British cinema has often found hard to master. Everyone who sees it will have their own favourite moment, but it's Jones's performance as debt collector, Big Chris, that steals the show.'

Out in New York I was in the office of former *loaded* fan, Graydon Carter, editor of *Vanity Fair*, and he was raving about the film and in particular Vinnie. When I explained he was a former hard-man soccer player and a cult legend at my club Leeds United he looked totally confused.

'Really?'

'Yes he's not an actor at all, which is probably why he's so good. And he's used to waving shotguns around. He once pulled one on the manager to get in the team.'

Meanwhile Vinnie was experiencing the same amount of confusion about *Vanity Fair*. Graydon decided to have Vinnie on the English cover of the magazine, which was a big deal to the film-makers Guy Ritchie and Matthew Vaughn, as at that time *Vanity Fair* was the bible in terms of helping break young actors and actresses. After a shoot with Mel Gibson hadn't done well, Carter told me he was never going to put a man over forty on the cover again. Vinnie wasn't bothered about showing up for the photo shoot and Matthew had to incentivise him. Even on the morning of the shoot he had to call him and plead with him to get there. Vinnie eventually replied, 'OK Vaughny, I'll go. But it's not like *Hello!* magazine, is it?' Worlds collide.

On a boat in Berlin *American Psycho* and *Less Than Zero* author Brett Easton Ellis asked me what was the most basic skill an editor must have. Condé Nast really was a global entity and this was at a global conference for its editors outside of America, where he was guest speaker. I'd met him once before, on my first night in New York, out in a club called the Light Lounge with my friends Joe, Maddy and Shelly. He was with Jay McInerney, and although I really liked his books it was a quick chat, nothing more. Now was an opportunity to spend a little more time with him on a river cruise. As he flicked through a magazine, wondering what he was going to say in his talk, I pondered his question and then replied: 'I think it's to have the ability to make the reader turn the page and definitely read the next one. And the next.'

It was a simple answer but he used it in his speech. And it's something I still think holds true today.

The magazine was going very well but suddenly my head wasn't. One night at a restaurant with my wife and Sarah Beck, a friend from school, Sarah said something that triggered some memory and I just broke down in tears. It was totally unexpected, like a wave just hit me. Sarah and Kaz just looked at me, shocked. One minute I was fine and the next I was crying into my arrabiata.

I went home and just couldn't stop, I felt terrible. I called Alex and left her a message saying I couldn't come in the next day and in fact I wasn't coming in again. She was shocked too because the title was in a really good place, the team were happy and buzzing and she thought I was fine at work. They very quickly shuttled me off to see Clive and the psychiatrist and once I'd explained what had happened and how much I just felt overwhelmed by emotion and grief they told me that this sometimes happens. That six months after I'd quit, my nerve endings that created the serotonin weren't functioning. That they had become overpowered by the coke and were all still clagged up by it, that I'd ceased to be able to create enough of it naturally. They gave me some antidepressants called sertraline. Suddenly I felt like I was walking on Spacehoppers.

I went back to see Clive a week later and told him, 'This feels amazing. Is this what normal people feel like, just upbeat and happy? I feel like I'm flying. It's better than coke because there's no comedown.'

'How many are you taking?'

'You said two a day.'

'OK, maybe come down to one a day and after a while a half and then ideally off.'

Four months later I was fucking terrified of stopping them, they'd become like a handrail, but eventually I did and found I was OK. My head felt OK again and I didn't need anything internal to bring me down – I had the biggest shitstorm of my life looming over the horizon.

All in all things had been relatively fine between the upper echelons at Condé Nast and myself; they seemed happy that the sales were driving up so well and Man of the Year had been a success. They'd say things like they'd like to see people like Martin Amis featured, but I explained we had Irvine Welsh. There was a sense that the magazine wasn't quite aspirational enough. 'I like these guys in the top hats in the hot tub,' Nicholas said pointing to Flowered Up, who were holding an illegal rave in a squatted mansion – there'd rarely been a bigger gang of drug fiends. Jonathan suggested I call the editor of the *New Yorker* and ask him to write a piece about Mohammed Ali. We already had a feature on Prince Naseem Hamed. In a sense it felt like they wanted it to be a bit more welcoming to guys in their fifties. We'd had a big disagreement when they asked me if I would create a section in the awards for a Man with Allure, sponsored by a fragrance to the tune of £30k. They should have just done it and run it as an advertorial. I didn't know any men with allure. It felt like a feminine take.

At the start of 1999 I was flown first class to New York to meet James Truman and Si Newhouse, the editorial director and the owner of CNP, to talk to me about moving to New York to take over at *Details*. *GQ* and *Details* had been overshadowed by *Maxim* and *Stuff* which were both absolutely flying and they wanted to move their younger title towards that part of the marketplace. I felt it would be better to just make it a sharper, younger *GQ* with people like Brad Pitt and

Edward Norton on the cover. Talking to James it felt like they were asking me to dig another title out of a hole again, like I'd just been doing. Getting rid of people is fucking exhausting; you ruin their lives for a while when you fire them. Getting people to understand how to change was also a hard, gradual process. I didn't fancy another Red Adair job. I wasn't sure how my sobriety would hold up, I wasn't sure if my wife would want to come; she wasn't seeing much of me anyway as I was out all the time. I felt I probably had a better job in London.

The offer just didn't seem as intriguing as when Jonathan had offered me *GQ*. I was up all night with jet lag and flu and then I met Si at a small, discreet restaurant. Yoko Ono was the only other diner in there. I knew I wasn't setting the world on fire and they didn't offer me the job. Only afterwards when I met up with Glenda Bailey, ex-*Marie Claire* and now *Harper's Bazaar* editor in the States, and my mate Steven Daly, a contributor to *Vanity Fair*, did they make me realise I should have bitten their hand off and worried about how to sort it later. I regretted not seeing them before my meetings.

Back in the UK the MD seemed desperate to find out if they'd offered me the job – I really think he saw it as an opportunity to get me out of his hair. The increasing sales were proving I knew what I was doing. My thinking was: make it solid, build on it. I thought I'd get to two years and then think about starting my own business. Felix Dennis had sent a load of faxes not long before saying *Maxim* in the States had sacked their editor; fuck knows why he hadn't called me and just talked it through. Alex had wandered in and said, 'This seems to be quite a poor attempt to poach you by fax.'

But fate had other plans for me.

The news-stand sales were going up and I was banking my bonuses, especially after we found some amazing-looking images of fashion models and actresses shot by Antoine Verglas. These really made the sales jump up to a point where they were 50,000 more than when I'd started just eighteen months before. And then we fucked up and they sacked me.

I'd turned the magazine around and re-staffed it; we'd redesigned it and won the first PPA award *GQ* had had for five years. But none of that would have been an issue if we hadn't been sloppy and included the Nazis and Rommel in a staff and writer vox pop and list about the best-dressed men. A number of writers had mentioned how cool the Germans' WWII uniforms were but it just didn't sit right when in the intro we were describing those on the list as 'cool' and 'movers and shakers'.

I was in New York for fashion week when the 'best-dressed men' shit hit the fan in the *Observer*. A big half-page news story with a load of goose-stepping soldiers alongside a picture of me and Si Newhouse. The same day I'd missed a Calvin Klein show where I had a front-row seat next to Jonathan's wife, Ronnie, who had worked on the collection. I'd just got caught out in failing to factor in the length of time it would take me to get across Manhattan but that certainly didn't help.

That night I was flying down to an American resort island off Mexico to go on an aircraft carrier for a story the next day and I was called back to London from there and whacked. They'd had one written complaint and probably calls from the Jewish business and fashion community. It didn't look good.

Ironically, not long before, I'd done a well-attended talk for Jewish Care in a central London hotel which had raised £4,000 in ticket sales for elderly Jewish people who needed support. They dropped me a line saying they knew I wasn't a fucking Nazi. That this was even being suggested made me feel sick. I'd stood and faced them in Leeds as a teenager at Elland Road; my great-grandparents had left Germany because of their Anglo-German marriage. I was embarrassed that something like this could have appeared; I understood the offence it had caused.

Still, it was my responsibility. I was in New York discussing *Details* when it had passed but I was the editor; the staff should have known it was not all right.

My lawyer let me sit in on the phone meeting to negotiate the formalities and financial aspect of my departure, so long as I didn't comment, and it was a brilliant scene. The MD was being chased about all over the place and with all the targets I'd hit and the time I'd served they had to pay me more to leave than they had to hire me. Months later, Susannah called me to ask if they could have my lawyer's number as they'd like to use him.

A number of weeks later Jonathan Newhouse called me and invited me to be on his team at the River Café charity quiz hosted by Jeremy Paxman – strangely, Michael Gove was one of the other team members. He was also quite keen for us to have our photo taken together for *Hello!*, although we didn't. He didn't mention my departure but he was a good man for inviting me, letting me know we could stay friendly despite no longer working together.

Graydon Carter from *Vanity Fair* suggested he had a job idea for me. He was a great Condé Nast editor and I wasn't sure what he was going to suggest and then he just laughed and said, 'Hey, how about German *GQ*?'

Paul Smith called me, as did Tony Parsons. A good friend pointed out to me that something wasn't a failure just because it ended badly but I wasn't happy inside about the impact of publishing something like that.

On the day it all happened my senior staff joined me for a farewell lunch. Years later Claire Grant, the managing editor, said, 'Tarantino in Disneyland was never going to last for long,' a brilliant summing up of my time there. A month later I saw my deputy Bill who had been holding the fort and his hair had turned grey. 'The first thing the circulation lady said to me, whatever you are going to do please don't change what James was doing, the sales are just booming.'

And they were. In the space of eighteen months the same woman, Caprice, had appeared on the cover of the issue that cost the previous editor his job and then cost me my job, and the actual real news-stand sales had increased by 55,000. Publishing houses had the opportunity to include two issues' projected sales which meant the official audited figures were often bumped up. But this change in figures was the real increase in the number of issues we were actually paid for. I knew them all month by month.

Luckily I had another job and office waiting, just down the road on Regent Street, *Leeds Leeds Leeds* magazine – the official club magazine of the team I supported which Hayden and I had started in my copious amounts of spare time when I'd stopped drinking. With professional journalists who were all Leeds fans, some of the skills I'd perfected on the men's mags were flying, as was the team under David O'Leary. I used the security and revenue of the contract with Leeds United and my payoff to start my own company. Which was where we came in on Mustique with Felix Dennis. Who put money in and became chairman.

The twentieth century ended and Internet IPOs were all the rage. Get a rose or tie delivered by a motorbike dot com. People thought we were mad starting a print publishing company, something tangible not purely digital but backed by Felix Dennis and former LUFC chairman Chris Akers and some high net worth individuals like Gary Speed and Vinnie Jones from the worlds of film, sport and media. We were able to launch it onto the Alternative Investment Market and I unexpectedly become a chief executive officer of a public limited company.

I loved raising the money. There was such a buzz to it and we were able to launch a movie mag, *Hot Dog,* and a mini men's mag called *Jack* which I named after Jack Nicholson after spending time at a fireworks party in London with him, Jonathan Newhouse and Jack's friend Nona Summers. *Jack* took a million a year in ads and was voted Magazine and Launch of the Year by *Campaign* and won a prestigious PPA design award. IFG was a good place to work and we had a lot of fun.

The best moment was raising more money to acquire *Viz Comic*. At a post-lunch meeting with twelve executives from our German investment bank business cards were flying around the enormous table like tracer bullets and our FD was opening his laptop to start the financial presentation when I closed it. He looked really alarmed and I then handed everyone a copy of *Viz* and asked them to open page three which featured a box ad for the British Starters Society that said something like 'Don't Make Space for the Main Course – Real Men Have Starters' and then on page five a same-sized advert for something like the Puddings Marketing Board 'Don't Be a Puff, Have a Pudding' and finally at the back of the mag an ad for 'Jesus's Crazy Christmas Discount Sale: Bags of Nails Just £9! Crowns of Thorns 3 for a Tenner'.

The bankers were all pissing themselves and the lead just asked me how much we wanted. I upped it from the required £6 million to £8 million and they just said yes. They gave the nod of confirmation to our broker and we got up and left. The whole meeting had taken ten minutes to settle down, start and finish, and when we got outside Jason, the FD, just said, 'What the fuck just happened?'

'They're drunk,' I replied. 'I recognised the atmosphere.'

And they were as good as their word.

I'd worked out that if we increased *Viz* from six issues a year to ten and positioned it on the shelves next to the men's mags, the cartoonists and IFG could both make more money from both ads and sales, which is what happened. I convinced a Murdoch title to pay £1,500 a week for the right to syndicate old, inoffensive, single-box jokes. Boris

Johnson took me for lunch to see if I could convince the *Viz* founder to do cartoons for the *Spectator* but he'd had some sort of breakdown and sadly he and the *Viz* staff had ended their relationship awkwardly. No one else had wanted to buy it so it was nice to help it on its way.

Five years on Dennis Publishing bought the company and I'd turned my *GQ* pay-off into a figure ten times greater. In many ways Condé Nast felt like the gift shop I'd exited *loaded* through. I have been forever grateful for their support in getting clean; it was a great swap – they got their title relaunched, re-staffed, their sales turned around and *GQ* Man of the Year started, while I was able to sort out my life, my lifestyle and my bank account. Working with so many great people at IFG was the second reward.

Fruit that doesn't ripen can rot

Winchelsea beach, East Sussex, 2022

Whereas editing *loaded* so often felt like the restaurant scene in *Goodfellas*, now my life feels a little like Ray Liotta's character Henry Hill in the closing shot of the movie – a normal everyday guy who takes his kids to school, rides his bike and plays football twice a week. For most of the twenty-first century I've been a dad; that's the most important thing in my life, looking after my two sons. They are the best thing that has happened to me. And so long as I don't sing in front of them in public they seem to like me.

The most rewarding thing is when people come to me about their own or their loved one's drink problems and I've been able to listen and share my experience, sometimes sending them off to see Clive. Six months later they'll call me and I'll have forgotten about the chats we had but if their lives are back on track then that's a great feeling. I spent years celebrating drug and alcohol use, and I do believe there are great times to be had doing that, but it's no longer an option for me and I feel I owe it to people like me to offer any help I can. If I ever want a reminder of the crazy times I can open *loaded* and laugh at what we did. It's a diary of my second childhood.

I've got enough things sorted not to have to work but I really miss the cut and thrust of a publication. I come alive when I've consulted or worked on ones I like. I've done over fifty business talks, sharing platforms and billings with Al Gore, David Cameron, Kofi Annan, Terry Waite and others. I have appeared a lot on news, sports and cultural

TV and radio shows and documentaries. The content company I had, Sabotage, ran for eight years and did work with many leading ad agencies and their clients JD, Scotts, Adidas, Puma, Foot Locker, Top Man, Cadbury, Stella, Enterprise, MSN, Triumph, Aston Martin and many, many more brands. There are only so many conversations you can have with new brand or account managers who think their client is a religion to be worshipped and marketing jargon the word of God. I packed that in to write this book.

I've consulted for many of the top magazine and newspaper publishing companies and occasionally now write for some of them too. I was mentor to the late and terribly funny Peaches Geldof for an MTV series on how to produce a magazine, of which she was editor, which was sadly cancelled after a shoplifting incident. The littlest things. She was brilliantly hilarious company.

As a gun for hire occasionally the phone goes and something like this happens. I was sitting in my car and the phone went and an American woman on a withheld number asked:

'Is this James Brown?'

I assumed it was a cold caller.

'Who is this?'

'Am I speaking to James Brown?'

After three goes around I sensed it wasn't a call centre.

'Yes, this is James.'

'Hello James, this is Mrs Ritchie.'

Which was a shock. I had once reviewed Mrs Ritchie for the *NME* when she was Miss Ciccone, or better known as Madonna, at Wembley Stadium way back. It was a good review so I figured she couldn't be ringing to give me some feedback.

'Guy tells me you found him two really good development writers for *Sherlock Holmes* and he suggested you might be able to do the same for me. Could you come over this week and talk about it?'

Which I did, and we spent a couple of days considering possibilities, which was really interesting. She had a great idea for the opening titles of her film *W.E.* featuring the sounds of thundering hooves over the Pistols' 'God Save the Queen'. I've never sat one on one in a room with someone with such a powerful sense of self.

In September 2018 the advertising trade bible *Campaign* magazine asked me if I would get the original *loaded* staff line-up together for a photo shoot for their fiftieth anniversary. They were choosing iconic brands that had changed the media, things like the Guinness white horses surf campaign. We would be the sole magazine involved. Having had years of seeing the glory of my *loaded* lumped in with the shit that followed into the market place and its content critiqued by those that had never really even read it, it felt good to have some of the recognition and acclaim it had enjoyed during the mid-nineties.

It was only the second time some members of the team were all together in the same place since I'd left in 1997. Michael Holden, Jon Link, Adam Porter and Christian Smyth were abroad; Wildey couldn't make it; Adam Black was at the synagogue for Passover; Mick Bunnage chose not to do it. In typical fashion Reece Sandell rang at the end of the shoot and said, 'I've missed this, haven't I?'

Tim Southwell, Martin Deeson, The Loafer, Steve Reid, Beth Summers, Graham Greig and I all met outside the innocuous door to our first proper editorial office on Upper Ground on the South Bank. Everyone was pleased to see each other. *Campaign* took some posed photos and for most of the hour-long shoot we were laughing and holding our stomachs in.

It was especially great to see Beth. It was the first time I'd seen her since I'd bumped into her at fashion week in Paris just after I'd joined *GQ*. Not long after that she was involved in a motorbike accident. Her dad Alan, daughter Eden, and her carer came with her. I hadn't seen Alan since he'd kindly secured our Phil Tufnell interview for issue two. Eden was four when we launched the magazine and would often spend Friday nights running round Studio 6 with us. She was in her mid-twenties now. Beth admitted a large part of her memory had gone but she was smiling and happy and curious for us to fill in certain blanks. Most of the guys who couldn't make it later asked how Beth was. 'Largely like she was after the first drink,' I replied. 'Happy, smiley and pleased to be with us.'

Beth was one of the key members of the editorial team, bringing some female perspective and balance. Proportionally we had a higher ratio of women on the team than any women's mag had men. And she was just the same as the rest of us: good at her job, funny, bolshy, loved drinking and hanging out. I was really glad she'd been able to make it.

When we finished the shoot she headed home and the rest of us went straight to a bar and didn't move for six hours. It was a brilliant afternoon – really, really funny – and we had so many stories to happily retell, remember and clarify. No one suggested doing the magazine again and no one was maudlin. There was a fair bit of discussion about Christian's gender identification change in Australia. 'Well good for him. I wouldn't shag her though.' Twenty-year-old conversations continued as if they'd ended yesterday. By four o clock, predictably, someone felt compelled to announce, 'We better get back to the office – we've got to finish the issue.'

No one in the media seems to have four- or five-hour lunches any more, lunches that wipe out the afternoon and leave you working or boozing, or both, late into the night. That had been perhaps the greatest thing about *loaded* for the staff. Knowing we had the most amazing job, where we got to produce a magazine we loved doing about subjects we talked about for free, and no one was ever telling us when we had to be in or out of the office. Knowing that we would get the work done well and the readers would love it. The whole magazine was like a functioning alcoholic.

If you can do what you genuinely love doing every day then you are ahead of the game. For thirty-six months, for me anyway, we had the best time ever. Beyond being in a great band or playing professional football, I can't really think of anything I'd rather have done. Somehow I assembled a great team of people and we collectively created this magazine and moment that we'd remember forever.

There were times – like when I discovered Martin Deeson had as a teenager actually briefly been trained by the Pope to be a priest only to end up in South America with Ozzy Osbourne for *loaded* – when I figured we were probably working for the devil, and it seems his work is never done. Approaching 6 p.m. on the South Bank I noticed some vaguely familiar activity I hadn't seen for a long time. The much-loved but most incompetent clandestine operator of the bunch was fussing about, going to a cash point, collecting crumpled notes, coming in and out of the bar making phone calls.

Me: 'What are you doing?'

Escobar: 'Getting some gear.'

Me: 'How much?'

Escobar: 'A gram.'

Me: 'A gram? What is the fucking point? Why don't you just buy some decent drink?'

Walter White: 'You're not in charge of us any more! We can do what we want.'

Me: 'When did I ever stop anyone buying drugs? Anyway, I couldn't give a fuck what you do, I'm just surprised. A gram of shitty, stepped-on gear? We used to be good at this, we bought big bags of the stuff. We went to South America to get it.'

Escobar (looking up): 'We're four quid short.'

If you should die before you awake

Prague, summer 2018

> *'Your face lights up when you talk about music.'*
> – My girlfriend, Em, while I was explaining why
> Sparks's 'The Number One Song in Heaven'
> is almost a reason to look forward to dying

Thirty-one years after I joined the *NME* I was stood on the temporary bleachers on a pocket-black night behind an out-of-service airport near Prague, looking out at 80,000 people dancing and singing along to the Rolling Stones performing 'Jumping Jack Flash' and 'Miss You'. To the right of me were two teenagers who knew all the words and behind them a good-looking sixty-plus-year-old woman and her friends. Imagine being able to entertain both. Like everyone else I was waving my phone about filming the crowd singing 'oooh eeee ooowee ooowee ooooh, oowee oowee oowee ooh, cos I miss you'. At other times I would have been more self-conscious of how I was moving – like a kid trying to grasp a balloon just out of reach – but I couldn't give a fuck. Life felt great. I was thinking about my new girlfriend and watching this amazing band defying age expectations and musical trends and delivering so many exhilarating songs that had defined special moments in so many people's lives.

In addition to this, at this point the England football team were unexpectedly advancing on the World Cup semi-finals in Moscow. Football, music and love. Day after day, another unstoppable hit of life – it was one of the best weeks of my life. There was such a heightened sense of excitement, possibility, hope and reassurance, and right at that moment as the skies had darkened and the stage glowed like a giant orange wall of fire, it was being soundtracked by the band that had been around my life since year zero. The intensity of the moment reminded me so much of what it felt like leaping about at the front of gigs when I was following the Redskins and the Three Johns around the country or was down the front at the Ramones, Cramps, Jesus and Mary Chain, the Jam, SLF, the Specials or the Undertones. As a teenager that was the only time I'd felt pure exhilaration, back before I drank too much, when music was my life, my only high. The compulsion to feel this way again made me realise: 'I need to go to Warsaw to their next gig.' Not out of any underlying desire to eat dumplings, trek wide streets and circumnavigate huge 1970s Communist housing blocks, but to follow the Stones to the last night of their tour. To have that sense of chasing the band, going into the unknown, geographically, and discovering new places, but achieving that expected hit again.

It would be the perfect ending to the book for me. I wanted to bring everything up to date. I like telling these old stories and am happy to discuss the effect drug use and later getting clean has had on my life but there've been two things nagging away at me for a while. One, I wanted to go on the road with a band again to document it. And two, I didn't want everything in this book to be about the past, I wanted to create new memories. For about three years I've just had this yearning to go back to the carnival, to see the set-up and take-down, to sense the build-up for band and audience, to be able to walk between the two. The intimacy uniting the band travelling to the stage and the community uniting the audience, both closing in on each other until the showtime brings them together. I wanted to see an empty, dark-walled, sticky-floored room with its day lights on transform into a reeling, feeling, seething, moving mass of music fans.

What I didn't expect, when that bug finally struck, was that that feeling would be ignited into action at a Rolling Stones gig. Their performance was just so fucking good, so lean, so hungry, I dialled up my teenage cynical self and said, 'Come on, it's the Stones, they've always been there. Allow it.'

So as Mick prowled and spun, defying both age and the heat of the night, and Ronnie and Keef shot up the skies with their howling guitar tracer and Charlie sat all proper and erect and almost smiling behind the lot of them, I spent the rest of the set wondering how long it would take to hitch or get a train to Warsaw.

Some basic research suggested I'd be fucking stupid to try and get to Poland by thumb or train in a day. So I did what I couldn't do when I was seventeen and, having left my credit cards at home in England by accident, just called a travel agent I know and asked her to book me some flights and a hotel for Warsaw. And I spoke to Ronnie Wood, who I know because you meet a lot of amazing people when you don't drink, and he sorted me some tickets, and delighted I set off on the road again.

loaded: where are they now?

In autumn 2021 Alan Lewis sadly passed away of Parkinson's disease and cancer. He was a fantastic man who changed our lives but had not done much lately.

Assistant editor Tim Southwell is publishing a comic about pug dogs in space.

Production editor Kristen (formerly Christian) Smyth is a playwright in Australia and now identifies as a woman.

Staff writer Martin Deeson asked me not to mention too many South American adventures in case it affects his chances of doing Greta Thunberg's PR. He wasn't referring to long-haul flights.

Staff writer Michael Holden now lectures in film studies.

Commissioning editor Adam Black is a property developer with housing and retail interests in former East Germany.

Internet editor Adam Porter is an oil industry analyst and lives in Barcelona.

Fashion editor Beth Summers is cared for by a full-time carer, her parents and daughter Eden, who is no longer five years old.

Fashion swagman Reece Sandell works as an expert track fitter on the London Underground.

Subeditor turned second *loaded* editor Derek Harbinson is a keen amateur ceramicist.

Subeditor Danny Plunkett is in a punk band.

Staff writer Pete 'The Loafer' Stanton has fallen in with a bad crowd; he now works for the government.

Art editor Steven Read directed a documentary about Gary Numan.

Designer Little Graham is a recluse with his own online gaming crew.

Editorial assistant Little Piers is the senior PR for the Brain Tumour Charity.

Designer Jon Link and contributing editor Mick Bunnage produce the *Modern Toss* cartoons.

Contributing editor and lead interviewer Jon Wilde was last heard of living in a tent with a dog in a field outside Brighton in pursuit of mindfulness.

I now spend most of my time on a beach.

It is perhaps unsurprising that few of us have ever really worked full time in the media again.

Acknowledgements

From the off I need to thank Quercus Commissioning Editor Richard Milner for his patience, belief and support for *Animal House*. It was really difficult to disclose personal family things I've never written about before and then there was the enormity of so many *NME* and *loaded* stories and although I think I've missed too many great moments out he's kept me going, reassuring me that there are interesting stories here. He went well beyond the call of duty in getting me to finish the book. Thanks also to his Quercus colleagues Ben Brock and Hannah Robinson for their work on the title, to Seán Costello for the copyedit, and to Andrew Smith for the cover design. I'd also like to thank David Luxton at David Luxton Associates for his support and encouragement.

Two magazine editors changed my life significantly. Tony Stewart gave me my chance at *SOUNDS* and helped me become a features writer. He opened the door for me that I'd been banging on for what felt like ages. *SOUNDS* is long gone but that period in 1986 and the first half of 1987 was a brilliant time for me and the other young writers he encouraged.

Alan Lewis changed my life twice. He taught me how to build sales and relationships with the readers and how to get the best out of the staff. At *NME* he not only put up with me fighting, puking, being obnoxious, rude and confrontational but actually promoted me to the best position on the paper. At Alan's funeral in 2021, founding *Kerrang!* editor, Geoff Barton, told me that not long after he'd joined *NME* Alan had told him "there's this kid I've got and he really seems to have something." I am so thankful he could see beyond my personality defects and was able to nurture my raw ability and enthusiasm. To give me control of the *NME* features and front cover choices aged

22 was a phenomenal thing to do. It allowed me to open the doors for so many great bands and writers in much the same way Tony Stewart had done for me.

He gave my colleagues and I the opportunity to enjoy a brilliant period on the *NME* when the paper was strong enough to champion a golden era of music. We were having the time of our lives but it was Alan's personality and ability that allowed that to happen. I told him all this when he was alive but I wish he was still here to say it again. It was only at his funeral that I realised just how much he really had influenced magazine publishing.

Five years later Alan suggested I create my own magazine and then managed to convince IPC to launch it. That he had the guile to change the so-so research results meant a generation of writers, readers, editors, publishers and advertising staff were able to enjoy brilliant times. We created a global genre of mass market lifestyle magazines for men. Alan knew fuck all about crisps though. If you are lucky enough to have bosses like Alan Lewis and Tony Stewart take the time to say thanks.

There were other people who helped me into print before these people. Anne and John from *Leeds Other Paper*, Mick Mercer and William Shaw at *Zig Zag* and Tony Fletcher at *Jamming!* who all printed my raw copy when it probably didn't make much sense. The fanzine scene is covered at length in the book but thanks to Mikki and Emma, Peter Hooton, Rom Ron and John Robb for chatting about those times. And also Bobby Gillespie and Douglas Hart.

I also want to say thanks to Steve Elvidge, Neil Howson, Choque Hosein, Elizabeth Conway, Keely Hollingworth, Geoff Storer, Gary Lovelace, Kengi, John from Nag Nag Nag, John Anthony Lake and many more about life, clubs, music and school in Leeds.

Thanks to the various bands who allowed me into the back of their vans and gave me floors and sofas to sleep on during the fanzine years. Particularly the Three Johns, Serious Drinking and Big Flame and the residents of Parfett Street, Whitechapel.

Ron Scalpello, Neil Perry, Paul Elliot, Billy Mann, Chris Roberts, Edwyn Pouncey and Tony Stewart all happily looked back at our time together on *SOUNDS*. Thank you to Len Brown, Adrian Thrills, Alan Jackson, Stuart Maconie, Quantick, Sean O'Hagan and Brendan Fitzgerald for talking about our times on *NME*, to Adrian Tierney Jones who sent me his daily diary of our time there, and to Simon Bendell (@nothingelseon) for further *NME* research. Thanks to all the staff on the titles and the bands I enjoyed writing about who made going to the office something I looked forward to everyday. I intend to write another book about many more of my music adventures.

I also want to pay tribute to the late Steven 'Seething' Wells and the reclusive Chris Dean of The Redskins, aka 'X Moore', who both encouraged me and showed me it was possible to get onto the *NME* in a brilliant way. Chris in particular was a huge inspiration and I miss him. Wherever you are I hope you are happy.

loaded, where do I start. Tim Southwell obviously for being the first on board when I started assembling the staff, so many fantastic articles and such passion for the mag. Steve Reid for coming up with a brilliant logo, Mick Bunnage and Jon Wilde for creating key parts of the magazine, Christian (then)/Kirsten (now) Smyth for helping define the irreverent self-deprecating tone of voice, Michael Holden for keeping everyone older than himself on our toes, Fashion Editor Beth Summers was a brilliant colleague, her assistant Reece Sandell was the much loved life and soul of our adventures at large. Thanks to Beth's daughter Eden Summers. Adam Black, Rowan Chernin, Irvine Welsh and the legendary Howard Marks. The Loafer Pete Stanton, Adam Porter and Mike Karin who were more bothered about me getting their computer games and cuddly toy columnist's names right than worrying about the references to the stench of weed that floated around their end of the office. All the other subs, designers and picture people: Danny Plunkett, Derek Harbinson, Jason Barlow, Marcus, Martin Deeson, Jon Link, Jim Parry, Robbie Martin, Les Rowley, Miles English. All the staff and freelance writers - you know who you are. Andy McDuff, Karen Swann, Chris West and the rest of the publishing and advertising teams.

All the photographers I worked with on *NME* and *loaded*, in particular Derek Ridgers, Kevin Cummins, Steve Pyke, Lawrence Watson, Tony Barrett, Martyn Goodacre, Grant Fleming and Chris 'I'm in The Hamptons again' Floyd.

For taking the time to talk about *GQ* my friends and former CNP colleagues Tony Chambers, David Gyseman, Sarah Lavelle, Natasha True, Bill Prince, Chris Sullivan, Claire Grant, Ash Gibson. I had such a brilliant time there.

Special thanks to Karen Walter at *NME*, Alex Hearn at *GQ* and Paula Davie at IFG who were regularly the thinking part of my life. They looked after me when I couldn't look after myself. Gaynor Perry had to look after the whole office at *loaded*. God knows how she managed it.

I want to thank Hunter Davies, Tony Parsons, JJ Connolly, Jeff Maysh and my dad Ray Brown for all giving me good advice when I was losing my way with the writing. Which was frequently. I did literally lose huge chunks of writing about *loaded*. For the Fabs, IFG folk and so many bands I had a good time with there'll be other books to come.

Thanks to Jim Moir and Bob Mortimer, the laughs between *NME* and *loaded* were endless.

If you want to find a way ahead in publishing I want to tell you about two inspirational people I met later in my life who always believed there was something great in writing, editing and publishing magazines and papers. One was the late Tony Elliot from *Time Out* who I wish I had spent more time with. He was a kind and inspiring man who had the ability to mirror the good in people in a way that pushed aside doubts or problems we might have faced. The other I only met once, the man widely regarded as the best British newspaper editor ever, Harry Evans. I visited him at his home in New York and we had a fantastic two hours together chatting about journalism, his career and other things like his love of table tennis. I was prompted to contact him after reading his superb book, *My Paper Chase*, which I found in Bequia in 2013 which made me want to be an editor again. It's a brilliant autobiography of a man in love with the power of news and the printed word. If you are a writer or an editor, aspiring or already successful, I suggest you get hold of a copy.

I misplaced so much writing for this book between Bequia, Japan and Winchelsea Beach but thank you to the people who put me up in those far flung places. If I've missed anyone out I apologise, I'll get you into the paperback.

Sir Paul Smith, Trevor Beattie, Jay Pond Jones, Kevin Sampson, Hayden Evans, Gerry O'Boyle, Vince Power have all helped me at various times and frequently given me good advice.

Susannah Amoore, Clive Meindl and Paul Roberts helped me immensely. It sounds too grand to say the first two saved my life but they certainly helped me find a less self-destructive life. I'm not sure where or what I would be without you. You know how much your help has meant to me. A special thanks to Corey Seymour and Manya Bartick.

Thanks to Mark, Jess, Wynn, Maurice and especially Chrissie, who have given me something extremely special in my life, your cake. Finally my good friends, you know who you are, you have to put up with me in your living rooms, beds, on the way to football matches and at gigs. My family, Dad and Ros, Alex, Tiff, Kaz, Lisa, The Bakers, Julie, Kait, Cheryl and Roger, Christine and Tony, Simon and the

Whittakers and the close friends and girlfriends who were around during the crazy years and since. Letting me in at all times of the night in all sorts of states and then seemingly being pleased to see me (alive) when I re-emerged the next day. Listening to me bang on endlessly about Beastie Boys, Leeds United and *loaded*.

Most importantly to Em who is funny and kind and cares about me more than I do myself. The last few years have been brilliant. Calm and happy are two words I would rarely associate with myself but you've made me both. And finally Billy and Marlais who now know more about football than me and are both better players too. You replaced what I lost when my mum went.

When James Brown's Sunday morning five-a-side game
organiser died suddenly it prompted the author to consider
how little the players who gathered each weekend in a variety of
questionable football shirts to overhit passes, fire balls out
of the pitch, and score goals that will live in their memories
forever actually know about each other. In *Above Head Height*
he goes in search of the true bonds of amateur football, what
draws people to small-sided games, and discover who
actually started organised five-a-side and why.

A must-read for anyone who has ever ever rattled a
four-foot-high crossbar with a ferocious volley and
accidentally tipped tiny black rubber pellets out of their boots
onto the hall carpet, this is the autobiography of an
everyday amateur player. The book has topped
the football bestseller charts.

QUERCUS

Reader reviews of *Above Head Height*:

'Captures every single essence of joy, challenge, pain, friendship and fun . . . and has actually improved my game!'

'Full of laugh out loud stories . . . the passion shines through.'

'Anyone who has played 5 a side or Sunday league regularly will love it.'

'This book is fantastic & I don't even read books!'

'Possibly the best football related book I've ever read.'

'A great and funny read.'

'Wonderful read, touching, funny and poignant in all the right places.'

'So much to love about this book.'

'My husband plays 5-a-side every week and he loved this book.'

'A great great read even if he is a Leeds fan.'

'A very funny memoir of a life in the football trenches.'

'This book had me in stitches.'

'A brilliant read.'

'It has inspired me to start playing again.'